365 Manners Kids Should Know

365 Manners Kids Should Know

Games, Activities, AND Other Fun Ways
TO Help Children Learn Etiquette

Sheryl Eberly

THREE RIVERS PRESS • NEW YORK

Published by Three Rivers Press, New York, New York. Member of the Crown Publishing Group.

Random House, Inc. New York, Toronto, London, Sydney, Auckland
www.randomhouse.com

THREE RIVERS PRESS and the Tugboat design
are registered trademarks of Random House, Inc.

Printed in the United States of America

Design by Susan Hood

Library of Congress Cataloging-in-Publication Data
Eberly, Sheryl.
365 manners kids should know : games, activities, and other fun ways to help children learn etiquette / by Sheryl Eberly.—1st ed.
p. cm.
1. Etiquette for children and teenagers. 2. Child rearing. I. Title: Three hundred sixty-five manners kids should know. II. Title.
BJ1857.C5 E24 2001
395.1'22—dc21
2001034065

ISBN 0-609-80637-8

10   9   8

This book is dedicated to my own

generally well-mannered children,

PRESTON, CAROLINE, AND MARGARET,

with

much pride and affection.

Acknowledgments

There are many who helped with this book. Carol Turkington, author of forty books, has my sincere thanks and unreserved awe. She kindly introduced me and the idea for this book to her agent, and made helpful suggestions all the way through. When I thought I had exhausted every possible topic, she had 110 more. She answered the mundane questions of a first-time book author, organized material, made it readable, and assured me there was never a reason to panic. Because of her help, there wasn't.

My deepest thanks go to Bert Holtje of James Peter Associates, who believed in the book and found the perfect publishing match, and to Carrie Thornton, my editor at Three Rivers Press, who patiently guided the publication and marketing of the book.

I can't thank each of my etiquette students over the years because they're in the thousands, but I couldn't have done this without them. They enthusiastically learned their manners at recreation centers, schools, churches, homes, country clubs, and resorts, and let me know which topics helped them: "I met the new principal at our school and I wasn't afraid to shake his hand!" They also explained things to me: "At a formal dinner you have three forks in case one of them falls on the floor!" Their valuable feedback helped shape my thinking as well as this book.

Finally, and most importantly, my heartfelt thanks to my wonderful husband, Don, and our children, Preston, Caroline, and

Margaret. Don is particularly understanding of publishing projects, having written a half dozen books of his own; his support is the single greatest reason for any of my accomplishments. And the children deserve medals. They've endured impertinent questions because of their mom's work ("Are you allowed to burp at your house?") and have listened to their friends being threatened by parents ("If your manners don't improve, you'll have to go live with the Eberly kids' mom"). They've borne it all with good humor.

Contents

Contents

Family Time

Getting Along with Other Kids

Contents

Introductions

Telephone Talk

Contents

You Are What You Say

Contents

The Written Word: Letters, Thank-you Notes, and E-Mails

Table Manners Made Easy

Contents

Stay Out of Sticky Situations with Food!

Contents

Just for Boys

Just for Girls

Invitations: Giving and Receiving

Out on the Town

Contents

At Church or Religious Services

Contents

Birthdays, Weddings, Receptions, and Other Special Occasions

Gifts—Giving and Getting

Great Holiday Etiquette

Contents

Vacation Time

Be a Great Guest (and Host)

Contents

Be a Good Sport

Be a Model American

Being Considerate to People with Special Needs

Body Basics

Contents

365 Manners Kids Should Know

Introduction

❧

If you have kids, you've probably experienced that sinking feeling when you notice your child doing something you never dreamed he or she would do in public. Whether it's inserting fingers into a water goblet or pulling her flower-girl gown over her head in the middle of a wedding, odds are that there will be moments you've wondered whether your manners instructions will *ever* sink in.

Actually, there's simply no way to anticipate every challenge you'll confront in your years as a parent. But knowing the proper thing to do isn't an impossible goal—for kids *or* for parents. Sometimes parents just need some help in teaching their kids manners, because often today's parents aren't sure of the right manners to teach.

Recently a mother called me to register her daughters for an etiquette class I was giving. "I often feel uncomfortable in social situations when I'm around people with social grace," she explained. "There is a lot I don't know about etiquette. I'd like my daughters to learn good manners, because I want more for them."

No matter how well educated you are about etiquette, most of us can always learn more. I'll never forget my first White House luncheon: I wore my new blue spring suit and arrived in the East Room in plenty of time. The event was designed to introduce

1

community leaders from across the country to First Lady Nancy Reagan's projects. Mrs. Reagan had hired me several months earlier to work in her office in the East Wing, and this was my first opportunity to attend a major White House function.

I was fascinated at how effortlessly the waiters wove in and out among the tables in that beautiful gold room, serving each of us roast spring lamb. I chatted with other guests and was pleased with how everything was going until an exotic clear soup appeared on the table. What could this be? I grew up in Pennsylvania Amish country, and our soups were far more substantial. Not a single vegetable was to be found in this bowl!

Because I was a bit unsure of myself, I checked what the others were doing. And then I spied a well-dressed woman across from me putting her fingers in the soup! Of course, then I realized instantly that I was looking at a finger bowl, not a soup bowl. I set it aside and thanked my lucky stars I hadn't tasted it!

With this book, I want to help readers and their children avoid the kind of anxiety I felt at that luncheon, even if they're simply dining at a friend's house. Knowing what to expect in a social situation eases the mystery and anxiety for children. Knowing how to *teach* children how to act in social situations makes every parent's job easier, too! For at least a generation, manners training in many homes seems to have been neglected. As parents, we've concentrated on developing our children's talents and self-esteem; we want our children to be creative and honest about how they feel. Some of us question the validity of the rules of etiquette themselves.

But I think the finer points of etiquette really are important for a child to know. Good manners involve more than simply knowing the rules about forks and finger bowls in formal situations—they include good attitudes, respect, and consideration for others every day. If we want our children to be confident, poised adults, we need to teach them the rules of etiquette today. Knowing proper behavior is an essential part of being prepared for life.

As a parent, I wouldn't think of sending my child off to a soccer game without soccer shoes, or to school without lunch money and homework. In the same way, you do your children a disservice if you send them into the world without good social habits. Other people form an impression of what a child is like by observing her manners. What an advantage to have the grace and self-control that enable a child to make a good first impression!

Parents can teach the very youngest children rules of etiquette, long before they truly appreciate why. A child can learn to say "please" and "thank you" even while he still believes the world revolves around him. He can learn to write a thank-you note to Grandmom for birthday gifts even though he thinks gift giving is just what Grandmom does. Even if—at the beginning—good manners mean just going through the motions, eventually a child will understand how important they are in showing others the respect they deserve.

Twenty years ago, a family I know decided they wanted to teach the six sons at their dinner table manners so they would grow up not just to be adults, but to be gentlemen. They were not allowed to sit at the table until their mother or grandmother had taken her seat. Elbows were not allowed on the table during the meal. Through the years—and it did take years—as the boys' manners slowly improved, their parents often said, "If you don't learn good manners, you'll never be invited to the White House."

As remote as the possibility seemed, the oldest son took the admonition to heart. When he was selected at fifteen to be a youth representative for a drug-free program, he found himself seated at a luncheon beside the nation's First Lady. He could only think: "At least I know which fork to use!" And his elbows never left his sides.

We all have high hopes for our children, and we have an obligation to help them prepare for their grown-up years no matter what their future will hold. When my then-two-year-old son got to meet President Ronald Reagan and show him his yellow Matchbox car, he liked the gentleman who gave him jelly beans. When we left the Oval Office, he announced that when he grew up he would either work at the White House or be a garbage collector.

His father and I are prepared for almost any eventuality. We've insisted that he learn his manners, because we know it will help him reach his full potential—whether that's riding on the back of a big green trash truck or in a long black limousine.

This book is designed to help parents develop a vision, as well as a practical plan, for raising well-mannered children. Far more than a simple rule book, it provides anecdotes, advice, and activities for turning rules into habits.

Sheryl Eberly

A Great Beginning

~

$\mathcal{L}$earning good manners will help your child act toward others with respect and take into account their feelings. Your child will also gain the confidence that comes from knowing the proper thing to do. As a parent, you're sure to discover it's a gradual process. While your children will put into practice a few good manners, you'll need to remind them often of others. Start with the basics, and enjoy the journey together!

JANUARY 1

How early should you start teaching manners?

Parents begin teaching manners by example as soon as a child is born. While our children might do what we say, they are more likely to do what we do. First-time parents may find it shocking to hear their child spout an off-color phrase she learned from a parent. Whether we like it or not, learning usually takes place in the home, through imitation.

It's a good idea to teach your child one new chore each year. If a child learns to make a bed at age three, at age four he can begin emptying the wastebaskets, and by five start to set or clear the table. Try a similar approach with manners. Teach your child a few manners—and when he's mastered those, start on a few more. Lay a foundation and begin to build on it. Expect basic manners from a five-year-old, and more from a ten-year-old. You'll be amazed how many compliments you'll get by the time your child reaches adolescence.

A three-year-old should:

- Establish eye contact when speaking to another.
- Say hello.
- Wash hands before and after a meal.
- Stay seated during the meal.
- Use utensils at the table.
- Say "please" and "thank you."

A ten-year-old should:

- Be able to hold a conversation with an adult.
- Use good table manners.
- Answer the telephone properly and take careful messages.
- Show self-control in public places.
- Take responsibility for keeping the bedroom neat.
- Stand when an adult enters the room.
- Know how to be on time.

A fifteen-year-old should:

- Initiate conversation and show interest with adults.
- Pick up after herself and her friends at home.
- Maintain a noise level that is acceptable to the family.
- Be protective and kind toward younger siblings.
- Express appreciation to parents and others.

JANUARY 2

There's no place like home

Some families are on their best behavior when they go out but like to kick back at home. They also let this philosophy govern their manners. Sarah Ferguson, the duchess of York, once told a reporter about her formula for good manners at the table. She and her daughters have A, B, and C manners, she explained. When they're dining with the queen at Buckingham Palace, they use their very best A manners. When they're at a restaurant, they're more relaxed, so they use their B manners. And at home? They're even less proper; C manners are fine.

Contrast Fergie's philosophy with pre–Civil War Eliza Farrar's. "Would it not be more refined and honest," she wrote in *The Young Ladies Friend* (1834), "to live a little better every day and make less a parade before company?"

There may be some value in being relaxed at home, but at what cost? One of your goals as a parent is for good manners to become *habits* for your child. If chewing with his mouth closed is necessary when he's out but not when he's at home, chances are he won't chew properly at home *or* when he's out. Having different codes of manners can be confusing to your child and not very practical in the long run. It's a bit like telling a pianist that how he plays at home doesn't matter as long as he performs well at a recital.

Parents can save themselves some headaches and teach children that the family deserves to see their best behavior. Here are a few ways parents can encourage children to help make home a nice place to be. Suggest that they:

1. Talk to their parents. Say "good morning" and "good night."
2. Respect the privacy of others. Don't listen in on phone conversations, read others' mail, or snoop in their closets.
3. Knock gently on a closed door before entering.
4. Use good table manners.
5. Borrow items only if they've asked to do so. Return them in good condition.
6. Spend time with their siblings. Don't hibernate in the bedroom.
7. Ask family members how things are going.
8. Use an "indoor voice" when they're in the house.
9. Pick up after themselves.
10. Don't let their goodbyes be accompanied by unkind words.

Activity

Post the above list on your refrigerator and compliment your child when he puts one of the rules into practice. If your child likes to create things on the computer, have him design the list for the fridge.

"Please," "thank you," and "I'm sorry"

Sometimes a child's good manners reveal a naturally sunny, kind disposition. This isn't always the case, but practicing good manners helps a child begin to develop consideration for others.

By following good manners in daily life, we learn to control ourselves and become aware of how our actions and words affect others. At some point, with enough practice, the learned formalities become second nature.

This is certainly the case with saying "please," "thank you," and "I'm sorry."

As soon as a child is able to extend a chubby little hand and ask for a cookie, you should encourage him to say "please." As soon as he is old enough to be given a gift, prompt him to say "thank you." As soon as he can offend another person, "I'm sorry" should become part of his vocabulary. Your child may still believe he's the center of the universe, but his words should reveal a person who cares for other's feelings.

"Please" should be part of every request. Insist that your child say, "May I please have a drink?" If the child is very young, "Drink, please" is okay.

"Thank you" should always acknowledge receipt of an item, favor, or kindness. Children should use it when they are handed a cookie, when they've been given a gift, or when they've visited someone's home.

"I'm sorry" (*not* "I didn't mean to!"): These two words can calm rough tempers, smooth hurt feelings, and give everyone a fresh start. Children should say this when they break something, make another child cry, or forget to do a chore, for example.

Activity

Use the prompt-and-praise method for reinforcing the use of the kind words in this lesson. Prompt your child in private about when to say "please" and "thank you." Praise him in private after he puts your suggestions into action. Also, always say "I'm sorry" to your child when you're wrong about something.

JANUARY 4

Apologizing

Children should be encouraged to make "please" and "thank you" a daily part of their vocabulary. But two other small but powerful words belong there, too: "I'm sorry."

When a child inadvertently bumps into another child in the hall at school, "I'm sorry" is the right thing to say. When she realizes she's taken a second brownie before someone else has had a first, "I'm sorry" helps her appear polite. When your child is late, forgets to bring her uniform, or lets her pet dig in the neighbor's garden, "I'm sorry" shows she can take responsibility for her actions. Little offenses stay little when they are acknowledged and apologized for. When nothing is said, they could ruin a friendship.

At times an apology needs to be written. Your child doesn't need to apologize in writing for small offenses if she's had a chance to apologize verbally, and she shouldn't apologize too much or if she's done nothing wrong.

But if your child breaks something or betrays a friend by revealing a secret, a short note of apology can accompany the replacement of the broken item or a bag of candy for the wounded friend. A note of apology might look like this:

Dear Alicia,
I am so sorry I told Kelsie that you're getting glasses. You told me to keep it a secret and I went and blabbed it anyway. I know you're worried about what it will be like and I only made

matters worse. Please forgive me. You're my best friend and I feel terrible that I hurt your feelings.

Jenna

Activity

Tell your child about a time that you apologized to someone. Explain how you felt and how things worked out.

JANUARY 5

Addressing others properly

Children should address grown-ups by their surnames and proper titles unless the adult instructs them not to do so. "Hello, Mrs. Smith." "Thank you, Dr. Bell." This is a fine mark of distinction for any child, and it far surpasses getting an adult's attention by saying "hey," by calling the adult by a first name, or by simply omitting the name.

Who is an adult and who is a child? According to etiquette, your child is considered an adult when he reaches the age of eighteen. Before that, he should call his neighbor by his surname, address his father's brother as uncle, and generally refrain from using the first name of anyone over eighteen. As a parent, you can reinforce this with your child by referring to other grown-ups by their titles and surnames when you speak with your child.

There are adults who want to be on a first-name basis with children. Although this could be confusing, children seem to be able to sort these things out and usually remember who the first-name people are.

Activity

Ask your child to tell you the proper way to address each of the following:

A married neighbor, Mary Flower	(Mrs. Flower)
A dentist, Sam Tooth	(Dr. Tooth)
An uncle, Bill Green	(Uncle Bill)

10

An unmarried teacher, Sue Book   (Miss Book)
A grandmother, Emma Goodheart   (Grandma Goodheart)
A neighbor, Ken Wall   (Mr. Wall)

JANUARY 6

Bow, kiss, or shake hands?

If you find an etiquette book that prescribes a curtsy for little girls and a bow for little boys, you can bet its pages are beginning to yellow. There was a time when these practices were mandatory for the well-mannered child, but today they've been replaced by a handshake or a nod and a smile.

Upon meeting an adult, your child may offer his right hand for a handshake. The hand should be empty, clean, and dry (a quick brush on the clothes makes sure).

Encourage your child to shake firmly but not to crush fingers or squeeze hands too hard. And keep the handshake brief—two pumps will do the trick! Your child shows tremendous social confidence when she doesn't hesitate to offer her hand.

If she's just too shy to reach out, a slight nod of the head, a smile, and eye contact is very gracious, too. This is today's version of the bow.

Sometimes, however, an old-fashioned bow is truly appropriate. You can help your child be prepared for that rare occasion, such as after your child's performance at a music or dance recital. A boy bows by bending slightly at the waist, hands by his sides; a girl tilts her head forward slightly while also slightly inclining her body, hands also by her sides. A curtsy is cute only for girls under the age of four.

As for kissing, a few children will kiss some people automatically, such as attentive grandparents. However, children shouldn't be prompted against their will to kiss people for whom they don't naturally feel affection.

_____ **TIP** _____

If your child picks up only one thing from this lesson, it should be *eye contact*. This is the most significant way to

acknowledge the presence of another person. In fact, if your child does shake hands or bows but neglects to look at the person, he really hasn't made a connection.

Activity

Practice shaking hands with your child, prompting her not to grab your fingers or hold her hand limp. Clasp your hands firmly, with the web between her thumb and index finger meeting yours. Encourage her to look at your face. You can make the practice more fun by using her teddy bear—ask her to shake the bear's hand and say, "Hello, Mr. Bear." Then respond on behalf of Mr. Bear by saying, "Hello, Mrs. Peacock."

JANUARY 7

Respect for the feelings of others

There's a difference between a child who offends someone else and feels remorse when he realizes it, and a child who offends others and doesn't care. The first has empathy for others.

Learning empathy takes a while because it covers a host of situations, but it's a fundamental part of good manners. When a child laughs at another child and then realizes that laughing hurt the other's feelings, he should apologize. If he borrows something from a friend and breaks it, help him replace it. In effect, he'll begin to feel some of the discomfort or inconvenience that he's caused another person. And he'll try not to make the same mistake again with someone else.

You can help your child be sensitive to the feelings of others by demonstrating sensitivity to his feelings. Do this by listening when he speaks to you, speaking to him in a kind tone of voice, and leaving some room for childish imperfections. No one is perfect, not even adults, and you shouldn't be too hard on your child when he isn't. When your child feels accepted, he'll know how to show acceptance to others.

You can also remind him about the feelings of others if you see him offending someone. Don't speak to him as though his offense were intentional, but give him the benefit of the doubt. You might say something like "I know you didn't mean to hurt Carly's feelings, but I think she's sensitive about her freckles." Try comparing it to something your child understands. "Remember how self-conscious you felt before you got braces on your teeth? That's how Carly feels."

You can also tell your child about times when someone has been empathetic to you. "I was all by myself at your sister's soccer game today, and Mrs. Bell asked me to sit with her and her friends. She must have sensed how lonely I felt."

JANUARY 8
Accept compliments

It's nice to receive a compliment. The best response on your child's part is to smile and thank the other person. There is no need to contradict kind words—they should be taken as sincere. Your child shouldn't point out, for example, that the only reason her sports team did so well was that the opposing team wasn't very good. If your child argues that she really doesn't deserve the compliment, the other person will probably feel uncomfortable, so remind her of that. Encourage your child to feel free to add a word of praise of her own when someone has complimented her. A child who accepts compliments freely and gives them as well shows she accepts herself and likes other people. Make sure that you as a parent set the right example.

Activity
Read these conversations with your child and discuss why only two of them reveal good manners.

CONVERSATION #1
Heather: "I thought you played your song beautifully at the piano recital."

Jamie: "It went terribly. I was so nervous and I forgot the third stanza and then I ended up doing the second ending first. It was really too hard. I should never have tried to play it."

Heather: "Well, I didn't hear any mistakes. I thought it sounded really good. I wish I could play like that."
Jamie: "I don't know why I ever agreed to take piano lessons."

CONVERSATION #2
Kristie: "I like your new haircut. It looks great on you."
Carrie: "Thanks. This shorter cut is easier to take care of. I was thinking how nice you look, too. Red is a great color for you."

CONVERSATION #3
Kelsie: I like your shirt.
Brittany: I don't. It's so old and out of style. My sister used to wear it.

CONVERSATION #4
John: "I thought you did a great job in the school play. You had great expression, and you were able to project your voice so the entire audience could easily hear."
Tim: "Thanks so much for saying so. You're very kind. It was my first time on stage, but I loved doing it. And thank you for coming to see the play. The audience was really responsive, which made our job a lot easier."

JANUARY 9

Give sincere compliments

Giving compliments can be tricky, so when your children are very young, it's better to encourage them to hold back their comments about the personal qualities or actions of others. The parent who encourages children to tell Grandma what they think about her Christmas dinner is as likely to hear "These brussels sprouts make me want to throw up" as "You make the yummiest homemade candy."

As your child gets older, encourage him to say the nice things he's thinking about his friends. The simple rule to follow is: Be sincere and truthful.

It may help to tell your child to focus on something specific. For example, if your child is admiring a friend's sweater, she should say, "I think that sweater looks really nice on you." She shouldn't say, "You always look gorgeous"—it won't ring true. And she shouldn't ask where the friend bought the sweater.

Compliments and words of appreciation sound sincere if they start with *I* and acknowledge specific actions: "I loved the story you wrote. It made me laugh." Gushing statements that start with *you* sound more like flattery ("You are so talented" or "You're the best writer in the class"). People like to hear specific good things about themselves, not sweeping positive statements that they know aren't true all the time.

Children should also be aware of who may overhear a compliment. If a friend was just chosen for the cheerleading team and another friend who tried out unsuccessfully is standing nearby, reserve congratulations for another time. At the very least, keep the congratulations short, so the other friend doesn't feel self-conscious about her disappointment.

Encourage your child to begin using compliments by addressing their peers. There's no need to direct personal compliments to adults unless the person has been kind to the child. Saying to an adult, "I thought the party you planned for all of us was a lot of fun" is okay, but "You look like you've lost weight" isn't good.

A compliment is a verbal hug. Although there are potential pitfalls in giving compliments, with practice children can learn to give them gracefully and truthfully.

Activity

A good place to start on this one is at home. Play a game called Who Gets the Compliment? One person comes up with a compliment and states it—for example, "I was so impressed by how neatly you wrote the report" or "When you hang your coat in the closet, the family benefits because the house stays neat." The rest of the family tries to guess whom the compliment is intended for. The one who guesses correctly comes up with the next compliment.

Be on time

Our time is limited. We can't stretch the length of a day, and we can't make time slow down. This makes it very important to use well the time we have been given. But it's also important that your child doesn't steal the time that belongs to others. Being late does just that—it steals from another person, something very precious that can never be replaced.

Being late can be a matter of poor planning: You didn't start getting ready early enough, or you didn't give yourself enough time when you left the house. But you can also be late because you don't care about being on time. If that's the case, you've decided you don't care whether you're rude. Others might not tell you right away how much your lateness bothers them, but they'll soon stop making plans with you. Here's how to get your child into the habit of being prompt.

1. Give your child *more* time than you think he'll need to get ready. If you usually give him a half hour, start getting ready an hour earlier than you need to leave the house.
2. Help her organize her things so that she has what she needs to get ready. Have your child put her shoes in the same place so she isn't running around the house trying to remember where she kicked them off the last time.
3. Get ready the night before: Have your child put his books in his backpack the night before school. Make sure all clothes are laid out the night before.
4. Some youngsters need help to get organized. Have your child list on a piece of paper all the things that need to be done to get ready to go somewhere. Give each item a length of time, and then add up how many minutes need to be allowed.
5. Of course, everyone is late sometimes. If your child is going to be more than fifteen minutes late, have him call and explain.

Respecting others

No one likes to be poked or hit, either because someone wants to get their attention or because someone's upset with them.

Siblings need to develop habits of respect for their family members. Encourage your child not to jab your arm with her index finger when she wants to get your attention. Saying "excuse me" works much better. And an older sister shouldn't whack her little sister's head, nor should her brother jerk her arm, when she does something that provokes them. These gestures humiliate. It's better for the older child to talk about the annoying behavior either with you or with her sibling than to deal with it physically.

Using words to solve problems instead of hitting, pushing, or slapping is an essential component of self-control.

Opening doors

Your son should let a girl or woman go through an open door ahead of him. If the door is closed, he should pull it open, then hold it while a girl or woman goes through. He should be careful not to pass in front of the girl in order to get to the door. If the door is heavy and opens inward, he may push it open and go through first, holding it for the person behind him.

When elevator doors open, a girl enters before a boy and exits the elevator before him. The boy may also push the buttons to indicate floors. If the elevator is packed with people, the person closest to the door leaves first, boy or girl.

A boy may enter a revolving door first to get it started. A girl enters first if it's already moving.

Boys might be confused about whether or not girls want to have doors held for them at a time when equality is emphasized. Assure your son that socially it is the right thing to do. And remind your daughter that if she is miffed when someone shows her this consideration, she is the one who is being rude. On the other hand, girls should hold doors, too, particularly when they see someone with arms full of packages, pushing a stroller, or alone in a wheelchair.

In the end, holding the door for someone else—no matter what gender—is simply basic good manners.

JANUARY 13

Anticipating the needs of others

Most adults make a daily habit of anticipating the needs of others, whether it be the demands of a boss, customer requests, or the needs of a child or a friend. Many children, however, find that anticipating the needs of others is a trait that takes time to acquire. You may see this kindness emerge in your children only in the teen years.

When your child can anticipate, he'll be able to recognize the needs that will arise in a certain situation and will know how he can meet them.

Your child can anticipate the needs of others by:

- Opening a door for others, stepping aside, and holding the door.
- Offering to help carry bags when a parent returns from the grocery store.
- Bringing extra chairs into the room when Grandpa and Grandma visit.
- Offering beverages to a visiting friend.
- Offering help to someone with a disability.
- Offering a seat on a bus or train to an elderly woman or a woman with small children.

JANUARY 14

Borrowing

A leading national psychologist has said that the greatest cause of sibling rivalry is not showing proper respect for the possessions of others—something to which any parent of more than one child would attest. Junior borrows Missy's markers and doesn't return them. Missy goes into Junior's room without permission. Before long Junior simply looks at Missy and there is an explosion. How can this bone of contention be buried?

Start by establishing some rules for the borrowers. Here are a few that might help save your children some squabbles:

- *Never borrow without asking permission*. That applies to even the smallest thing—such as a roll of tape. The important thing is that Junior places value on his tape, and Missy needs to recognize that.
- *Return the item in a reasonable amount of time*. The idea of what constitutes "reasonable" varies. The library says two to four weeks, but the video store says two to five days. Your child should ask her brother when he expects to get his CD back or when her sister wants the sweater returned.
- *Allow the borrowee to hand over the item*. Missy might not mind if little sis uses her nail polish, but she probably doesn't want her going through her cosmetics to find it.
- *Get permission a second time*. Just because Missy borrowed the CD once doesn't mean she's now entitled to it anytime she chooses.
- *Replace something that was used up*. Or replace the used item with something similar. If your child borrowed a cassette player and depleted the batteries, she should replace them. If she mooched her sibling's Halloween candy, she should reciprocate with some of her own. If she borrowed a dollar at the movie theater, she should pay it back or treat the lender to a movie.

Activity

Ask your child to do an inventory of what she has in her possession that has been borrowed from someone else. Is it in returnable condition? If not, what should be done? Did she agree to return the item at a certain time?

JANUARY 15

Breaking items

Ask your child if he has ever broken something at a friend's house and then hidden it, and you'll probably get a knowing smile. It happens to everyone at one time or another. Something is broken or spilled, or someone gets hurt in the middle of innocent play. A child's first response may be to deny it, hide it, or run away.

Most accidents aren't that serious, and your child's best response is to go ahead and fess up right away. If he's visiting at a friend's house, it may be easier for him to tell his friend first; then the two of them can tell his friend's parents together. Let your child know the importance of saying he's sorry for what happened. A sincere apology diminishes the natural negative reaction elicited by the accident.

Some adults set the wrong example by apologizing too much. Overapologizing demands extra smoothing of the feathers, draws unnecessary attention to oneself, and looks like a ploy for attention. A simple apology and offer to help solve the problem is the best approach.

Does your child have an obligation to replace what was broken? If it's possible, he should try.

JANUARY 16

When you don't know what to do

No one is expected to know everything, especially a child. If your child finds herself in a situation where she feels clueless, she can:

- *Look around.* Take a minute and see how someone else is sweetening their iced tea or using the gauze-covered lemon on the side of their entree.
- *Do a little research.* If she's attending a bat mitzvah, do some reading on the meaning of the ceremony and what to expect when she's there. Talk to others who are familiar with Jewish traditions.

- *Ask someone.* There's nothing wrong with saying, "This appetizer looks delicious, but I don't have a clue what it is. Can you help me out?"

Remind your child that after a faux pas (literally, "a false step"—an etiquette mistake), she should remember the lesson, but there's no need to keep punishing herself. Apologize once and then drop it.

Family Time

~

Encourage your children to consider how their actions affect others at home. Learning to treat family members with respect is a good goal. As a parent, be sure to talk about and model courteous behavior yourself. Children are excellent imitators and they'll follow your lead, but it'll require consistency and selflessness on your part and theirs! Your reward will be a happy, nurturing environment at home, and your child's good manners with family will translate into good manners elsewhere.

JANUARY 17

When Mom and Dad come home

Your child can show consideration for you by greeting you with courtesy when you arrive home from a trip or even just a day at work. Everyone is sensitive to how they're greeted upon entering the house. Children don't want to be nagged, criticized, or given chores the minute they come through the door from school. This is buffer time—time to relax and make the transition. They want the courtesy of a cheerful greeting and your calm interest in the events of their day.

In the same way, they should understand that you hope for courteous treatment when you come through the door. Tell your child that to a parent, courteous treatment means:

- Greeting you with a pleasant hello: "Hi, Mom. How was your day?"
- Holding the bad news until you've had some time to relax.
- Not begging for gifts if you've been on a trip.
- Accommodating some of your likes and dislikes. For example, you shouldn't have to look for sections of the newspaper or find that your mail has been opened or scattered.

JANUARY 18

How are we related?

Interest in who is related to whom is an adult preoccupation for the most part; children don't seem to have the same fondness for figuring it out. That may be because you have to reach adulthood to understand how important good relationships with relatives can be. Here are some definitions that your child should know to identify his family:

Aunts and uncles—the brothers and sisters of your parents
Grandparents—the parents of your parents
Great-grandparents—the grandparents of your parents
Cousins—the children of your aunts and uncles
Second cousins—the children of your parents' cousins
Cousin once removed—the child of your cousin
Second cousin once removed—the child of your second cousin
Stepbrother (stepsister)—the child your stepfather or stepmother had before marrying your parent. You and your stepbrother or stepsister do not share a birth parent.
Half brother (half sister)—a child of your parent and stepparent

Activity

Help your child visualize how generations are related. Get a genealogy tree and fill in the names of the relatives you know off the top of your head. If your child finds it interesting, do some more research together.

JANUARY 19

Stepparent dos and don'ts

Children can show a stepparent respect in some practical ways. Treating a stepparent courteously doesn't mean your child loves his own parents any less. The way people treat each other at home sets a pattern for how they will relate to people outside their home as well. It also affects whether or not your home is a nice place for others to visit. Some things your child can do:

- Acknowledge the stepparent's presence. That makes the atmosphere much nicer than when your child acts as though the person doesn't exist.
- Call the stepparent by the name he or she chooses. "Mom" or "Dad" probably won't feel right—a child can ask the stepparent if he prefers a first name or a nickname.
- Celebrate birthdays and other accomplishments of the stepparent. It's also very generous to acknowledge Mother's Day and Father's Day.
- Share uncomfortable feelings. It'll help other family members realize they're not responsible for your child's bad temper.
- Avoid comparing the two families and making the stepparent look bad in comparison.

JANUARY 20

Stepsibling dos and don'ts

Blending families is very difficult for children, and if there ever is a time that requires courtesy, compassion, and communication, this is it. The best way for your child to get along with stepsiblings is to put the Golden Rule into practice—he should think about how he would like to be treated and try to treat his stepsiblings in the same way. He'll find the respect he is giving others will be returned to him. Getting along is possible when everyone in the family makes a personal commitment to family harmony. It won't be easy, but compromise and a great deal of give-and-take will help.

Your child should:

- Try to accept the fact that the family has changed.
- Communicate with her stepsiblings, letting them know what is going on in her life and asking about theirs.
- Express her preferences and be willing to hear theirs. Talk about family habits and how you can compromise on bedtime, bathroom, and television schedules.
- Remember that she is a person of value, with special talents.
- Go overboard in showing the same courtesy all siblings should show to one another—knocking on a bedroom door, getting permission before entering, borrowing only with permission, speaking with a kind tone of voice.

Your child should *not:*

- Lock herself in her room, locking stepsiblings out.
- Act as though their friends don't exist.
- Act as though the stepsiblings don't exist.

JANUARY 21

When your child has a baby-sitter

Most parents of young children feel a need to have several baby-sitters lined up whom they can rely on when they need to go out. The best way to cultivate a good relationship with a sitter is to pay her a good rate, give her clear instructions about your expectations for the children while you're gone, and help your children develop a cooperative attitude toward the sitter.

25

It's a good idea to speak to your child about how you expect them to behave when you're gone, and reward them for a good report from the sitter. Let your child know that:

- The same household rules apply whether you're home or not: They don't eat in the TV room, play in Mom's office, jump on the furniture, or stay up past 9 P.M.
- Family information is private. Junior shouldn't tell the baby-sitter that Missy is being punished for breaking a tape player or that Dad can't quit smoking.
- Baby-sitters should be treated with respect. Children should help out by putting toys away, letting the sitter have time with other siblings, showing where things are, speaking kindly to her, and following directions.

Activity

Your baby-sitter might appreciate a list of your rules of the house. This helps her know what is acceptable to you and what isn't. Go over the list with your child.

JANUARY 22

When friends are more interested in siblings

As your kids become teens, a new challenge can emerge when friends come to visit. Your child's friend may want to come to your house *because* she hopes to see your child's older brother. Or she may think one of his friends is pretty special and ask your daughter to have your son invite him over while she's at your house.

That isn't good manners on the friend's part, but how can you help your child solve the problem? One family eased the pressure on their kids by establishing a household rule: When their daughter invites a friend to sleep over, their son does not. The children simply told their friends the rule and were happy not to have to divide their attention between their friends and their siblings. Your child might also want to invite a friend over when siblings are away.

Teen siblings shouldn't miss the opportunity occasionally to have a group of their friends over and let them mix. It can be fun for everyone.

When friends don't want to be with siblings

When your child invites a friend over, she's probably hoping to have some uninterrupted time with the friend. Siblings don't always respect that desire. A little sister may tag along and ask to be included in the activities.

Not only does your child have the right to some private time with her friend, but she's courteous if she tries to make the visit fun for her friend as well. Her friend probably doesn't want to entertain little siblings any more than your older child does.

To keep a younger sibling happy, invite a friend at the same time for her or make sure she has an activity that occupies her attention. Monopolizing her sibling's special time with a friend is as disrespectful as borrowing one of her possessions without asking. Help her respect boundaries for family members. This eases tensions between siblings.

_____ TIP _____

Every now and then, encourage a big sister to ask her little sister to join in an activity with just the two of them. Maybe she'll take her along to the mall or play a game with her. That lets the little one know how much her big sister likes her.

JANUARY 24

Frightening others

Ghost stories designed to be told around the campfire in the middle of the night somehow make their way down through the generations. The stories raise goose bumps on the skin but often have surprise endings that aren't scary at all.

Children love to tell stories like these when they feel safe. The stories are frightening, but it's okay to tell them if there aren't children in the group who find the stories truly horrifying. Laughing or screaming at the end relieves the tension.

Storytelling is an entertaining pastime, but there are other ways of scaring each other that kids should avoid. In the movies, these are called "jump scenes." This is when something completely unexpected and frightening happens. At home it could be when a big brother waits under the basement steps, knowing his younger sister will be coming down to play. As she passes him, he jumps out with a roar, scaring her.

While creating a jump scene seems humorous to the big brother, it can be profoundly disturbing to the younger sister. She may never be comfortable walking down the basement steps again.

Frightening another person is a sure way to get a reaction, but it certainly isn't good manners. Remind your child to be sure that everyone is okay if ghost stories are told, and urge him never to try to truly frighten someone.

JANUARY 25

Slamming doors

Slamming doors may be intentional or simply careless. In a fit of anger, and being unwilling to address a situation with words, your child may retreat and slam a door behind her.

Teach your child that slamming doors isn't an acceptable way to settle conflicts. It's okay to retreat from an upsetting situation (and hope to talk about it later when tempers have cooled), but not with the slamming of a door. The sound is jarring, and it's too aggressive, like shouting or swearing. Simply put, it shouldn't be allowed.

Sometimes kids slam doors because they just don't think about how loud it sounds to others. Show your child how to close a door gently, and let her know that it will help your home to be a more peaceful place.

JANUARY 26

Television

If someone has been invited to visit, turn off the television when they arrive. Guests should not have to compete with the TV for your child's attention. Even if your child isn't watching the program, the background noise of television can be distracting. If yours is a home where the television is on most of the time, be aware that many other people prefer a quiet background, especially during a meal.

When a visitor comes unannounced during your child's favorite program, he doesn't need to turn off the show. Encourage him to ask the friend to join him for the remainder of the program, or he might take a minute and put a tape in so that he can record the show to watch after the visitor leaves.

If your child is in the middle of a favorite program when someone comes to visit you, he should say hello and then return to the program if you are visiting in another room. He should lower the volume so that only he can hear it.

Some occasions are planned around a television program—the Super Bowl, a favorite movie rerun, or the Olympics, for example. When this is the case, everyone in the room should focus on the program. Remind your child not to take the best chair, but to make sure all of the guests are comfortable. Some may need pillows for the floor, and everyone should have a good view of the TV.

If your child isn't a sports fan, he shouldn't expect to play in the television room when everyone else wants to watch a basketball game. When watching a movie on television or a video, he should remember some of the same limitations of the movie theater—no talking, asking questions, or telling what happens next.

Activity

Suggest that your child and his friends videotape their own "television show." Provide them with costumes, props, and a video camera and let them come up with the script. When it's finished, watch it together and let your child's friends have the best seats.

JANUARY 27

The family computer

In some homes, each family member has a separate system, but in most cases sharing a family computer is still the practice. Family members may need to juggle computer time and wait in line to do a school project.

Your child can help keep tempers in the house from flaring by remembering that when he gets up from the computer, someone else will sit down. He should leave the desk cleaner than he found it and get rid of empty soda cans, chip bags, and candy wrappers. No one wants to have to take out the garbage before starting to type. In fact, *kids shouldn't eat or drink at all* at the computer. No one wants to type on frosting-covered keys, and the minute a drink is spilled on the keyboard, trouble starts.

Children should respect the privacy of others. If she's not allowed to go into a sibling's room, why would it be okay to snoop in her brother's computer files?

Keep the computer your children use in the family room. This will make it more difficult for them to look at sites you don't approve of, or to escape for long periods of time without interacting with other family members.

JANUARY 28

Cards and board games

Kids play cards on long bus rides and board games on the family room floor with their friends. Your child will be a welcome participant in these games if he plays by the rules. (If he doesn't know them, he should ask.) When he's playing an old game with a new group of kids, it's good to check if they play by the rules he knows. Sometimes people change the rules, and he won't want to insist that everyone must play his way. Some good-natured discussion about the merits of one rule over another is fine, of course.

Games are more fun when everyone plays with the same level of seriousness. Tell your child not to crack jokes and chat if the rest of the players want to keep track of cards in their heads. On the other hand, if everyone else is talking, knitting his brows and playing competitively doesn't endear your child to anyone.

Sometimes there are too many players. The child who is the host volunteers to sit out the first game.

It's also good for your child to admit if he's never played the game before. That's a good time to watch—until he's sure he can play without disrupting the game or annoying his teammates. Above all, he should be a good sport.

JANUARY 29

Books

How unpleasant it is to borrow a book from the library only to find its pages marred by childish scribbles. Children should learn from their earliest years that books are not to be treated as toys or coloring books.

When you first expose your child to books, teach her that they should be handled carefully. If she tosses a book to the floor, pick it up and gently tell her: "We don't treat books that way." Don't allow her to write in books, bend or tear out the pages, or handle them with sticky fingers. Buy your child her own bookplates for her name and the date it was acquired.

If you want to write a message in a book you're giving as a gift, write on the flyleaf. The title page is reserved for the author's autograph.

Some adults would never make a note in a book, while others enjoy comments from previous readings. Some like bookmarks, while others just turn down a page corner to mark the place. Adults may feel entitled to some idiosyncrasies since they can buy and replace their own books. Children don't have that luxury; being impressionable, they may think that handling books the way their parents do is acceptable. Encourage your child always to respect the value of a book, especially when it belongs to someone else.

Activity

Keep a basket in the family room for books that have been borrowed from friends or from the library. This will make it easier to keep track of books that don't belong to you.

Allowance

Giving your child an allowance can be a useful tool in helping him learn how to handle money responsibly. It can also make it possible for him to enjoy his social obligations.

An allowance should be viewed as an important learning experience rather than as pay for work. A well-mannered child will do chores without the expectation of being paid and without complaining, and will make an effort to contribute to the orderliness of the household.

When you give your child a regular amount of money, however modest, he should wait until he has enough money to pay for something he really wants. He learns the very grown-up principle of deferred gratification, and he also learns that it's often easier to spend money he doesn't have than money he has. How much easier it is to ask Mom to buy something than to finally decide to purchase it with allowance money he has saved.

Allowances also help children to give charitably. Educate your child about the benefit of giving to charity by picking an organization that you and your child feel is a worthy cause.

Activity

Get your child a small ledger book and help him keep track of how he spends his allowance. Help him set it up and then let him keep the records himself. You may remind him about the importance of keeping records, but allow him privacy with his ledger.

When your child is home alone

Most children at about age ten or eleven enjoy the feeling of independence that staying home alone gives them. They shouldn't be left by themselves for long periods, but an hour isn't too long if they know when you'll be home. Discuss guidelines together so that your child will feel safe and will know what you expect of him while you're gone. (Also, check your local laws. In some areas it is against the law to leave a child under age eleven home alone; this age varies.) Here are a few areas to discuss with your child:

1. Ask your child to keep the doors locked.
2. If someone rings the doorbell, he shouldn't answer it unless he can see that it's someone he knows. He shouldn't let a stranger into the house, even if the person says he is a repairman.
3. He should leave the house only if you've given him permission to do so.
4. Give him a list of phone numbers to call if he feels scared.
5. Give him suggestions for activities while you're gone.

Little things around the house

The mayor of New York City has been trying to develop a nicer New York. He wants the people of New York to take care of little things. Taxicab drivers were given a supply of air fresheners. People were urged to clean up glass on the streets. The mayor believed that a lot of little things add up to something much bigger—he's hoping people will want to visit his city if it's a nice place.

Little things around the house add up, too. Here's a list of little things to share with your child that will add up to being a big help to the whole family:

- Carry your plate from the table to the dishwasher.
- Make your bed when you crawl out in the morning.
- Hang up the towels right away.
- Put the newspaper pages back in order when you've finished looking at it.
- Put a new toilet paper roll on the holder and throw away the cardboard from the old roll.
- Put dirty clothing in a hamper.
- Hang your coat up as soon as you come inside.
- Throw away candy and snack wrappers.
- Put your shoes in a neat row with others just inside the door.
- Change a lightbulb that has burned out.
- Express appreciation for dinner or being picked up after a sports event.
- Feed and exercise the family's pet.
- Put your toothbrush in the proper container when you're finished.
- Throw away empty containers of food rather than putting them back on the shelf or in the fridge.
- Get the mail or bring in the paper.
- Pick up toys and put them away.
- Put the TV remote or portable phone back where it belongs.
- Throw the empty soda can in the recycling bin.
- Take toys, books, or food wrappers from the car when you get out.
- Flush the toilet.

Activity

To make white socks easier to sort, have your child place a smiley face inside the top of each pair of socks. Give each person in the family his own color for the smileys.

May I have your attention, please?

When your child is with others, he should focus on them and not operate in another world. This is true at the table, in conversation, when traveling with others, in church, or at a program. If your child needs solitude, it is better that he spend a quiet day at home rather than join the group at the beach only to avoid conversation, wander off on his own, or bury his head in a book all day.

It's nice to focus on another person. While some children just like to be alone, others like to be with people but are easily distracted. Like a butterfly flitting from one flower to another, they start a conversation but begin talking to someone else while the first person is in midsentence. Or their attention just wanders. It's frustrating for others to be describing something to this kind of child only to finish and listen to him make a completely unrelated remark.

It's also nice to focus on the group. The parent who reads the newspaper or watches television at the table sets a discourteous example for the children. Adults have no obligation to make every moment at home revolve around the wishes of children, but mealtime should be a group affair. Each person should be willing to give his attention to the others at the table.

It's respectful to focus on the event. Your child might think that the priest won't see him reading a book during the Sunday lesson. One way for your child to evaluate whether or not his behavior is appropriate is to ask himself, "What if everyone did what I am doing?" Of course, it would be extremely insulting to the minister if everyone read the latest novel during the service. Whether or not the speaker notices your child's lack of interest, those sitting nearby won't be able to ignore it.

Your child shouldn't be preoccupied with projects at a public event. Let your child know that when she's attending the symphony, it isn't the time to make a beaded necklace or add stitches to a sampler.

Activity

Play a game called High-Low at dinner. Each person gets to tell the best and worst things that happened to him that day. Family members who aren't talking should give their undivided attention to the one who's talking about his day.

FEBRUARY 3

Your child's bedroom

There is something about seeing a royal mess in a child's bedroom that can nearly send a parent over the edge. Even though the rest of the house is in order, looking in on a room that appears to have been hit by a tropical storm can make you feel as though order elsewhere is merely an illusion!

Parents often think how embarrassing it would be if a friend came to visit and saw the mess. But it's possible to raise a well-mannered child whose room almost always looks cluttered and messy.

Start by relaxing about the subject. Remember some elementary psychology: Nagging is a big turnoff. Some children are able to organize their possessions and keep things neat, and others aren't. Some get better at it over time, while others seem to get messier.

A messy room isn't a sign of what your child will be like as an adult. When your child grows up, she'll probably organize her home much the way you organize yours.

Periodically work alongside your child to put her room in order. She wasn't born knowing how to do it, and following your lead may give her the tips she needs. Plus it's always easier to do a job when someone else helps. Help her develop a plan— all clothing on hangers or in designated drawers, trash in the wastebasket, books on a shelf, used tumblers in the dishwasher, A+ homework papers in a file, and special artwork framed for the wall.

Do what you can to encourage neatness, and then relax. Until your child develops the same craving for order that you have, walk by her room, take a deep breath, and close the door.

Getting Along with Other Kids

~

Friendships make the world go round, and manners make friendships possible. Teach your toddler to treat playmates kindly, help your high-school-age child be a loyal friend, and pay special attention to friendship at every stage in between. Encourage your child to look for ways to get along with others. A variety of friendships will enrich your child's life and help him feel part of his neighborhood and community.

FEBRUARY 4

Friendship

Friends listen, do things with us, show us things about ourselves, introduce us to new experiences, make us laugh, and are there when we just want to hang out with someone. But they also let us down sometimes. You do your child a kindness by helping him develop the good manners that contribute to good friendships.

Your child needs to take responsibility in a friendship. Remind your child to think about his friendships and take the lead sometimes. He shouldn't always expect the other person to call first, suggest an activity, share a secret, or write him a note. If this doesn't come naturally for your child, help him to make a conscious effort. A one-sided friendship lasts about as long as a potted plant that doesn't get water. Friendships need attention in order to grow.

Your child can take responsibility by inviting the friend to come to your house, smiling and waving when he gets off the bus, remembering his birthday, saving a seat at the lunch table, introducing him to another friend, making him a gift, or thinking of news to tell him.

Sometimes the other child will take too much responsibility. Not only shouldn't your child expect a friend to take the initiative all the time, he shouldn't allow it. It isn't friendship, and it isn't healthy, if another child takes over your child's life. If your child is constantly responding to the demands, bossiness, and manipulation of another child, there are courteous ways for your child to set some boundaries.

Taking responsibility means learning to strike a balance between your child's preferences and those of his friend. It isn't discourteous for your child to express his preferences.

Activity

I language sounds a lot less threatening than *you* language. Help your child understand the difference between the two and practice talking about different topics in both.

Good: "I don't mind sharing clothing sometimes. Let's do it once a week and keep the outfit for three days."
Bad: "You borrow my clothing too often and keep it forever."

Good: "I like to spend time with you, and I try to spend time with other friends as well. I hope you'll understand if I can't join you at the pool every day."
Bad: "You expect way too much. You aren't the only friend I have, but you act as though I should only do things with you."

Best friends

If your child has a best friend, she has a friendship to be treasured. Maybe the friendship developed over time, or maybe something clicked the first time the two children met. Whichever the case, best friends can't be made or broken quickly.

Your child may take her time in developing such a friendship so that she can really know the person. Some best friends are like two peas in a pod—they look and act alike. Others are as different as night and day—one is dark-haired with brown eyes and is thoughtful and steady, while the other has red hair and blue eyes and is bubbly and outgoing. Even the closest of friends shouldn't forget that there are other people in the world. Sharing secrets and telling jokes that they alone understand is a fine thing when they have a sleep-over at one child's house. But if they're with a group, they should look for ways to include others.

Remind your child that doing something with another friend doesn't mean they aren't best friends anymore; rather, it shows that they are confident enough to give each other freedom. Becoming possessive of each other's time or jealous when one of them makes plans with another friend can kill a friendship.

Is it okay for your child to have a best friend? Of course. They might be best friends for one year or for many years. But it is also okay if your child doesn't have a best friend—maybe that lies down the road somewhere. Help your child remember that friendships can be nurtured but should never be forced.

When it becomes necessary to end a friendship, it's better to go slowly—don't dump a best friend quickly. It's okay to recognize that friends can drift apart, but it's always better if both friends feel the same way.

Activity

For a wonderful experience of true friendship, rent the video *Anne of Green Gables* or give your daughter the Betsy-Tacy books to read. Or choose the story of David and Jonathan's friendship in the Old Testament of the Bible (1 Samuel 20). Discuss what makes these friendships special.

Is your child a good friend?

Let your child take the following quiz and think about what it means to be a good friend. It probably isn't difficult for your child to name a few things she wants in a friendship, but sometimes it isn't as easy to know if she's a good friend. Answering these questions might help.

1. Are you happy when something good happens to your friend?
2. Do you listen to your friend talk without changing the subject to something about yourself?
3. Do you give your friend the benefit of the doubt, knowing that everyone has a bad day every now and then?
4. Do you introduce others to your friend?
5. Do you sometimes give up a favorite activity of yours so that you can do what your friend wants to do?
6. Do you write a nice note to your friend every now and then?
7. Do you feel sad when something bad happens to your friend?
8. Do you let your friend know the real you?

The best answer for each one is yes!

Four yeses: Try to put yourself in the other person's shoes a bit more.
Six yeses: You're doing great!
Eight yeses: A perfect best friend!

A loyal friend

Your child's friendships will thrive if she learns to be a loyal friend. Loyalty doesn't mean exclusivity—a child can have a number of friends (in fact, it's good if she does). But she should be reliable with each friend. For example, when she makes plans with someone, she should keep them even if a better invitation comes along.

Your child should give the other person the benefit of the doubt. If her friend buys the same sweater she wanted to get, she shouldn't immediately assume that the other girl did it on purpose. Maybe her friend just saw the sweater and liked it. If your child does discover that her friend rushed to the store to get the sweater before she had a chance to buy it, she'll express her disappointment, but she shouldn't stew over it forever. Loyal friends offer each other their honest feelings and their forgiveness. They know that friendships have ups and downs, so they don't dump each other at the first offense.

Your child can also show her loyalty by being genuinely happy when her friend succeeds. Maybe her friend is the fastest runner in the class or her drawing takes first place at the fine-arts festival. These are reasons for a loyal friend to celebrate, not feel jealous. Help your child understand that different people have different talents. As you help her identify her own gifts and strengths, you'll help develop your child's self-esteem and ultimately her ability to be a good friend.

Bullies

Your child should never let someone else be abusive to him. Treating others with respect doesn't include letting them walk all over him. If someone hits your child, shoves him, pulls his hair, is verbally abusive, or steals or destroys your child's property, he should ask you or another adult to help handle the situation. Not only will he be protecting himself, he'll be doing the bully a favor by giving him a reason to stop his bad behavior.

Explain to your child that acceptance by peers is so important that sometimes kids use the wrong means to try to achieve it. A bully may believe that when everyone is afraid of him, he's achieved a certain status. Or he may have been bullied by others, so he thinks bullying is acceptable behavior. Whatever his reasons, it's wrong to bully, and your child should never put up with it. He may think that by going along with the bully's demands the abuse will stop, but he'll find that he's only inviting more attacks.

That said, remind your child not to taunt or deliberately annoy older children. There's a certain pecking order among kids—on the school bus, for example. If younger children typically sit up front, your child risks raising the ire of an older child if he insists upon sitting near the back. The younger child's time will come for a backseat.

TIP

As a parent, you should get involved if your child is being bullied. But listen to both sides.

FEBRUARY 9

When your child wants a new friend

If friendships begin to feel routine for your child, encourage her to look outside her regular group of acquaintances. Friendship might come from unexpected places if she takes the initiative. Making a new friend can keep your child from having unreasonable expectations of a single person.

Friends don't always have to be the same age. A third-grader hosted high-school students from another state who came to learn about the history of her area. Three girls stayed in her home for a week. The third-grader was a good friend all week—she played games with the girls, laughed with them, listened to them, and just hung out with them. She was very accepting and was truly happy to have them in her home. When they left, they promised to write. A pen pal relationship developed that lasted several years, in spite of the age difference.

One family with young boys adopted a ninety-year-old woman in their church. They invited her to their home occasionally and took her out to lunch on her birthday. Being with the family helped her cope with loneliness. The boys benefited, too. They learned to listen and express interest in another person and discovered what life was like nearly a century ago.

Making new friends takes effort. Your child can explore possibilities in the community—one place to start is any kind of lessons, such as art, swimming, or riding lessons. She can be aware of others who aren't part of a tight group of friends and who may be hoping for a new friend, just as she is. She can keep her eyes open for new friendship when your family is on vacation. Sometimes friendships develop that last for a week and are picked up every year after that if your family returns to the same vacation spot. Tell your child not to be afraid to introduce herself to other children and that it's okay to be friends with older kids, adults, and members of the opposite sex.

FEBRUARY 10

New kid on the block

People who move often cherish friendships from a distance. They learn to use e-mail, write letters, or catch up on the telephone. And they understand that true friendship doesn't happen overnight. But they also turn their focus to their new neighborhood and start over, realizing that people are the same everywhere—they want to have friends.

If your child is new at school, encourage him to be friendly but to relax. If he feels lonely sometimes, that is to be expected. If others don't immediately include him in their circle of friends, it doesn't mean they don't like him—they might be so focused on the friends they've had for a while that they aren't yet aware of what fun it could be to get to know him. Making new friends often takes some time.

Your child appears friendly when he expresses interest in the activities of the children in his new neighborhood. He learns to play soccer if that is the sport everyone enjoys. He doesn't talk endlessly about how much he misses his old neighborhood, where everyone likes to go to the beach on weekends.

Your child shouldn't be pushy in trying to get new friendships started. Encourage him to take natural opportunities to get to know others—such as by inviting them to your house to work on a school project or attending a party at school.

Activity

If your child can write, recommend that she develop a pen pal. Help her think of a person she knows but doesn't see very often. Be sure she has a ready supply of stationery, and suggest that she respond to letters within two weeks. Get her a pretty box in which to keep the letters she receives.

FEBRUARY 11

When your family moves

When your family moves, there will be many details that preoccupy everyone's time. Don't let that get in the way of your child's saying a proper goodbye to friends. Your child may be overwhelmed with feelings of sadness and may feel like having a pity party. But he shouldn't forget that his friends are feeling sad, too.

Encourage him to tell them about the move. It may be too painful to go into detail the first time he breaks the news. Some children, including teenagers, can't talk about things such as this without crying, so it's embarrassing for them to discuss it at length right away. But ignoring the subject doesn't help, either. Even though it's painful, your child should tell each of his close friends as soon as he knows you're moving. They won't appreciate it if they find out this important news from someone else.

When his emotions are under control, he should tell his friends why he's moving, how long it will be until he has to leave, and that he'll miss his friends. They probably have invested a great deal of time in the friendship and truly love your child.

Hearing that he's leaving can make them feel abandoned, hurt, or angry. As much as they realistically know he isn't leaving because he doesn't like them, they may still feel that way. While your child feels that he's the only one who will experience a change, that isn't true—his friends will experience loss, too.

Activity

If you know your new address, make copies of it or help your child print it out on the computer to give to each of his friends.

FEBRUARY 12

When a friend moves

Children have little to say about whether their family will make a move, but this doesn't mean they're not affected by it. When your child's friend announces she has to move, be sympathetic to your child and give her a chance to talk about how she feels. Encourage her to tell the friend how much she'll be missed. Allow your child to spend time with the friend just as usual until she leaves. Dropping her company because it's too painful to think about leaves bad memories in the minds of both children.

If the children are very close, encourage your child to make a gift or buy something that will remind her friend of your community or school. A collage of snapshots in a picture frame is a nice keepsake, as is a gift that is linked to things the children enjoyed doing together—a new basketball if they played on a team together, or some unique lures if they enjoyed fishing together. Or let your child have a party and make a scrapbook with snapshots brought by friends.

Encourage your child to ask for the friend's new address and help her keep in touch. If a visit the next summer is possible, either at your home or the friend's new home, making plans for it can ease the sadness when your child's friend leaves.

Talk about the fact that even though friends sometimes move away, all of the good times were well worth it.

FEBRUARY 13

Public playgrounds

Going to a playground can be a marvelous training ground for your child. If he stays at home in his backyard, he may never need to share, wait in line, or rub shoulders with someone who looks different. Many communities have pulled together and built elaborate playgrounds for their youngsters. Help your child preserve neighborhood unity by being considerate of others at the playground.

He should take only his fair share of time on the swings, slides, or rides, particularly if others are waiting. If he is waiting, he shouldn't sigh or ask if the other child is almost finished. Nor should he push a child who might be ahead of him in line.

He should assume that everyone who is at the playground has as much right to be there as he does. He shouldn't indicate that he's bothered by another child's presence, and he shouldn't stare at or ask questions about children who are different from him. Let him know you'll be happy to answer his questions but that it shows respect for others if he keeps such questions until he is alone with you.

If your child eats at the playground, he shouldn't take food on the swings or slide. That way things won't get sticky and he won't choke. He should throw every piece of paper away as well as bits of unfinished food.

Activity

Have your child adopt a tree at a park near you. Each time you go to the park, notice how the tree has changed. In the spring look for the first bud; notice the shape of the leaves when they emerge; study the seeds and bark. Look in a book about trees to learn the name of the tree, and suggest that your child give it a nickname as well. Have your child invite a child from the playground to share a snack on a blanket under the tree.

FEBRUARY 14

A good neighbor

Getting to know his neighbors is not only good manners for your child, but also contributes to his safety and sense of well-being. Interacting with neighbors helps your child learn to relate to others, deal with differences, and help out when others are in need. The inevitable broken window and trampled shrub provide opportunities to apologize and make restitution.

Neighborhood picnics and bicycle parades are delightful enrichments for summer days. And the child who's lucky enough to play under the kind and watchful eye of neighbors enjoys an extra amount of security. Help your child understand that good relations in a neighborhood require the efforts of everyone; even the very young can share some of the responsibility.

Activity

Take your child along with you when you deliver cookies to someone new on your street or when you take some food to a shut-in. Your example will show him how to be a good neighbor.

FEBRUARY 15

Neighborly manners

People may disagree about the need to fence in their property, but whether your child sees a white picket fence, a row of evergreens, or nothing at all between his yard and that of his next-door neighbor, he should establish a fence there in his own mind. No matter how generous and welcoming his neighbors may appear, they still want their property and privacy to be respected.

Your neighbors will be happy your child lives on the block if he:

- Asks permission if he crosses their property on a regular basis.
- Occasionally visits uninvited, but keeps a balance between playing in another child's home or yard and inviting that child to play at his home.

- Stays to play for a short period of time and goes home for meals.
- Treats younger children in the neighborhood kindly.
- Looks at or waves to a neighbor who passes by on the road.
- Addresses grown-ups on the street by their title and surname.
- Jumps on his neighbor's trampoline or swims in his pool only when invited, and understands that there are dangers with both.
- Willingly takes care of a neighbor's paper and mail if they are on a trip.
- Is conscientious about caring for a neighbor's pet when the neighbor is away.
- Keeps the outdoor noise level low in the evening and after dark, especially if he has elderly neighbors.
- Doesn't trample his neighbor's landscaping.
- Keeps his pet at home and apologizes if his neighbor has to call about his pet.

Activity

Take a walk on your street and be sure your child knows his neighbors. Tell him their names and something about them. Introduce him to those who are outside.

FEBRUARY 16

Swimming pools

Swimming pools are great summer fun, but your child shouldn't treat her neighbor's pool like community property. Wait for an invitation to swim, and encourage your neighbor to let you know when they want the pool to themselves. Some families put up a flag as a signal to their neighbors that the pool is open to others. Children should swim only when there are adults at home.

Help your child be a good guest by reminding her to take a towel each time she swims and to bring it home again. She should never put a wet towel on wooden furniture because it ruins the surface of the wood. Give her a plastic bag for her wet suit if she will change before coming home. She shouldn't go in her neighbor's house with her swimming suit on.

Your neighbor has a right to establish her own pool rules. Even though they may seem excessive to your child, they must be followed. Families who have swimming pools become keenly aware of the need for safety precautions.

Your child shouldn't expect the neighbor to provide snacks. Make sure she contributes chips and sodas. Always consider the use of a neighbor's pool a privilege. She shouldn't invite friends to swim there. Remind her that it's all too easy to wear out her welcome. Your child should thank the neighbor every time she goes swimming.

Activity

If your child gets to swim regularly at a friend's pool, talk with your child about how your family might reciprocate. Invite the friend to spend a day with your child at the beach or an amusement park.

FEBRUARY 17

Your pets

Someone has said that there is no such thing as a bad dog, just bad dog owners. Owners have primary responsibility for training their pets to have good behavior. Your child should know that a happy pet is often a calm pet. If your dog's needs for nutrition, exercise, and affection are met—and children are great at meeting the needs of pets—he'll be less demanding and much more pleasant to be around.

At the start of each day, your child should greet, hug, and feed her pet. After school, she should make sure the pet gets exercise, and help keep her pet clean. It's just plain bad manners to expect her friends to be nuzzled by a dog that smells terrible because it hasn't been bathed recently.

No one—not even a dog lover—enjoys having a dog jump up. If your child's pet insists on jumping on visitors, it should be removed from the room when visitors arrive.

Prompt your child to be aware of fears that her friends might have. If her friend is afraid of dogs, the dog shouldn't be around when that friend comes to visit. Another person's fears may not seem rational to your child, but they are to be respected. Your child's friend may have been bitten by a dog when she was small and has now transferred that terror to all dogs.

Your child should also be sensitive to her friends' allergies. The courteous thing to ask a friend visiting for the first time is "Are you allergic to any pets?"

Activity

When your family is together, begin a conversation about your own pet and those of your friends. Let everyone tell a story. Include humorous incidents as well as times that pets caused problems. Tell your child how you handled a troublesome encounter with a pet.

FEBRUARY 18

Pets as gifts

Children may think pets make great gifts, but in reality they don't. For example, one mother I know loved pigs and collected them in many forms, from jade to needlepoint and ceramic. But her children took her love of pigs too far when they decided to bestow upon her a live Vietnamese potbellied pig. Three months and a mountain of manure later, the children asked the mother what she wanted for her birthday. "Only to be divested of my Christmas gift!!" she cried. They found the pig a happy home on a farm.

The gift of a pet can be a burden to the one who receives it, but it can also be the wrong thing for the pet. Giving a pet to a child (a chick at Easter or a rabbit) can sometimes mean a life of deprivation or danger to the animal.

FEBRUARY 19

The pets of others

For many of us, pets are considered part of the family. Their physical needs are a priority, they receive excellent health care, they are loved and cuddled, they sometimes sleep with a member of the family, they often travel with the family, and when they die they are sorely missed. Others wouldn't dream of fussing over an animal this way.

No matter what your family's attitude toward pets, your child should know it's never acceptable to be cruel to animals. He should take no pleasure in teasing his friend's pet. He should not urge his friend's pet to break household rules by calling it upstairs or offering it candy. Learning to show kindness toward animals reinforces your child's understanding of the need to show kindness and consideration to those who are weaker and dependent.

Even so, your child doesn't need to feel the same affection his friend feels for the pet. When he visits a friend he may simply greet little Fluffy and go about other activities. If the pet insists upon being the center of attention, your child may acknowledge that he hopes Fluffy isn't offended if he doesn't hold him, but he's never been one of the world's great animal lovers.

If your child is allergic to animals, he should by all means say so and tell his friend if taking a dose of medicine will help or if he needs to stay in a separate room from the pet.

FEBRUARY 20

On the school bus

School buses will probably never be bastions of genteel conversation spoken in hushed tones. But civility can be elevated a bit by a few basic manners. Go over these rules with your child:

- Proceed to the bus quietly. Walk, don't run.
- Say hello to the bus driver and smile.

- Sit in your assigned seat (if you have one).
- Stay in your seat when the bus is moving.
- Keep your hands to yourself.
- Keep your feet and backpack out of the aisle.
- Don't insult others or shout at them.
- Get off at your stop promptly.
- Don't clown around near the bus.
- Walk straight home.

FEBRUARY 21

Interrupting

Interrupting causes frustration and resentment. Your child might interrupt your conversation with another adult with an insistent "excuse me." Although "excuse me" is a polite thing to say, when it's repeated it becomes an interruption. Let him know it's better if he waits quietly for a minute; you'll acknowledge him soon.

Abruptly changing the subject is another way to interrupt. Maybe a friend is discussing something your child finds boring—she's talking about ballet, and your child prefers to talk about sports. It's polite to give the friend a chance to talk about her hobby. The friend will become frustrated if your child is immediately reminded of her own hobbies and switches the subject to herself.

It's also considered to be interrupting if your child is so eager to be part of the conversation that she finishes the other person's sentence or asks questions while her friend is still talking. The other person might not say it, but she'll be thinking, "Let me finish!"

Finally, if your child is conversing with a group, she shouldn't turn to one of the people and start a separate conversation. When part of the group breaks away in this manner, it's distracting to the others. They may want to continue with their topic but can't avoid hearing the other conversation that has begun.

Changing the subject politely

No one is obligated to stick with the same subject until they're bored senseless, but neither should your child change the subject by blurting out, "This is boring. Let's talk about something else."

A good way to switch subjects is by asking a question. It's best for your child to "interrupt" herself to change the subject. A good conversation has a balance of listening and talking. When it's your child's turn to talk, she may close one subject and start another. She might end a discussion about a book with: "The book sounds fascinating. I hope to get a chance to read it this summer. I hope there's time, though. What are you doing over the summer months?" This helps the conversation to change smoothly from books to vacation plans.

Activity

Go around the dinner table, letting each person bring up a topic of conversation with the others joining in. When it's your turn to bring up a new topic, rather than abruptly changing the subject, come up with a closing remark about another person's topic.

Dating turnoffs

In the early teen years, it's hard for most kids not to look wistfully in the mirror and wish they could change some of their physical features. They're sure they'd be more attractive if they had blue eyes instead of brown, had a nose free of freckles, or were tall rather than short. While they can't change these things, there are other things that are under their control. Working on social skills is one example of something that can improve their friendships.

When kids are asked, they'll tell you that poor social skills are dating downers. Here are five of the top turnoffs:

1. Poor conversation skills
2. Being late
3. Using foul language
4. Bad table manners
5. No sense of humor

When a friend loses a loved one

When your child's friend experiences a death in the family, the family's very closest friends go to their home and offer to be of help. They may take food or help make phone calls. Acquaintances offer their sympathy in other ways—visiting at the funeral home, attending the funeral, or sending a letter of condolence, depending on their closeness to the family—but do not visit the family at home.

Don't say too much. Your child may fear he won't know what to say to the bereaved. While children aren't expected to offer condolences, your example can help prepare them for later years. Keep your words sympathetic and brief.

Explain to your child that going to a funeral expresses your concern for those who are grieving. If your child says he didn't know very well the person who died or didn't like her, tell him that you go not for the sake of the one who passed away but for those who have lost a loved one. It would be unbearable for them to go through this time alone, so family and friends gather around to remember the life and the good qualities of the person who died.

When a friend has bad news

What should your child say when a friend has bad news? This can be a difficult situation. How your child might wish he could wave a magic wand and make everything okay! But that isn't possible—there really might not be anything in her power to change the situation. There are many kinds of bad news your child might hear from a friend:

- I got cut from the soccer team.
- My family is moving.
- I broke my leg.
- My grandmother is dying.
- My parents are getting a divorce.

Remind your child that if he hears this news, it isn't the time to give advice; it's a time to be supportive, which could mean just being there and saying nothing at all or saying something simple, such as "I'm sorry about what happened. This must be a hard time for you." It should go without saying that your child should never be glad when a friend has difficulties.

When a friend's parents are getting a divorce

It's hard to imagine more difficult circumstances for a child than when his parents are getting a divorce. As much as his parents may want to provide him some comfort—and there are those who do a heroic job—they can't help but be preoccupied with their own problems at this time.

There are no words that will make a child's pain go away, but if your child has a friend in this situation, it's important for your child just to be there for him. Being understanding will mean a lot.

Children whose parents are getting divorced often feel that it's their fault that their family is breaking up. They remember times they were disobedient or angry with their parents and think that this wouldn't be happening if they had been a perfect child. They sometimes think they could have prevented the divorce, and they may still think there is something they can do to keep their parents together. They feel abandoned, angry, scared, and ashamed. It's a time of great confusion and heartache.

It's also a time when your child can be a true friend. He won't be able to solve his friend's problems, but he'll be able to listen while his friend unloads. Sometimes kids keep their pain to themselves, but that isn't a healthy (or happy) solution. When your child's friend wants to talk, your child shouldn't ask questions about all the details of the parents' problems, but he should be willing to listen. Your child will never want to share with people other than you the details he's heard. To let his friend know he can trust him, your child might say, "You can talk to me anytime about what you're feeling. I won't spread it around to everyone else." Encourage your child to invite his friend to stay involved in normal activities. They might go to the movies or shopping or have a sleep-over. Continuing the normal activities of daily life helps relieve some of the pain.

Introductions

~

Help your children make a positive first impression by teaching them when to introduce themselves and when to make introductions. Encourage them to use these social skills often. This gets new friendships off to a good start and helps develop a sense of confidence. Others will appreciate the thoughtfulness!

FEBRUARY 27

Introduce the more important person first

The job of making an introduction isn't just for grown-ups. Here's how to make it easy for your child.

The notion of "precedence" is a way of figuring out how to show honor and respect. Don't worry about who gets introduced to whom. If you say the name of the more important person first, you'll automatically be handling the introduction properly. The more important person is established this way:

- *An older person takes precedence over a younger person.* Say the name of the older person first: "Grandmother, I'd like you to meet my friend Kathy. Kathy, this is my grandmother, Mrs. Kindheart."

- *A woman takes precedence over a man.* Say the woman's name first: "Mrs. Jones, I'd like you to meet my neighbor, Mr. King. Mr. King, this is my piano teacher, Mrs. Jones."
- *A dignitary (elected official, church leader, etc.) takes precedence.* Say the dignitary's name first: "Mayor Good, may I present to you my sister, Karen Stanley. Karen, please meet Mayor Good."

Activity

Role playing helps kids learn how to make introductions—make it fun! Assign identities: "Preston, you're the president of the United States and Caroline is the queen of England. Please introduce me to the queen." When your child performs the introduction, you can then murmur something like, "It's a pleasure, Your Highness." Make up other identities and have your children practice introductions. Give them extra praise if they come up with a topic of conversation of mutual interest. Find a few props: a paintbrush and easel for the art teacher Mr. Burnt Umber, some colorful fabric and scissors for Grandmother Patchwork. Remind your child to hold props in the left hand so that the right hand is free for a friendly handshake. Compliment your child if she smiles.

FEBRUARY 28

Remembering names

A name is very personal, and children and adults alike want others to know their name and pronounce it correctly. Tell your child she should say the other child's name as soon as it's learned.

Suggest that your child connect the name with something by making a mental note. Maybe the connection will be a rhyme such as "*Rose* has a freckled *nose*," or "*Bill* better not *spill* a drink on that sweater," or "*Jean* is as beautiful as a *queen*."

Try to help your child remember the name the next day. Take a minute to review the rhyme or simply rehearse the new name. This will help your child remember.

Activity

To practice making connections, come up with a rhyming word connected to the name of each person in your family. Also ask your child to recall any new names he has learned over the past week.

MARCH 1

Include names in introductions

It's easy for a child to be so worried about what others think about him that he doesn't remember the new name he has just heard. Tell your child that he should pay attention during the introduction and repeat the person's name. Say, "It's nice to meet you, Jordan." Remind them that if they repeat the person's name, odds are they'll remember it later on.

MARCH 2

Introducing parents with a different last name

When your child introduces you to a friend, it's easy to call you "Mom" or "Dad," but it's proper to say your title and surname. That sounds pretty formal, but it's the best way for a child to give a friend the information she'll need so she won't be embarrassed later. Learning this skill is especially helpful when you and your child have different last names.

If your child's friend is certain of your last name, she'll feel more comfortable later when she calls on the phone or meets you. And you'll save her the embarrassment of discovering down the road that she's been calling you by the wrong last name.

Here's what your child should say: "Mother, I'd like you to meet my friend, Kelly Gold. Kelly, this is my mother, Mrs. Kline."

If your child hears a friend referring to you with a wrong last name, it's fine to say matter-of-factly, "My mother and I have different last names. Her name is Mrs. Kline."

MARCH 3

If you forget someone's name

It happens to everyone—we learn a name and within minutes have forgotten it. When your child's memory fails, the best thing to do is ask to have the name repeated. Suggest that she say, "I'm sorry, I've forgotten your name." The other person will automatically refresh her memory.

It's trickier if your daughter wants to introduce two people but can't remember one of the names, even though she definitely met the person before. She can leap into the introduction by asking a question, hoping that the person will help her out. She might say, "Have you met my friend, Cathy Wells?" With a little luck the other person will say, "Nice to meet you. I'm Jan Kent." If Jan doesn't help out, either your child goes on with the conversation or she admits her memory lapse.

MARCH 4

Meeting a group

Sometimes your child won't be introducing two individuals to each other, but one friend to a group. In this case, your child should introduce someone to a group of friends by saying the person's name to the group. For example, "Kristie, I'd like you to meet the soccer team. Go ahead and tell Kristie your names, everybody."

Teach your children that if no one tries to make an introduction when she encounters a group, it's acceptable to make such an introduction herself. Encourage her to smile and say, "Hi! My name is Kelly Smith. What's your name?"

Stand to show respect

Standing when another person joins you is a simple gesture of respect. Because so few children hop to their feet to show deference anymore, the child who does will be head and shoulders above the rest! If it feels natural for your children to stand when Grandma comes to visit, it will feel natural years later when she meets a college president or is being introduced to a potential employer. A child should stand:

- *During introductions.*
- *During hello and goodbye.* When an adult visitor arrives or leaves, encourage your child to stand up, come to the door, and say hello.
- *With older people.* A child should always stand when an adult stops to talk. If your family is at a soccer game and your child's teacher comes by to chat, your child should stand up to say hello.
- *During certain ceremonies.* Your child should stand during a religious or civil ceremony, such as during the "Hallelujah Chorus," the national anthem, pledging allegiance to the U.S. flag, or to show respect when a foreign country's flag is presented at a formal event.

Discuss with your child what you expect ahead of time—it will spare you having to nudge your child in front of guests. If your son doesn't stand up at the appropriate time, talk to him about it later.

Telephone Talk

～

The telephone creates endless possibilities for communicating instantly with others, but some know-how is required to use it well. Remind your child to use words and tone of voice to communicate interest in others, since you can't see your caller. Encourage your whole family to use good telephone manners—everyone who calls your home will appreciate being met with courtesy on the line.

MARCH 6
Placing a telephone call

When your children graduate from two cups and a string to the modern telephone, they'll need to learn that although it seems simple, using the telephone well requires some knowledge and discipline. At first they'll think only of calling friends, but eventually your children will want to use the phone to place an order, get information, or make an appointment. The more confident they are on the telephone, the more capable they'll become with this useful tool.

Tell your child to hold the telephone close to the chin without touching the face. It shouldn't be smashed against his mouth or dangling by his shirt collar. And he should smile—friendliness transmits through fiber optics.

Here are telephone basics for your children:

1. *Dial the number carefully.* If you get a wrong number, apologize. Don't say "oops" as you slam down the phone.
2. *Call at the right time.* Don't call after 9 P.M. or during the dinner hour.
3. *Hang up after six rings.* Not everyone has an answering machine.
4. *Give your name immediately.* Say, "This is Jeremy. May I please speak to Peter?" This sounds much better than blurting out, "Is Peter there?"
5. *Get a snack* after *you make your call.* The sound of pretzel munching comes through loud and clear.
6. *Turn off the radio or TV.* The telephone is meant to amplify your voice, but it also amplifies background noise as well.
7. *Have a reason for calling.* It's okay to call to visit, but if that's the only reason, take charge of the conversation and keep it brief. The burden of what to talk about shouldn't fall on the person who picked up the phone.
8. *If you reach an answering machine, leave a brief message.* Give your name, the purpose of your call, and your telephone number. If you're already asking someone to call you back, don't make that person look up your number as well.
9. *Take responsibility to say goodbye.* That job belongs to the person who made the call.

Activity

If your child is at least ten years old, help her place a call requesting information. For example, if she's been asking for jacks, have her call the toy store to see if they have jacks in stock. Practice the conversation and stay with her when she places the call in case she needs help.

MARCH 7

Receiving a call

Discuss your family's policy about how the telephone should be answered at your house. Some acceptable ways of answering are:

"Hello" (with a bright voice).
"Hello, Klines'."
"Hello. This is the Kline residence."
"Hello. This is the Kline residence, Brandon speaking."

Some unacceptable ways of answering are:

"'Lo" (mumbling).
"Yeah?"
"Who's this?"

If your child answers the phone and the call is for her, remind her to respond to the question "May I speak to Sue?" by saying, "This is Sue." Don't say, "Speaking." That sounds too abrupt.

When your child repeats her name, it immediately confirms that the caller has the right person, and it also gives your child the opportunity to correct the pronunciation of her name if necessary.

If the call is for someone else in the house, your child should say, "Just a minute, please. I'll see if he is available." (Don't say: "Hang on!") Then she should:

- *Put down the phone,* go to the person, and tell him about the call rather than yelling into the mouthpiece or through the house.
- *Ask to take a message* if the person can't come to the phone. She should say, "Dad isn't available right now. May I take a message and have him return your call?" Don't reveal where Dad is—the caller doesn't need to know he's in the bathroom or sleeping. *Important:* Make sure your child knows she should never tell a caller that no one else is at home.

- *Let the person who called say goodbye* unless she needs to go because dinner is being served or someone else needs to use the telephone.

Taking a telephone message

Your child should take a message if he answers a call for someone who isn't at home or who can't come to the phone. If your child is too young to write, allow him to answer the telephone only when you are available to take the call or take the message. It's frustrating for a caller to get a chatty four-year-old on the phone when she wants to go over some quick business details with you.

If the caller wants his call returned, your child simply writes down the person's name and telephone number. Tell your child to ask the person to spell his last name if he isn't certain what it is. After he's written down the number, he should repeat it to the caller to check its accuracy. Remind your child always to take a phone number—it is a great time saver for a busy parent with a stack of while-you-were-out notes waiting for him.

Establish a family message center (a bulletin board, magnets on the fridge, or a place on the desk) so that messages don't get lost.

If a caller wants to give your child a detailed message, encourage your child to say you'll call back. If he writes down the topic, however, it will give you an opportunity to think about an answer before returning the call. It sounds disrespectful for a child to screen calls, so tell him not to ask a caller what his call is regarding. Kids should also make notes for a family member if they've saved messages on voice mail.

When kids take reliable messages, parents can be prompt in returning calls. Returning a call within twenty-four hours is a courtesy, and your kids will learn by your example.

Activity

Give your child practice in writing a telephone message. Make up a caller's name and telephone number and give her a short message. Show her where you keep a supply of paper and pencils that she may use, and tell her where to put the message so other family members will find it.

Handling call waiting (yours)

Let your child know what she should do when she's talking with a friend on the phone and a beep announces another call coming in. Some families let the second call go to voice mail; others want every incoming call answered.

If you want all calls answered, tell your child that if she's on the phone and a second call comes in, she should get permission to answer. Suggest she say to the first caller, "I have another call coming in. Do you mind if I answer it? I'll be right back." When she picks up the second call, she either takes a message or asks the person if he wants to hold while she quickly finishes the first call.

Some parents tell their children that calls from adults take precedence over chatting on the phone with a friend. If the second caller is an adult, your child should say: "I'm on the other line but I'll quickly say goodbye and tell Dad you're holding." When your child gets back on the first line, she says: "I'm sorry, but my dad has a call holding on the other line. I'll have to say goodbye and call you back." Holding time on the phone seems endless, so your child should try not to keep the second caller holding for more than thirty seconds.

If Dad can talk, when your child hangs up the first call she should tell the second caller that she's going to get Dad.

Handling call waiting (theirs)

Your child might realize the importance of handling second incoming calls quickly only if his calls to a friend have been repeatedly interrupted by call waiting and he's been forced to hold for long periods of time. Call waiting shouldn't be used to take time with the second caller while the first caller holds. It should be used to take a quick message or to get back to the first caller and say goodbye.

If a friend asks your child to hold too often while he chats on incoming calls, your child may say he's sorry that he can't hold and ask the friend to call him back.

Home alone: answering the phone

During their elementary-school years, many children enjoy the independent feeling of staying home alone for an hour or two. Sometimes parents will tell their children not to answer the telephone while they're out, or they will establish a signal—if it rings twice back to back, go ahead and pick it up because it is the parent calling.

If your child does answer the phone while he's alone, he doesn't need to let the caller know that no one is there with him. He may simply say, "Mom isn't available to come to the phone right now. May I take a message for her?" If the caller persists, your child may simply repeat himself: "Mom asked me to take a message for her. Would you like her to call you back?"

This kind of response is fine when your child doesn't know the caller. Let your child know that it's okay to say he's home alone if Grandma or an aunt calls. He will sound coy if he refuses to give out any information to someone close to the family.

When your child doesn't want to talk on the phone

When a friend calls on the phone every day just to see what's up, your child might be perfectly happy. But she also might be bothered. Some children can chat endlessly with their friends face-to-face but freeze up when they have to talk on the phone. They feel shy, don't really know what to talk about, and find that conversation becomes an ordeal. You'll know this is the case when the phone rings and your child immediately pipes up: "I'm not home!"

Be glad that your child is well liked, but give her some guidelines for limiting the calls. You might get an egg timer and let her keep her conversations to three minutes. She can tell the friend that she isn't allowed to tie up the phone for long periods and that she has to go. Or you might tell your child that she's allowed to receive calls a couple of days a week. She can tell her friend that she'd like to talk on the phone, but because the family phone gets busy, she's supposed to get calls only on Wednesdays and Saturdays.

The first attempt to solve the problem should be between the children. When a parent intervenes right away, it seems heavy-handed.

MARCH 13

Answering machines: your recorded message

Grandma might be happier without an answering machine, but your child will have few friends who don't have one. While answering machines may seem impersonal at times, most people will agree that it's nicer to be able to leave a message than to be forced to dial repeatedly before finding someone at home.

Your child may record the message if he's mature enough to speak clearly and can do it without giggling. A long, cutesy message recorded by a laughing child or one that includes every member of the family adding a word or two of greeting is usually entertaining only to the family recording it—callers find messages like this tiresome, especially when they've heard them before.

If your child wants to record the message, have her write it out (keeping it as natural as possible), practice it a number of times, and *smile* when she records it. Have your child speak with a normal tone of voice—there's no need to be overly exuberant. Keep the recorded message short (about ten seconds) so that busy people who call won't get fidgety while they wait for the beep.

If you have a simple, businesslike message, you may keep it for a long time. If it's humorous or seasonal, you'll want to change it periodically.

MARCH 14

Answering machines: leaving a message

When your child reaches a friend's answering machine, he should leave a message. He shouldn't dial repeatedly, hoping to get someone to pick up on the other end. Each time he dials and listens to the answering machine message, he leaves a click on his friend's recording when he hangs up. It's much better to leave one message than a series of clicks.

When he leaves a message, he should include:

- His name.
- His telephone number.
- A *brief* message.

When your child leaves a message, he should speak slowly and clearly, especially when he's giving his phone number. He should *always* leave his phone number, even if he believes his friend knows it. It's a good habit to get into, and it saves the person receiving the message the time it would take him to look in the phone book. After he leaves one message, your child should wait until it's returned. He shouldn't call again to see if his friend got his message.

Remind your child not to leave confidential information on an answering machine—there's no guarantee the person it's intended for will be the only one listening to the message.

Activity

The next time you're out doing errands with your child, let him call your home and leave a message. When you get home, listen to the message with him and discuss what he did correctly.

MARCH 15

When to call

Ill-timed telephone calls are disruptive. While people don't have an obligation to answer the phone during dinner, for example, there are times when they might need to answer the phone even if it's inconvenient for them because they are expecting an important call, or because another family member is away from home at the time. Some parents *always* pick up the phone if their teenager is out.

Your child shouldn't call a friend during the dinner hour (between 5:30 and 7 P.M.). He wouldn't think it was right to walk into a friend's home and stand by the table while the family was eating—nor should he disrupt a meal with a telephone call. If he absolutely must call during dinnertime, it's courteous to apologize for interrupting dinner. Because just about any time could be inconvenient to take a call, it's always nice to begin a phone conversation by asking if the person has time to talk.

Most people follow the rule that you should call before 9:30 P.M. It depends on the habits of the family, however. If there are young children in the home, calling after 8 P.M. might be too late; if there are teenagers, calls will probably be taken until 10:30 P.M. The key when calling other kids is to ask what is convenient for them.

MARCH 16

Ending a call

The person who called should say goodbye first. The caller who is courteous will chat a bit, discuss the business she had on her mind, and then say goodbye. Ending the call isn't only her option, but her responsibility. If she's considerate of the other person's time, she won't let the conversation drag on endlessly.

Unfortunately, there are some callers who have no idea when enough is enough. Apparently they have no one waiting to use their phone, no homework to be done, and hours of free time on their hands. They love to visit on the phone, even though there isn't any pressing matter to discuss. When the caller says goodbye, she should mean it. Not being able to get off the phone is like standing at the door and taking ten minutes to say goodbye. The other person can't push her out, but that's what she'll soon feel like doing. Callers need to be decisive—say goodbye and hang up.

If your child finds herself on the phone regularly with a caller like this, your child may end the call herself. Although she is tempted to say, "Well, gotta go!" and hang up, she can soften her words by saying, "I'd like to be able to talk longer, but I need to give the dog some exercise." Sometimes it's easier for a child to say goodbye if she can say that her mom wants her to get off the phone. If you recognize the problem of the long-winded caller, you can give your child an excuse for ending the call by asking her to please not tie up the phone.

Maybe it sounds like common sense, but teach your child to actually say goodbye. Some adults end calls by finishing a sentence and hanging up: "Thanks for sending me the estimate. I'll call you when I've made a decision." *Click*. That's too abrupt. The final word should be *goodbye*.

Activity

Give your child practice in looking up numbers in the telephone book. He might look up Grandpa's number the next time you are planning a visit. Or suggest he look up the number for the movie theater and call to get the times for a movie he wants to see.

MARCH 17

Getting a wrong number

Children can be caught off guard when they dial a wrong number. Their first inclination may be to hang up immediately when they hear a strange voice on the line, but it's important to apologize first. Your child should say, "I'm very sorry. I've dialed the wrong number." The other person will probably respond, "That's okay." Dialing a wrong number isn't a huge offense unless it happens in the middle of the night.

Your child needs to be sure not to dial the wrong number a second time, however. That's even worse than hanging up without an apology. If your child dialed a wrong number, he either took the wrong number from the phone book or accidentally hit a wrong button when he was dialing. To find out what went wrong, it's okay to say to the person on the other line, "I'm sorry. I've dialed the wrong number. Did I dial 123-4444?" If the person says yes, your child has the wrong number and needs to look up the number again in the phone book. If the person says no, your child's finger probably hit the wrong button and he simply needs to dial the number again, this time more carefully.

Activity

Put a small container on a shelf in your home and label it with your child's name. Each time you see her use a new good manner, put a dime in it. At the end of the month, let her spend the money.

MARCH 18

Cellular telephones

Cellular telephones are convenient to use, and they've become as common as crocuses in the spring. Parents keep cell phones with them so their kids can easily reach them, and some even tuck a phone into their kid's coat pocket for extra peace of mind.

Cell phones have made life easier and safer in many ways, but they can also become a public nuisance. When your child uses a cellular phone, tell her to talk in a low voice. She may find it hard to believe that such a little device can convey her voice clearly, and may end up speaking too loudly without thinking about it. She should find a private spot to talk when she places a call and when she receives a call if she's with a group. If possible, she should always show regard for others by not talking on a cell phone within earshot of them.

Children also may believe that because a cell phone works like a regular telephone, it is a regular telephone. But it's not. Explain to them that cellular phone use is priced differently than regular telephone calls. When one cell phone calls another, both phones pay for the time used. If you want to keep your cell phone charges low, urge your child to use it briefly and only when necessary, not to chat. Let her know when free minutes are available. She shouldn't ask to borrow a cell phone from a friend, except in an emergency. It isn't like making a call from a friend's house, and it costs her friends' parents money.

Activity

Show your child how your cellular phone works and discuss with her when she should dial 911. Don't have her carry in a backpack or pocket a phone programmed to dial 911; emergency services have been overwhelmed by 911 calls with no one on the other end because phones were dialed accidentally when they were pressed against something.

MARCH 19

Phone tricks and pranks

Your child shouldn't use the phone to amuse herself at the expense of others. Remarks such as "Can you guess who's calling?" and "Is your refrigerator running? Well, you better go catch it!" may be annoying to the person on the other end of the line, even though they're harmless.

Playing pranks that truly worry others isn't harmless, however, and it's inexcusable.

Using 911 for any call other than a true emergency is much more serious than a simple prank. It ties up the line and may prevent someone who really needs help from getting it. Be sure to have this discussion with your children as soon as they are old enough to use the phone.

You Are What You Say

❧

Don't hesitate to get started early with your children on conversation skills. As they begin to understand the reciprocal nature of thoughtful conversation, they'll develop sensitivity toward others and be confident in new situations. Your child will be able to make others feel heard, come up with something to say, and avoid saying things that hurt others. Even very young children can grasp the importance of conversation courtesies.

MARCH 20

Positive use of humor

Your child can use a sense of humor in many positive ways. It can take the edge off an embarrassing situation and help make friends. But your child needs to learn the importance of combining his sense of humor with a kind heart.

Humor can hurt others; a mean joke that mocks others draws everyone down, whether it's a racist joke or a joke about the opposite gender. While these kinds of jokes may elicit a laugh, they leave a bitter aftertaste.

If your child makes fun of others, those who are listening will wonder what he says about them when they aren't around. They'll lose their trust in him. Remember that children and adults react differently to humor. While an adult may enjoy teasing, children generally don't.

Your child's sense of humor can get him through embarrassing situations. Remind him always to laugh at himself but never at others. If his friend spills soda on his pants, for example, your child can help by getting a towel and assuring him that everyone will know it's soda.

Activity

Tell your child about a time when someone used humor in a way that made you feel uncomfortable. Ask him if he has an example of the same thing that he could share with you.

MARCH 21

When your child is funny

Humor should also be used in moderation. If your child has a talent for remembering jokes and for being able to deliver a punch line with punch, let her know you enjoy her entertainment. If she readily sees the funny side of a situation, laugh when she comes up with a good one-liner. But always encourage your child to use her sense of humor in moderation.

Even if a child is truly amusing, she shouldn't get into the habit of being funny all the time. The person who is constantly cracking jokes becomes tiresome to others. If they aren't funny themselves, they may feel inadequate or boring. They'll begin to find ways to avoid the jokester.

Don't hide behind humor. Friendships are easier when people let others know them. It's irksome to habitually get a funny answer to a serious question. Sometimes funny people need to give straight answers and be willing to let others get to know their true feelings.

Activity

Buy a new joke book and enjoy it with your child. Encourage her to find appropriate times to let her humor shine.

MARCH 22

Swearing

Children hear swearwords in a culture that peppers its streets and entertainment with them, and they may want to mimic the bad language. Even if your child doesn't hear swearing at home, you might catch something foul coming out of his mouth. Don't overreact—some of the appeal of using the words is the strong reaction they draw. Your child actually may have no idea what the words mean.

When you hear swearing, calmly ask your child if he knows the meaning of what he has said. Tell him that some words are very offensive to others and should always be avoided. If he isn't sure what the word means, he shouldn't use it.

When swearing becomes frequent, a child might not even hear himself swear. Just as the teenage girl who uses *like* in every sentence ("I was, like, so surprised!") doesn't hear herself saying it, a child who has made swearing a habit might not even be aware he is swearing. Tell your child that while most people aren't going to say anything to him about his bad language, they won't like it at all.

Encourage your child not to have a double standard. If he tries not to swear when he is with adults but thinks it is okay when he's on the playground, he's bound to be embarrassed sooner or later when a swearword slips out at the wrong time. It's never too early for your child to start choosing polite and pleasant words.

MARCH 23

Discussing money

Some families freely spend money, while others count every penny. Their habits aren't necessarily a reflection of how much money they have. Help your child understand that people's opinions about money are strongly held. He can easily offend others if he talks about money.

First of all, encourage your child to talk with you about money, not with friends. When he talks with a friend about money, he may sound as if he's bragging, or if he confides a financial concern, he'll be discussing a problem his friend can't help with.

Children shouldn't ask others what they paid for things, nor should they volunteer that information about their own purchases. While kids will probably compare in their minds their possessions with those of their friends, they shouldn't do it verbally.

MARCH 24

Accents

Your child will meet children and adults whose speech sounds different from hers. She shouldn't laugh at them or make comments about how strange they sound, but should make every effort to understand what they are saying.

Understanding a different dialect can take patience. It's okay for your child to tell the other person she doesn't understand what he has said and to ask him to please repeat himself. Your child should then repeat what she believes she understood. This is better than pretending to understand what someone else is saying.

Different speech patterns bring color to a culture. How boring it would be if we all sounded exactly alike! Yet when a person is repeatedly asked about his accent, he begins to think that people would be happier if everyone spoke with identical inflections. Remind your child that if she asks questions about why a person sounds different, many others have probably done the same thing. It's better to accept the way the person speaks without comment.

If your family has an accent that is dramatically different from most of those in the community, urge your child not to take others' remarks too seriously. While they may hurt, they are probably made more out of a lack of knowledge than from any malicious intent.

Activity

Rent the classic movie *My Fair Lady* and discuss the merits of Henry Higgins's efforts with Eliza Doolittle.

MARCH 25

How to just say no to drugs and alcohol

It's important for a child to be able to say no when he wants to. Drug and alcohol use among kids is so widespread that most school-age children will face the need to say no.

Counselors tell us that kids need to say no in a way that's effective. Saying no isn't effective if later your child feels uncomfortable about offending his friends and decides to go along with them after all. He needs to be able to stick with a decision. Counselors also say that when a kid says no, it shouldn't be so strident that it condemns and demeans the other person. The best way to say no isn't to tell the other person how stupid he is.

Saying no is most effective when your child has thought ahead about situations he might face and has a clear reason in his mind for saying no. When he says no, he talks about himself rather than attacking the other person. He might say, "I'm not going to drink because I don't want to get kicked off the soccer team," or "No, thanks. I've told my parents I won't take drugs," or "No, that's not my thing."

Activity

Hug your child often or pat him on the back. Tell him when you notice the good things he does. You'll help build his confidence in himself and help enable him to say no effectively.

MARCH 26

Whispering

It's good for your child to whisper if she needs to ask you for a tissue during a religious service. It's not good to whisper if she's confiding in the person beside her at the dinner table.

Tell your child if she whispers to one person when she's in a group, she'll give the others the impression she's trying to hide something. They'll believe that she's talking about them and that she's probably saying something mean, or they'll feel left out. Whispering makes others feel uncomfortable and excluded, and it's best to avoid it.

Activity

Discuss with your child what she can do when she joins a group where someone is whispering. What should she say if everyone gets quiet when she arrives? Should she ask if she's interrupting something and hope they include her? Should she just say "excuse me" and leave? Either approach might work—it depends on how well she knows the group.

MARCH 27

Correcting a friend

Only a bossy know-it-all corrects the grammar and pronunciation of a friend. At least that's how it can feel if you're the one being corrected. There simply isn't a way to do this in a normal conversation that doesn't make the other person feel small, especially if it's done in the company of others.

Help your child understand how to be tactful if she needs to correct a friend about specific information. Rather than bluntly stating, "You have it all wrong. That's not true!" your child can state it in a way that's much easier for the friend to accept: "I thought the teacher said our test was tomorrow, too, but I noticed on the chalkboard that it's the next day."

Sometimes your child will disagree with the opinion of a friend. Rather than saying, "That is the stupidest opinion! Why did you say that?" she might say, "I felt the same way about Kelsie—she seemed stuck up until I did the science project with her. Then I realized she's just quiet but really nice."

Remind your child that starting a sentence with *I* rather than *you* keeps it from feeling like an attack.

MARCH 28

Pointing

It'll probably take a few reminders, but you'll want to help your child learn that it isn't polite to point at other people. Kids also need reminders not to make personal comments about others. For some reason their pointing is often accompanied by statements such as "Mom, look at that lady's funny hair!"

Pointing isn't strictly forbidden, of course. It's okay to point at an object ("That's the prettiest ring in the case"). And pointing might be necessary if your child is telling someone how to find the school office, for example ("Go down the hall to the right").

It's also impolite to point with utensils during a meal, whether your child is using a knife, a fork, or chopsticks.

Activity

Your child might want to introduce you to his new friend. Show him an acceptable way of indicating another person. He may extend all of his fingers toward the person, with his palm turned slightly upward. That's much nicer than jabbing the index finger at someone.

MARCH 29

If someone is boring

It's no fun to be confronted with a bore. Help your child respond sympathetically when he's with someone who's boring. Maybe the person seems boring because the two simply don't have anything in common. Everyone is a bore sometimes.

If the other person won't stop talking, your child should find a courteous way to escape. If he's at a party, he shouldn't dart off immediately, nor should he look over the person's shoulder. But when there's a chance to make a break in the conversation, he may mention that he wants to get something to eat or play a game, and then leave. If he's in a smaller group and can't get away, he may begin a conversation with someone else close to him.

MARCH 30

When your child doesn't want to play

Children sometimes differ with their neighbors on how much time to spend together. One might want to be with other children every daylight hour, while another is content with time alone. Or *you* might be the one who is content with time alone— alone with your child, that is.

If your child loves the company of others, maybe you should count your blessings. When kids in the neighborhood come to play at your house, you know what activities they're into. You might have to provide more cookies than any other parent in the neighborhood, but you also have the opportunity to give the kids what they often need most—some loving adult attention.

If your child prefers time alone, help her to establish some reasonable boundaries and to communicate them in a kind way to her friends. Maybe she'll want to let others know they're welcome to visit your home most days, but that you have a couple of family days each week. It might also help to say that playtime is outside the house rather than inside.

It's never easy telling a neighbor not to visit, but it's better than becoming so angry about the situation that you either blow up or vow never to talk with the neighbor again.

Above all, try to keep things in perspective. Any parent of teens will tell you how quickly the years fly by. In retrospect, a yard full of kids from the neighborhood might not seem like a problem at all.

MARCH 31

If the driver has been drinking

Plan with your child how she should handle this situation. Make sure she carries change to place a call or knows how to call you collect. Or maybe she should use a taxi or ask another friend for a ride. What's important is that you discuss it.

Remind your child that her safety is the number one concern. This isn't the time to worry about hurting someone else's feelings. And she shouldn't worry that she'll inconvenience you. You'd rather give her a ride than meet her at the hospital.

She can tell the driver that she doesn't feel comfortable riding with him and that she's arranged for another way home. If she's really courageous, she might also tell him that she thinks he's been more affected by alcohol (or drugs) than he realizes and he should let someone else take him home, too.

APRIL 1

When someone speaks to your child

It's polite for your child to respond when someone speaks to her. That might sound obvious, but if a question hasn't been asked, sometimes children find it easier not to say anything. When someone makes a remark to her, even "I see what you mean" or "hmmm" is better than complete silence.

Family members are more likely to be guilty of this than others, because they can take each other for granted. With her friends, your child is usually tuned in. So at home, if you say, "We're going to the mall after dinner," she should respond with "Okay" or "Oh, good." She shouldn't wait until you repeat yourself and then respond with, "I heard you the first time!"

If you ask her a question, right away she should acknowledge that she heard you, even if she doesn't have an answer. Saying "I need to think about that" is better than saying nothing.

With kids, not responding is an innocent omission, but it's good not to get into the habit.

APRIL 2

Unfriendly words

While children seem to know intuitively that swearing is wrong (they may swear simply to test the power of the bad words), they're less likely to think about how degrading to others unfriendly words can be. Unfriendly, aggressive phrases such as "Shut up" and "Get out of my face" can become part of their everyday language because they're an easy way to deal with a situation your child doesn't like.

Rather than attacking the other person when met with unfriendly words, it's more respectful for your child to say, "I'm not interested in that subject right now" or "Would you come back later? I have to work on this project."

APRIL 3

Put-downs

Kids are still honing their conversation skills, so they might resort to an easy topic—other people. It's okay to discuss others in a positive light, but putting others down has its pitfalls.

Put-downs give the speaker a false sense of importance. There's usually an audience for someone who's willing to talk about others. Put-downs are also an easy way to get a laugh, but they're a misdirected use of wit. The group might laugh when a child mocks someone's haircut or athletic ability, but they'll worry that his comments will soon be turned on them.

Put-downs are used to make the speaker feel better about herself. Mentioning the weaknesses of others somehow makes her feel more successful, but the only person she's fooling is herself. Put-downs insult others and make the speaker look bad, too.

Activity

Role-play with your child possible responses she can use when her friends put others down. She might change the subject or mention something positive about the other person. Make sure she's comfortable with the response; she might simply choose not to join in the put-downs.

Making light of serious subjects

It's better to treat the subjects of death, funerals, mental disabilities, or physical handicaps with seriousness than to risk offending someone by making lighthearted remarks. Remind your child that people sometimes keep their difficulties to themselves, and he may add to their burden by joking about a sensitive topic. A child's friend at school may not mention that his sister is mentally handicapped, but it'll be painful to him when others laugh about someone with special needs.

If your child discovers too late that he let insensitive remarks slip out, it's good to apologize.

Distinctive speech

Slang will probably be a part of your child's language, but encourage her to make it a small part. The more distinctive the words and phrases she chooses, the more impressive and effective her communication skills become. Good speech patterns show refinement, and they certainly affect first impressions. Speaking well is a worthy goal. As one speech coach said, "It takes so little to be above average!"

Help your child develop the habit of respectful responses. When asked a question, it's better to respond with "yes," "no," or "certainly" than with "yeah" or "uh-huh." One-word responses are too blunt, so she should add a couple of words.

Help her weed out of her conversation words and phrases such as "um," "like," and "you know." These filler words are distracting and boring. There's nothing wrong with pausing in conversation. In fact, it's good to think before you speak. Encourage your child to articulate clearly. Mumbling is unimpressive. It masks wit and intelligence.

Body language

Your child communicates by what she says, but she also communicates through body language. Children easily understand what overt body signals are, such as giving a thumbs-up or clapping. But true body language is more subtle; most of the time we don't think about it. Help your child understand that her body language is read by others as it gives out messages about her feelings.

- *Folding arms over the chest* says your child is protecting herself from getting too close; she's not feeling at ease. She'll seem friendlier with hands by her side or clasped loosely in front.
- *Leaning slightly toward a person during conversation* shows your child is interested in what's being said. Drawing back indicates shyness, doubt, or lack of interest.
- *Smiling* communicates friendliness and makes people want to be near your child. Smiling might mean she is trying to understand something, but a frown seems disapproving or angry.
- *Nodding rapidly when someone is talking* tells the other person to finish up—it communicates impatience. An occasional nod expresses interest better.

Eye contact

There's hardly an aspect of communication more important than eye contact. When your child looks at someone with whom he's conversing, he shows he has two positive qualities: self-confidence and interest in others.

When your child drops his eyes during conversation, it might simply mean he hasn't been prompted about the importance of eye contact. But avoiding looking at someone communicates shyness, insecurity, or lack of interest.

Adults in particular respond favorably when children use eye contact. To them, it's a key way of showing interest and respect.

Maintaining eye contact doesn't mean staring. It's fine for your child to shift her eyes away occasionally, especially when she's speaking.

TIP

An "eyebrow flash"—briefly raising the eyebrows when greeting someone—communicates extra warmth and interest.

APRIL 8

Ask leading questions

If your child learns this skill, she's well on her way to being a good conversationalist. It indicates her interest in others and helps draw them out.

Leading questions need more than a yes or no answer. For example, "What did you think of the movie?" is better than "Did you like the movie?" Or try "Tell me about . . ."

Leading questions take some thought, both on your child's part and on the part of the one answering them. But the effort is worth it; they're a big help in getting a conversation going. They're part of listening well because they show your child wants to hear what the other person has to say.

A conversation continues when people use follow-up questions. This is a way to learn more about a subject. For example:

Jenny: "Tell me about your summer plans."
Lisa: "I'll be on the swim team again."
Jenny: "That sounds like fun. Which strokes do you like best?"

Activity

Help your child plan for the next conversation he has with a grandparent by coming up with a list of interesting questions. You might suggest some of the following: "What is the first major news story you remember?" "What were you doing during World War II?" "What was your first car?" Remind him to use follow-up questions during the conversation.

APRIL 9

Using positive words

A child who learns to use positive words becomes a cherished friend. Friendly words make others feel good; it would be hard to overuse them. On the other hand, negative words are hurtful and hard to forget. And most of the time they're unnecessary.

Urge your child to look for positive things to say. Here's how:

- When talking about people, be affirmative: "She put a lot of effort into her presentation."
- When talking about things, be upbeat: "The new bookstore has all of my favorite series."
- When talking about ideas, stay positive: "I'd like to see us find more ways to help homeless people."

Don't get into the habit of criticizing, complaining, or gossiping. Do get into the habit of accepting, appreciating, and being curious.

Activity

To keep conversation positive, encourage your child to balance his negative statements with positive ones. If he's complaining that a field trip was boring, ask him to tell you one thing he liked about the trip and one thing he didn't.

APRIL 10

Sloppy language

There was a child in ancient Greece whose dream it was to become a great speaker. He had a very weak, soft voice and stammered so badly that people laughed at him. Determined to improve, he went to the sea, filled his mouth with pebbles, and spoke above the roaring waves. In time this boy, Demosthenes, became one of the greatest speakers that ever lived.

Your child might not dream of being a great orator, but getting rid of sloppy speech will put him head and shoulders above the crowd. He shouldn't mumble or speak too fast, and he should aim for proper grammar and pronunciation. He should also listen to people who have perfected their speech. (Actor James Earl Jones is one. He overcame stuttering to develop some of the most beautiful diction in the world. Now he earns a living by using his voice.)

Activity

Practice the proper pronunciation of the words listed below.

SAY:	DO NOT SAY:
going to	gonna
let me	lemme
give me	gimme
don't know	dunno
can't you	cancha
don't you	doncha
want to	wanna
have to	hafta

APRIL 11

Tone of voice

Is your child's voice pleasant and friendly or loud and irritating? Does he speak clearly or mumble and trail off at the end of a sentence? Tone of voice and pronunciation can communicate as much as the words that are used. (One of the reasons a child loves to hear her mother read is because her tone is gentle. The child might not understand all the words, but the sound of the voice is comforting.) Here are some ways to help your child evaluate his voice tone.

WHEN YOUR VOICE IS:	YOU APPEAR:
Loud and harsh	Bossy and self-centered
Dull and monotone	Unresponsive and unfeeling
High-pitched and whining	Selfish
Pleasant and energetic	Friendly and fun to be around
Loud enough to be easily heard	Respectful

Activity

Have your child repeat the following sentences into a tape recorder, using the different tones of voice listed above.

"I would like to go to the shopping mall."
"How were you able to read so many books in one summer?"

Play back the tape so your child can hear the difference in tone. Encourage her to use a pleasant, clear tone.

APRIL 12

Asking none-of-your-business questions

"How much does your dad make?" "Do you like having such a little house?" "Why doesn't your mom have a job?" "How much did you pay for your dress?" "How much do you weigh?" These are questions that are too personal to ask. Kids often help each other learn where the boundaries are when it comes to questions that are inappropriate. They'll have a quick retort such as "Who

wants to know?" or "None of your business!" And that'll be the
end of the discussion.

Answering none-of-your-business questions

Let your child know she doesn't have to answer questions that
make her feel uncomfortable, even if an adult is asking in a social
situation.

Tell your child it's okay to say that she can't give that information or that she's forgotten. For example, if she's asked about the
price of something, she can just say she can't recall. A vague
response would be okay, too. She might simply say she paid too
much.

Some questions show kind interest in others, and some come
across as prying. Your own tactful conversation will be a model
to help your child understand the difference.

When adults do annoying things

Adults are anything but perfect, and kids notice. In fact, adults
break many of the rules that kids are expected to abide by. Does
that mean Junior has the right to point out that his uncle took the
last piece of cake? Or tell his teacher that she has bad breath? It's
better not to. Showing respect toward grown-ups means keeping
comments such as these to himself. Your child might often have
to hold his tongue—such as when his teacher changes her mind
and requires that a paper be rewritten, or when he's visiting
Grandpa and is told that he can't watch TV.

It's all part of showing deference. Older people deserve deference just because they're older, not because they're perfect. This
will take self-control on the part of your child, but he'll be revealing his own self-respect as well.

Show deference to older people

Children should learn to show deference when interacting with adults. Some nice ways for kids to communicate deference are:

- Stand when an adult enters a room.
- Take time to speak with an adult, rather than ignoring him in favor of peers.
- Greet the adult by name. Say "Hello, Mrs. Brown."
- Look at the adult when being spoken to.
- Say "excuse me" or wait for a pause in conversation before interrupting.
- Avoid walking between two adults who are talking (your child's teacher will appreciate this).

Deference is shown based on age or position, not on the child's fondness or regard for the adult. Upon learning about deference, one teenage girl immediately blurted, "But we're all created equal."

That's true, but there's also a place for respect. A grandmother deserves a place of respect in the eyes of her children and grand-children. A police officer needs the deference of the community to do the job. A teacher should be shown deference by the children in the classroom. The child who shows deference indicates inner character and self-control.

Correcting adults

Sometimes conversation with adults goes against the grain with your child. He may have to answer boring questions about his favorite subject in school. Or a grown-up will have ill-informed opinions on a subject your child knows a lot about, such as fly fishing. Grandpa's never done it, but he doesn't think it takes much talent. Your son, a fly-fishing fanatic, knows differently.

Or Grandma loves to eat sausage—all of her family enjoys it and not one of them was ever overweight, she says. Your daughter knows the fat grams of every item on the grocery shelf and would no more eat a piece of sausage than put a stick of butter in her mouth. Does she set Grandma straight on the dangers of eating fat? No.

Give-and-take is part of peer conversation and classroom discussion, but in social conversation with adults, flat-out disagreement is forbidden. It's better for your child to let a subject drop than dive in and slug it out.

Let your child have healthy give-and-take conversations with you at home. Kids develop logical reasoning abilities in middle school, so they find it thrilling to argue. Remind your child never to state his points in disparaging tones.

APRIL 17

Active listening is the first step in good conversation

Your child has two ears and one mouth, so she should try to listen twice as much as she talks; she'll probably learn something, and she'll put the other person at ease.

When your child gives others a chance to express themselves, it's likely they'll return the favor. When she's listening, she shouldn't just say, "Uh-huh . . . uh-huh" and hope the other person soon stops so that she can say something. It's better to give her full attention. *Active listening* involves looking at the other person, asking a few questions, and responding to what's been said.

Activity

Here's a good way to show your child how it feels when someone doesn't listen:

1. Ask her to tell you about the best party she ever attended. Don't look at her when she is talking; interrupt occasionally; change the subject.

2. Ask her to name her favorite amusement park and to tell you why she chose it. Listen attentively; maintain eye contact; ask a few leading questions.
3. Now ask your child to compare how she felt during the two conversations.

APRIL 18

Ten TNT Discussion Topics

There are ten topics you should tell your child never to discuss:

1. How much money parents make.
2. Funny stories about the mistakes of others.
3. A friend's physical features.
4. Foul or off-color stories.
5. Illnesses of others similar to that of the person with whom you are talking.
6. Very personal details about the lives of others.
7. Your own good fortune in contrast to another's misfortune.
8. "I told you so . . ." conversations.
9. Thoughtless or lighthearted references to handicaps or death.
10. Any topic to the exclusion of all other topics.

APRIL 19

Practice conversation starters

Think about topics your child likes to talk about; her friends will probably enjoy similar topics. Sometimes youngsters may need help in learning how to start a conversation, especially with a new friend. Give your child some samples:

"What's your favorite roller coaster?"
"What good books have you read?"
"Have you ever had stitches?"
"What kind of movies do you like best?"

If someone asks your child a question, have her answer the question and then ask, "What about you?"

Activity

Have your child come up with conversation starters for the groups of people below. Some hints are given in parentheses.

- *Elderly people (their grandchildren, their hobbies)*
- *People their parents' age (jobs, hobbies)*
- *Teachers (summer activities)*
- *New friends (sports, music, hobbies)*

The Written Word: Letters, Thank-you Notes, and E-mails

❧

Keeping in touch through old-fashioned letter writing should never go out of style. But with all of the new electronic ways for kids to communicate, you'll need to make a special effort to encourage your child to put pen to paper. A typed or handwritten letter has an impact that can't be matched electronically—it's treasured by Grandma, taken notice of by a community leader, and saved and reread by a friend. And when your child does choose to use e-mail, her letter-writing skills will probably improve the quality of her computer messages.

APRIL 20
Stationery

Thank-you notes are so important—but it will be hard for your child to write a note if she has to search the house for stationery or ask you to go out and buy some. Make the task more inviting by creating a special place for all the supplies that are needed to write the note.

There are many beautiful notes available to buy, but they can be expensive. A hand-decorated note is charming as well as fun for a child to create.

You can also make a trip to a craft store, where plain fold-over notes are available in every color imaginable, along with matching envelopes. Your child can have a great time decorating them. The sky's the limit with stamping, and a few stamps and different-colored ink pads are so much fun for some children, the note-writing task becomes almost painless.

Encourage your child to add to her collection by picking up note cards that reflect his interest when he travels. Dinosaur paper from a natural-history museum or "Starry Night" cards picked up at an art gallery beg to be used.

If you have a drawer available for notepaper, that's great. Check it periodically to be sure it is stocked. Keep pretty pens for the task, and add a sheet of stamps to the supply. A basket on a desktop also works nicely if the drawers are full.

Activity

After the holidays, spend an afternoon writing thank-you notes with your child.

APRIL 21

When to write a thank-you note

When should your child send a thank-you note? If in doubt, do—and sooner rather than later, preferably within a week. Sometimes writing thank-you notes is obligatory, not just courteous. Help your child get a note of thanks in the mail on the following occasions.

• *When she's received a gift from someone.* It's especially important that the note be written promptly if the gift came in the mail. Writing a note is a necessity whenever the gift giver wasn't there to see the package opened and to be thanked in person. Families differ in their expectations about thank-you notes within families. Make sure your child isn't needlessly offending Grandma by neglecting to write, even though Grandma knows she received the gift. Notes should also be sent when your child has been sick and visitors brought her gifts.

• *When she's stayed in someone's home overnight.* This applies to overnight visits with people other than relatives or close friends. For example, notes should be written if your child is an exchange student and stays with a family in another state, or if she's spent time at a summer cottage owned by a friend's grandparents.

• *When someone holds a party for her.* If she's the guest of honor, she needs to send thanks after the event. A friend might host a welcome-to-the-neighborhood party. A phone call the next day to say thanks is nice, but a note needs to be written, too.

• *When she's received a favor or special kindness from someone.* If an aunt has sewed her costume for the school play, an uncle has taken her camping with her cousins, or a neighbor fed her fish while she was away, their thoughtful efforts should be acknowledged in writing.

APRIL 22

What's in a thank-you note?

Thank-you notes are very easy to *send:* Slip them into an envelope, stick on a stamp, and off they go. It's the writing that's difficult. If it gets put off too long, it probably won't get done.

Verbal thanks are okay before a child can write his name, but after that, even if the parent writes the thank-you note and the child only prints his name in big, unsteady letters, he should send one. Encourage your child to have fun with the note and attempt to add a bit of his personality to the words. Thank you notes have three parts: thank the giver and name the gift, say something about the gift, and then use a nice closing and sign your name.

Activity

Get a poster-sized newsprint tablet and markers and let your child create a giant thank-you note. Let him decorate it with drawings if he chooses.

APRIL 23

E-mail or snail mail for a thank-you?

Since so many children are as capable sending e-mail as they are with a pen and paper, they may want to send their thank-you notes electronically. The most that can be said about that practice is that it's better than not writing a thank-you at all—but not much better!

Thank-yous are meant to embody a bit of the sender's personality, not only in the words chosen but in the stationery and handwriting. Often these notes are saved and reread. They may get posted on a family bulletin board or stuck on the front of the fridge. Is this likely to happen to an e-mail message? Probably not.

As eager as everyone has been to embrace new technology, some things never lose their appeal. Remind your child that a personal note is one of them.

APRIL 24

Writing letters with care

Everything about a letter is a reflection of the person sending it. The paper it's written on should be clean and neat, the message clear and succinct, the words spelled correctly, and good grammar used throughout. It never hurts to have someone look at your child's letter before it gets dropped in the mailbox.

Writing a neat social letter reflects well on the sender. While a pen pal will be glad to receive any message, even one on a scrap of notebook paper, it's especially delightful to open an envelope and find uniform handwriting on pretty stationery. Some people save every piece of correspondence they receive, only to mention this to the sender years later. Others pass the letters they receive on to others to share the news. Writing or typing a letter might not be the quickest way to communicate when e-mail is at our fingertips, but it does remain a very personal means of expression and one that is often read and reread by the one who receives.

Writing a letter to a famous person

Your child may want to write to the president, the pope, a movie star, or a famous athlete or author. Encourage him to write but not to send along a book or other item to be autographed. Busy people aren't obligated to return unsolicited items that are sent to them.

Address the letter correctly, title and all. This will ensure that the letter will get there and that it will be read. If possible, call the person's secretary if you aren't sure about spelling the name or whether for example, the person is a Dr. or Mr. Check in an etiquette book that devotes an extensive section to the protocol of letter writing to make sure you use the correct form of address.

Keep the letter friendly and to the point. Don't attack or ramble on, covering every topic that comes to mind. Most famous people have someone who reads the mail, gives a report on the topics that come up, and helps on the responses. The famous person probably only sees your child's letter when it's time for him to sign a response.

Be sure to include a return address on the letter. It's a rare child who has his own letterhead, and the envelope may be discarded. The return address helps make sure your child gets an answer. It's the first item on the letter, followed by the date.

Don't forget to add the proper postage to the envelope.

Activity

Allow your child to choose a leader, entertainer, or author she admires and help her write a letter to that person. She should address only one topic and, if possible, type the letter. This will make it easier for the person to read and respond to the letter.

APRIL 26

Writing a letter to ask for information

Maybe your child wants to write for information about summer camp or to express to a legislator her desire to see National Kid's Day placed on the calendar. These are considered business letters and are organized on the page differently than social letters.

Have your child place the letter in the center of the page. If it's a long letter, the margins will be narrower than if it's just two or three paragraphs long. Here's how it should look. Notice where it's double-spaced and where it's single-spaced.

123 Macadam Drive
City's Edge, Pennsylvania 17551

February 5, 2000

Camp Having Fun
200 Streamside Trail
Anytown, Montana 02120

Dear Camp Director: *(The title is used if your child doesn't know the person's name.)*

I read about your camp in a magazine and would like to have information on this summer's schedule and rates. I'm a fifth-grade boy and would like to go to a camp where I can *rough it* for a couple of weeks.

I've enclosed a self-addressed stamped envelope for your reply. Thank you very much.

Sincerely,

(Your child's signature goes here—first name if he knows the person, first and last if he doesn't. Leave four spaces between closing and typed name.)

Brandon Keller

Enclosure

Activity

Help your child write a letter asking for information. You might let him practice by writing to a grandparent or other relative asking for information about a school project. Give him the responsibility to get the mail from the mailbox each day until his answer arrives.

APRIL 27

Writing a letter of appreciation

Thank-you notes are great when your child knows the person to whom he is writing, but they're a bit too informal when he's writing to someone he doesn't know well.

Maybe your child is glad the school board voted against school uniforms or happy that his community built a new baseball stadium. Why not write a letter of appreciation to the school board president or to the mayor? Everyone likes to know he or she is appreciated.

Your child's letter may be typed or handwritten and follows the same format as a business letter. Using a plain sheet of stationery (not one with flowers or animals on it) gives it a serious look. The return address is at the top left of the page, followed by the date, receiver's address, salutation, body of the letter, closing, and signature.

Activity

Regularly scan the newspaper with your child. When there's an article about something he particularly appreciates, have him write a short letter to the person involved. Encourage him to look for a response.

APRIL 28

A condolence letter

Written words of condolence (sympathy) can be read and reread and thus offer great solace to someone who has lost a loved one.

101

If your child's friend loses a sibling, parent, grandparent, or someone else to whom he was very close, you may want to help your child pen a few understanding words. If you write them yourself on behalf of your family, let your child read the letter before you send it. Help your child:

- Choose plain stationery in white or gray.
- Write words of sympathy.
- Tell the person how sorry you are about the loss.
- Say some appreciative words about the person who died.
- Relay a fond memory of the person.
- Give a specific offer of help.

What your child should not do:

- Buy a commercial sympathy card and sign his name.
- Type a condolence letter.
- Call on the phone (unless he is a very close friend).

APRIL 29
Signing a yearbook

You'll probably know yearbooks have arrived the minute your child comes through the door. Yearbooks are made more special by the personal messages of your child's classmates, from acquaintances to best friends. She'll spend hours poring over the photos of smiling faces and the messages in diverse handwriting. Here are some tips for your child about writing something that can be read by others, even many years from now:

- Write something positive and appropriate.
- Write in the margins or on blank pages, not on a face.
- Don't write something embarrassing or too personal.
- Don't smudge or crease someone's yearbook.
- Don't take up too much space.
- Return the yearbook as soon as it's been signed.

Activity

Buy a stamp from a craft shop that says, "This book belongs to . . ." Help your child make yearbook nameplates by stamping the message in bright ink on white, adhesive-backed mailing labels. Let her offer one to each person in her class. Suggest that the children write their names on the plates and place them inside the front cover of their yearbooks.

APRIL 30

Netiquette: rules for your child

Combine the words *net* and *etiquette* and you get *netiquette:* manners for the way people relate to each other on the Internet. The Internet is effective only when people using it know the rules and honor them. Netiquette is meant to keep Internet activity organized and civilized. While the Internet seems huge, in a sense the resources are limited. Each person should be careful not to overwhelm the system by sending junk e-mail, by sending or requesting information needlessly, or by repeatedly posting the same message.

Newsgroups and chat rooms are meant to be visited by people who think similarly and who want to learn more from each other. If your child doesn't like cats, for example, he shouldn't visit a feline fans chat room and say every negative thing he can about cats.

If your child doesn't keep his interactions on the Internet positive, others will enforce netiquette. He might be "flamed" (flooded with negative, vulgar, and threatening messages), "mailbombed" (hit with so many messages that his system and his provider's system may crash), kicked out of a chat room, dropped by his Internet service provider, or—if things get really bad—sued by someone he's offended.

Activity

Using emoticons is a creative way to express friendliness on the Internet. Look for a smiley dictionary online or come up with your own smileys. Here are a few to get you started:

:-) Smiling
;-) Winking
:-# Smiling with braces

MAY 1

More Internet etiquette: keeping kids safe

Your child probably knows how to log on to the Internet, get information for a school report, and send e-mail messages to her friends. In fact, she may be more adept than you are. But she also needs to learn how to act online and how to protect herself from dangerous people and harmful information on the Internet.

Much material online is inappropriate for children. Because searches for information are rarely exact, websites may appear that aren't related to your child's search but reveal sexually explicit, violent, or hateful information or encourage illegal activity. She won't need to search for such sites to find them.

Your child may also meet dangerous people in chat rooms. Adults who want to harm children may pose as other children in order to befriend your child and get information about where she lives. Your child may also be tempted to use your credit card number to purchase items on the Internet.

Help your child have a positive experience on the Internet by staying in touch with his Internet activity as a parent. Place your computer in a much-used room in the house, rather than in a bedroom. Express interest in what she does online. Ask her to teach you some shortcuts she may have discovered for getting around, or let her show you some of her favorite sites.

Encourage your child to tell you if she encounters troubling material or individuals. Let her know that you will check her browser history occasionally so that you know what sites she has visited. Encourage her not to spend most of her free time online—she still needs plenty of sunshine, exercise, and face-to-face contact with people.

Use a filtering service for children that is available from an Internet service provider; some services automatically filter things that are inappropriate for children. Others provide passcodes so that children have access only to certain sites, while other family members have broader access. Remember that no filtering service is 100 percent effective. There is no substitute for parental interest and involvement.

Nine nevers for Internet safety

Here are some rules to keep your child safe online:

1. Never ignore troubling information you come across on the Internet. Tell Mom or Dad.
2. Never give out your address or telephone number without your parents' permission to someone you've met on the Internet.
3. Never agree to meet someone you've met on the Internet unless your parents know about it.
4. Never download an attached document if you don't know the source.
5. Never send a picture of yourself to someone you haven't met in person.
6. Never spend most of your free time online.
7. Never keep mean or bad messages that arrive through e-mail. They aren't your fault. Let Mom and Dad know.
8. Never use your parents' credit card number on the Internet without asking their permission.
9. Never write inconsiderate, mean, or threatening messages online.

E-mail

For many children, e-mail has become the preferred way of communicating with friends. It's easy to send off a message and exciting to see if you've got mail. But it has some pitfalls, too. When your child isn't actually talking with someone, she might say things she wouldn't say to the person face-to-face. Later she could regret it. Here are a few e-mail guidelines you can review with your child:

- Write positive things. Don't criticize others or gossip about them.
- Limit the number of messages you send. Don't flood another person's mailbox with forwarded material every day.
- Remember that others may read your e-mail. Don't write anything you wouldn't want your friend's family to read—or anyone else, for that matter. Remember, too, that your e-mail message travels to a central location and your friend retrieves it from there. When your friend deletes your message, it's only deleted from his computer. It can still be retrieved from the central location.
- Don't type in all capitals. IT FEELS LIKE YOU'RE YELLING!
- Use your best spelling and grammar. Some people are irked by mistakes, or they might not be able to understand your message. It's also good practice for you to learn to write well.
- Don't use e-mail for messages that should be handwritten, such as thank-you notes.
- Be careful about new friendships online. Adults sometimes pose as kids to learn things about you that they have no reason to know.
- Never forward obscene material. Tell your parents if it is sent to you.
- Don't pretend to be someone you're not when you're online.
- Keep up the face-to-face conversations with your friends. E-mail should never replace them.

MAY 4

Graffiti

Graffiti might sound like an Italian appetizer, but there's nothing appetizing about it—it's defacement of public property. It's a civic duty and good manners as well to keep our environment clean.

That's true of public buildings, public parks, sidewalks, roads—any of the spaces we all share.

Remind your child that scratching her name on the door in a school bathroom or writing on a table at a restaurant ruins that property. But it does more than that; it lessens the respect others feel for the property as well. The more public spaces are damaged, the more people feel free to do damage. Even children should take responsibility to help keep their community clean. It's very public-spirited and generous, and it's also abiding by the law!

Activity

If you notice a public building in your community that is defaced by graffiti, volunteer to help clean it up. Check with a public official to get permission to do the work and discuss the appropriate method. Work along with your child.

Table Manners
Made Easy

∿

The family table is a place of such importance—not only do children satisfy their hunger, they learn self-control, family values, conversation skills, and how guests are welcomed. As a parent, your training at the table might include specifics such as forks and finger bowls, but you'll really be emphasizing that eating together is a significant cultural ritual.

MAY 5

Start the meal off right with proper posture

Proper posture for dining begins with sitting three to five inches from the table with both feet flat on the floor and the back straight. Legs shouldn't be crossed because the top leg is bound to start swinging and will hit either a table leg or the person dining across the table.

The back stays straight throughout the meal. If your child needs to get closer to the table, she should bend from the waist, but she should avoid "hunkering down"—rolling the shoulders and back and poking her nose into her mashed potatoes. She should bring food up to her mouth, not take her face down to her food. At the same time, she should avoid "guarding" food—

placing the left elbow on the table and wrapping the forearm up around the plate.

Elbows should hug the sides—they shouldn't rest on the table or jut into a neighbor's space. When your child holds her utensils the way she would hold a pencil, her elbows will naturally be at the correct place. If she grabs utensils as she would grab the handlebars of a bike and "shovels" her food, her elbows will fly out like wings.

When the meal is over and everyone is chatting, it's okay to rest an elbow on the table. Here's an easy way for youngsters to remember: Elbows off the table if you're holding a utensil, cup, or piece of food. Elbows on the table when you're between courses and your hands are empty.

It's best to eat with only one hand, keeping the other hand in your lap. But it's also acceptable to place your wrists at the table's edge.

MAY 6

Everyday table manners

Children take cues about table manners from their parents. They are far more likely to do what you do, not what you say. Resolve to make the family dinner a habit in your home. If you work late and eat dinner after the children have eaten, have the children join you for fruit and dessert. Nothing can replace this time together as a family. When your child masters the basic rules of dining, she'll be ready for any meal at your house or the White House. Here's the drill:

- Come to the table prepared. Before being seated, wash your hands in the bathroom, get rid of chewing gum in a waste-basket, and take out removable orthodontic appliances.
- Be seated and put your hands in your lap.
- If a blessing is said, close your eyes and sit quietly.
- Put your napkin in your lap.
- Begin eating when everyone has been served.

- Pass serving dishes to the right. If you start a dish, hold it and ask the person to your left if she would like some before you pass it to the right.
- Eat with self-control.
- Don't eat too fast or too slowly. Try to keep pace with others.
- Cut only a few bites of meat at a time. This not only appears gracious, but helps your meat stay hot longer.
- Butter your bread a small piece at a time. Place a pat of butter on your dinner plate or bread plate. Tear off a bite-sized piece of bread or roll, butter it, and eat it. Don't saw a roll in half and coat both pieces with butter.
- Chew with your mouth closed. No chomping noisily. This is easier to do if you haven't stuffed your mouth.
- Hold your water glass securely. While grown-ups grasp the stem of a goblet, children are free to cup their thumb, index, and middle fingers around the bowl.
- Thank the host at the end of the meal.
- Place your loosely folded napkin to the right of your plate. Push your chair under the table after you rise.

Activity

Make a bingo chart for each family member, including Mom and Dad. In the squares, write the manners listed above and post the charts close to the table. Each day, have family members choose a manner to work on. If they accomplish it, they put a sticker in the square. When someone gets bingo, serve the dessert of his or her choice.

MAY 7

Don't bring these things to the table

Children learn many important social skills at the table. They practice conversation, learn their place in the family, pick up values from their parents, and learn self-control and awareness of others. It's a time to focus on the people at the table, not on individual activity. Encourage your child to leave these behind when he comes to the table:

- Handheld video games
- The remote control for the television (keep the TV off during meals)
- A magazine or book
- The newspaper
- Homework
- The dog

Set the table properly

Sitting down to a table that has everything in its proper place helps the meal go smoothly. If your child has ever played croquet, she'll know that there is a special way to set up the lawn, a correct spot for each wicket, and a proper order for your ball to follow as it progresses through the wickets. Ignoring the game rules could be fun for a brief time, but soon she would tire of the confusion. The same is true of the table. Each item has its proper spot where it will be handy. If the table is set properly, everyone will know what to expect. The informal table setting contains a minimum of utensils and plates and forms the foundation for the formal setting. Formal table settings merely include more items.

The plate goes in the center with the knife and spoon on the right, with the knife closest to the plate and the blade side facing the plate. The fork is to the left of the plate. Utensils are straight, not touching each other or the plate, and not shoved under its rim. The bottom edge of each of the utensils is the same distance from the table's edge. The water glass always goes above the knife. The napkin goes to the left of the plate and, most conveniently, just to the left of the fork. It's easier to pick up a napkin if it isn't lying under a fork. If there is an extra little plate or bowl for salad or pudding, it is placed to the left of the plate above the fork.

Activity

Help your child set the table properly. To get the utensils evenly lined up along the table's edge, tell your child to use his index finger to measure. He should put the second joint of his finger at the edge and place the handle of the utensil at the tip of his finger. Then serve a fancy lunch for him and his best friends!

MAY 9

Formal table settings

If your child dines at a fancy restaurant or at a wedding, she'll see lots of silverware and many plates, both large and small. Formal table settings have the same pattern as for informal ones—there's just a bit more to it.

Although there are many utensils on a formal table, there shouldn't be more than three of any one kind. If four forks are required, a server should place only three on the table and bring the fourth fork when needed.

Explain to your child that the setting starts with a service plate (or charger) underneath all the other plates in the center of the place setting. Other plates (such as salad) are placed on top, and it will be cleared just in time for the main course. To the right of the service plate are the spoons and knives. The number of utensils you're given varies with the menu, but knives and spoons are on the right (just as in the informal setting).

Farthest from the right side of the service plate is a soup spoon, with a larger bowl than a typical spoon. Next to the spoon may be three knives—one for fish, one for salad, and one for the main course (entree). The knives will all be the same size (or the salad and fish knives might be smaller). Tell your child the trick for using the right utensil is simple: Use them in order, the outside utensil first, moving in toward the plate with each course.

To the far left of the plate will be a series of forks for fish, salad, and main course. (An exception to the forks-on-the-left rule is when there is a tiny seafood cocktail fork resting in the bowl of the soup spoon.) A spoon or fork above the plate means good news—dessert will be served.

The first goblet above the knife will be for water. There may be as many as three or four other goblets of varying sizes—for white or red wine, champagne, or sherry. To the upper left of the plate is a small bread plate and a small butter knife placed horizontally on the plate with the blade facing down.

Activity

Have your child plan a meal that includes soup, salad, entree, and dessert. Then practice using the correct setting, either with actual china or drawing them on a piece of paper. Make sure the setting has all of the necessary plates and utensils. When your child has mastered this, celebrate a birthday or other special occasion at a nice restaurant. Talk about what you find on the table in the restaurant.

MAY 10

Take formal table manners to dinner

Special occasions call for special meals—a wedding banquet, a holiday festival, a birthday dinner at a fine restaurant. A formal meal can throw your child curveballs unless he's thought ahead about what will happen.

Sometimes your child will be invited to special events because he's already demonstrated that he can handle himself in an adult situation. Other times he just finds himself at a formal event and gets to practice manners he's only read about or used at home. Whichever the case, the more he polishes his manners, the greater the number of wonderful invitations he'll receive. Here are some quick lessons to teach him. We'll have more in-depth explanations later.

• *Make sense of all of the silver.* Just remember to start with the utensils farthest from your plate and work inward. Knives and forks often come in pairs. You might have a fish knife and fork, a salad knife and fork, and of course a knife and fork for your main course. If you don't have as many knives as forks, be sure to save a knife for your main course.

• *Cleanse your palate.* Before you get the main course, a small scoop of fruit sorbet may be served. Enjoy its tart, refreshing taste, and begin the main course without lingering seasonings from the fish or salad course in your mouth. Sorbet is served in a footed bowl with an underplate and a small spoon. This is not a predinner dessert!

• *Wash your fingers in your finger bowl.* After your main course and before dessert, you may see a small bowl filled with lemon- or herb-scented water (it isn't thin soup!). Dip your fingers into the water, then dry them on your napkin. If the bowl of water rests on a doily on top of a dessert plate, use both hands to remove the doily and the bowl to your upper left.

• *Be ready for dessert.* Your dessert fork and spoon might be found lying above, and parallel to, your dinner plate. They could also arrive on either side of your finger bowl. In this case, place them on their respective sides of the dessert plate on the table-cloth. When you have removed the doily and finger bowl, you are ready for dessert. Remember, spoons are used for soft dessert. There won't be a knife at dessert, but if you need to cut a pastry and your fork won't do the trick, use the side of the bowl of the spoon to do the cutting and eat the pastry with your fork.

MAY 11

Blowing on food

Simply put, this isn't done. Your child shouldn't blow on food before it goes into the mouth, nor should she blow with her mouth open (or fan it with her hand) when she's already popped in something that's too hot. The sound is unpleasant to others at the table.

A quick drink of water will help put out a fire in her mouth; she shouldn't spit out the food. It's better to wait a few minutes and let the food cool on its own.

Paper trash at the table

Your child shouldn't let paper refuse clutter her area at the table. Cracker wrappers and sugar, salt, and pepper packets go under the rim of her service plate or her bread-and-butter plate. Simply tuck the paper under the plate. There's no need to crumple the paper.

There are fewer pieces of paper to deal with if the top is only torn off three-fourths of the way. If it's torn off the whole way, pour out the sugar and place the top into the empty packet.

Sometimes candy, nuts, petits fours, or hors d'oeuvres are served in small paper cups. The papers are taken along with the food. If they stayed in the serving dish, they'd create a mess. They're left on your own plate.

More tips for formal feasting

• *Sit at the table to which you've been assigned.* An alphabetical listing of guests will be posted on an easel at the entrance to the dining room. Find your name and check the number by it. This is your table number. Tables are usually numbered in rows, with the number displayed in the middle of the table. Or you might find your table number on your name tag. If all else fails, look for staff members with a list in their hands and give them your name.

• *Look for your place card when you've found your table.* This small card has your name on it and designates where you sit at the table. Never switch cards so that you can sit beside someone you think would be more fun. If there are no place cards, sit boy, girl, boy, girl. Your mother sits to the right of your father; a girl sits to the right of her date.

• *Be attentive to food that needs to be passed.* Send the salt and pepper around together. Pass cream and sugar as soon as coffee is served. Make sure the pats of butter follow the rolls. Be aware when things are passed to you. Don't let them get stuck by your plate, but pass them on to your right.

• *Keep your feet on the floor and your back straight.* Don't slouch in your chair or tip your chair back on two legs. Don't cross your legs at the knees or fold them under you on the seat of your chair. If your legs are too short to touch the floor, cross them at the ankles; if you can touch the floor, keep your legs side by side with feet on the floor and back straight.

• *Keep your plate until everyone at the table has finished.* Pace yourself to eat at the same speed as others at the table. You don't want to make everyone wait for you, nor do you want to inhale your food so rapidly that your plate is clean while others munch and converse. Don't push your plate away and groan with satisfaction when you've finished.

• *If you drop a utensil on the floor, leave it there.* Ask the server for another one. After you've used a utensil, place it on one of your plates. As you eat, your knife goes across the top of the plate with the blade facing you. Spoons for soup or coffee go on the under-plate or saucer. Never put a used utensil back on the tablecloth.

MAY 14

Grace: the art of giving thanks

Saying grace is the practice of offering a prayer of thanks at meal-time. It may have been more common for previous generations whose schedules weren't packed with soccer practice, art class, piano lessons, dance class, fund-raisers, and play dates, and whose families were able to enjoy regular evening meals together. But even in the midst of busyness, many families stop for this simple ritual of thanksgiving.

It's common for religious Jews to say grace after the Friday evening meal. Christians typically say grace before meals. The prayer may be as uncomplicated as "For what we are about to receive, Lord, make us truly thankful. Amen." Or it may be a verse that is easy for the children. In some families the father always says the prayer; in others, each family member takes a turn at praying. Grace may be a familiar song, sung by everyone at the table.

People bow their heads and close their eyes during grace. Parents often hold hands with young children, both to form a family bond and to keep them from snatching a piece of food. Although hand holding may be initiated for the sake of the preschoolers, it becomes a connecting ritual, and parents will find their teenagers continuing to reach for their hand during grace. It's thoughtful for you to let guests in your home know when your family says grace so they won't be caught off guard.

Activity

If you are comfortable with it, teach your child a traditional grace and allow him to say it before a meal.

MAY 15

Grace: when you're visiting someone else

When your child visits a friend, she should try to fit in with the customs of the friend's family as much as possible. If your child isn't accustomed to saying grace and she notices that her friend's family does, she may take a cue from them and either join them or sit quietly while they pray.

When grace is said, people either stand or sit; heads are bowed. To help everyone focus on the prayer, eyes are closed. Napkins aren't picked up until after grace is said. Your child may take her cues from the host about when to pick up his napkin.

MAY 16

Who gets served first?

The guest of honor gets served first. That means Grandma, the new neighbors, or Dad's colleague from work is the first one to get the serving plate of fried chicken and encouraged to help himself. A woman is served before a man, an older person before a younger one, a guest before a family member. After the first person serves himself, food goes around the table counterclockwise, so the guest passes it to the right and each person helps himself in turn. The host or hostess serves himself or herself last.

But what about everyday meals, those rare occasions when the whole family is seated at the table? For starters, children should make sure Mom has taken her seat. It is hardly a sign of respect for her to arrive at the table with the last serving dish of food only to discover that most of the food that was already on the table has found its way to people's plates. Since Mom is the woman at the table, Dad and the kids may treat her with dignity by recommending that she serve herself first. Then she passes food around to the right.

A parent may hear a child complain about being hungry and rush to serve him first. This is okay for a two-year-old, but as your child gets older, he needs to learn to practice self-restraint. He should wait his turn at the table. The same is true at a buffet meal. Children should not rush ahead of adults because they claim they are "starving." Honor grandparents at the holidays, the pastor and his wife at a church dinner, or the teachers at a class meal by letting them serve themselves first.

MAY 17

Passing food

When your child serves herself at the table, she uses the utensils provided on the serving plate and gives herself a modest portion—she doesn't want to leave the last person served with too little to eat. She may want to look around and do a quick mental calculation about the amount of food she may take if everyone is going to get an equal amount.

If there is a large spoon and fork on the serving dish, both are to be used. One is meant to scoop the food while the other keeps it from sliding across the serving dish.

Your child should take the portion closest to her. She shouldn't dig through the pieces of chicken, for example, to find the largest piece, nor scoop her macaroni from the center of the dish—any more than she would cut into the center of a cake to get her piece. When she takes her portion from the edge closest to her, she keeps the food looking presentable.

Asking for a drink

At the family dinner table, remind your child to ask for a drink rather than reach in front of others to grab the pitcher. He should always add "please" to the request, and "thank you" after. If he's old enough to handle a pitcher, it may be passed to him and he may fill his own glass, being careful to hold the pitcher's handle firmly and supporting the side of the pitcher with his other hand.

Your child should drink slowly and quietly, trying not to make a gulping sound and making sure his mouth is empty before taking a drink. A small bit of cookie remaining is fine, but others won't want to see a mouthful. The exception to this is if your child has mistakenly put something very hot or spicy into his mouth. A quick sip of something cold may be the only way to put out the fire!

When a friend comes to play, beverages should be offered first to him before your child serves himself. If there's only one soda left in the refrigerator, your child should divide it into two cups and share with his friend.

Removing plates during the meal

If you're eating at home, your child can help clear the plates from the table. If you're eating in a restaurant, that job belongs to the server. She has a system for doing it, and it's better not to begin stacking them or passing them to her.

Mealtime is nicer if you clear the table before dessert. There is no need to remove every crumb, but take the dinner plates and serving dishes away. Ask your child to help. Remind him to remove the plate *from the person's right* and carry only two plates at a time to the kitchen. Stacking plates is an invitation to an accident.

In a restaurant, plates will be cleared after each course. Utensils used to eat that course will also disappear, and clean silverware will appear for dessert. Remind your child that at home, the statement "You may keep your fork" isn't bad manners, it is good news—dessert is on the way.

MAY 20

Cutting meat

While it may seem efficient to cut a piece of meat into ten bite-sized pieces before popping one into the mouth, encourage your child to cut a piece or two at a time. Meat will stay warm longer if it is left in one piece, and cutting it all at once makes your child appear to be in too great of a rush to get the food into the stomach.

Parents, if you're cutting meat for your two-year-old, go ahead and do the entire job. But when your child seems ready to cut his own, he should learn to do it one piece at a time.

The drill goes this way:

1. Hold the knife in the right hand and the fork in the left. Neither utensil should be upright; both should be nearly parallel to the plate or at a slight angle.
2. Brace the back of each utensil with the index finger. This can be difficult for children, so don't be dismayed if your ten-year-old asks you to help cut a piece of meat. Encourage him to practice, and he'll pick it up.

MAY 21

If a guest is a vegetarian

What we eat is a very important—and personal—choice. Your child shouldn't comment on or try to change the eating habits of friends. If your child has a vegetarian friend who comes to your home often, it is a courtesy to make extra portions of vegetable dishes and salads available. You don't need to apologize for eating meat yourself, and neither should your child.

Don't be embarrassed if you find out too late that a guest is a vegetarian. You may notice he isn't eating meat and you didn't prepare anything special for him. That's okay. It's his responsibility to eat what he can in your home or eat something before he arrives so that he's sure to have what he needs.

If your child is a vegetarian

Meeting eating restrictions is the obligation of the one who abides by them. If your family has chosen not to eat meat, or if your family follows religious dietary prohibitions, don't ask your host to make a special meal. Eat what you can of the meal that's provided, or plan ahead and fortify yourself with something before the meal.

If your child has dietary restrictions, tell her she may want to quietly let her hostess know before the meal that she won't be eating everything that is served. Your child should assure her that she'll have plenty to eat, and urge her not to make something special.

When a person knows ahead of time that there will be nothing that she chooses to eat, she may want to skip the event. At the very least, she should consider bringing her own food, although it's difficult to do this and not offend a host. Under no circumstances is it appropriate for a child to lecture others on what is and isn't acceptable to eat. If asked about her eating habits, your child may simply reply: "It isn't something I would expect of anyone else, but I'm not able to eat meat."

If food is spoiled

The meat may smell bad before the first bite is taken. When this happens to your child, he should know that he has no obligation to eat spoiled food. Good manners don't require it, and it could make him sick. But neither should he make a scene by gagging or spitting the food back onto his plate.

If it's impossible to swallow, he should take it from his mouth with a fork or spoon and place it on the edge of his plate. He should not blurt out, "Yuck!" At a restaurant, he should tell you so that you can quietly ask the waiter to replace it.

Sometimes it's better simply to ignore the spoiled item. If it's a small part of the meal (a vegetable, for example), it can be left on the plate. It's impossible to ignore a spoiled main dish, and it should be replaced.

But remind your child that the most important thing about dining with others is the opportunity to converse and enjoy being together. It's not necessary that every aspect of the meal be perfect.

If your child is at a friend's home when he bites into something that is spoiled, he may ignore it or ask to have another serving. If he notices someone else asking for a new portion, he shouldn't ask what was wrong with the food.

MAY 24

Decoding spoons and forks

Utensils are arranged in the order in which they'll be used. If there's lots of silverware, your child will probably see more forks and knives than spoons. The basic rules are these:

1. Start with the utensils farthest from the plate and work inward.
2. Spoons are used for soup and soft desserts.
3. Knives and forks travel together and are used for everything else (even mashed potatoes and peas).
4. Utensils are held like a pencil, not like the handlebars of a bicycle. Holding them properly helps keep your child's elbows by his sides.

Here are some of the foods each is used for:

- *Spoons:* to eat soup, fruit cup with lots of juice, soft desserts such as ice cream, mousse, or crème brûlée; to stir iced tea, hot tea, or coffee.

- *Knives:* to spread butter on bread; to cut a sandwich in half.
- *Knives and forks used together:* to cut meat or fresh fruit.
- *Forks:* to eat salad, vegetables (even peas and mashed potatoes), meat, fish, and pasta; to cut soft foods such as lasagna and boiled potatoes; to eat pie and cake.
- *Spoons and forks together:* to eat dessert, such as an éclair or pie and ice cream (hold an éclair in place with the fork in the left hand, cut it with the spoon, then eat it with the fork).

A printed menu often accompanies a formal dinner. A quick comparison between the silverware in the place setting and the items on the table can help your child make sure he won't run out of utensils. He doesn't want to send off his last knife with the waiter before he's been served his entree. A well-trained waiter probably won't let this happen, but an ounce of prevention is good, too.

MAY 25

Using utensils correctly

Holding utensils correctly is a mark of distinction for any child, not to mention a confidence booster. There are two acceptable ways for your child to eat. The first is the most common.

American: Cut a bite-sized piece of food while holding your knife in your right hand and your fork in your left. To eat, place your knife on the top of your plate with the blade facing you. Transfer your fork to your right hand and pick up the food with your fork.

European: Hold the knife in your right hand and your fork in your left, just as you do in the American method, but don't transfer the fork to your right hand. When cutting food, your index finger rests on the back of the utensils, and they are properly held if they appear to grow straight out of the tip of your index finger. Never hold your fork like an icepick. It isn't necessary to lay down your knife when taking a bite. Eat by piercing food with the fork or pushing it onto the back of the fork. Bring the food to your mouth with the fork tines down.

MAY 26

Utensils: after the meal

Placement of utensils tells others what your child is up to. It's kind of like a secret code. There are two positions for knives and forks. When you pause during the meal to talk or pass food, place your knife at the top of the plate with the blade facing you and your fork on an angle on the left of your plate.

When you're finished eating, imagine the plate is a clock and put the handles of your knife and fork at the 5:20 position. Placing the knife with the fork in this way at the end of a course makes clearing the plate easier. If there is still food on your plate, discreetly move it aside. It's unsightly to prop utensils on top of food.

Activity

Have your child imagine he will be enjoying the following menu. Draw a diagram or arrange silverware on a table so that he will have exactly what he needs to eat the meal.

<u>MENU</u>

Cold Curry Soup (soup spoon)

Sesame Sticks (fingers)

Roast Spring Lamb (dinner knife, fork)

Fresh Mint Sauce

Vegetable Medley (fork)

Bundled Baby Romaine with Marinated Hearts of Palm
(salad fork and salad knife)

Raspberry Sherbet Ring Filled with Fresh Fruit (dessert spoon and fork)

Petits Fours (dessert fork or fingers)

MAY 27

Napkin etiquette

Napkins are easy for kids to forget unless they *really* need them. If a glass of water tips over, the first thing you'll probably reach for is your napkin, and maybe your neighbor's as well. But napkins should go on your lap as soon as everyone is seated, whether or not there is a dining disaster.

The first thing you always do at the table (after saying a blessing if that's your custom) is pick up your napkin, open it halfway (or completely if it isn't too big), and place it across your lap. There it stays throughout the meal. If your fingers are sticky, clean them on the napkin as it lies on your lap. If you drip sauce on your chin, pat your mouth clean with the napkin; *gently* blot the food from your face using a corner of the napkin. Then put it back on your lap.

Use your napkin just before you take a drink, to take care of crumbs—not a pretty sight for anyone else at the table! Here are some tips for your child:

- Use *your* napkin, not your neighbor's. You'll find it to the left of your plate, on your plate, or sometimes tucked into one of the goblets. If it's in a goblet, it's in the goblet at the upper right of your plate.
- Put your napkin on your seat if you must leave the table. Put it back on your lap when you return.
- Use the tip of your napkin dipped in your water to clean a small spot of food from your clothing.
- Don't blow your nose in your napkin—ever!
- Don't put a soiled napkin back on the table until the end of a meal.
- Don't ask "Who took my napkin?" If you're in a restaurant, quietly ask the server to bring you another one.

Activity

Get a book on napkin folding from the library or look through your cookbooks for ideas. Help your child fold the napkins in a special way for a family meal, using cloth or paper napkins. Emphasize napkin etiquette at the meal.

MAY 28

Ten things your child should never do at the table

Some behaviors should always be avoided at mealtime. Your child should never:

1. Take a bite so big that it changes the shape of her face.
2. Put a knife in her mouth.
3. Lean back with her chair resting on two legs.
4. Pick her teeth with a toothpick.
5. Fish around in a serving plate for the largest piece of meat.
6. Chew with her mouth open.
7. Lean one elbow on the table with her back to the person beside her.
8. Push the plate back when she's finished.
9. Point a knife at someone.
10. Talk about gross things.

Activity

Discuss the list above and demonstrate what each of the rules means. Then put a small bell (or buzzer from a game) by the table and ring it when someone breaks a rule from the list. Have your kids guess which rule was broken. Give them a chance to use the bell, too.

MAY 29

Second helpings

May your child have seconds? Yes—sometimes. It's okay to have seconds when:

- Your child is eating at home.
- Everyone else has had firsts.
- Seconds are on the table.
- She's dining at someone else's home and seconds are offered.
- She's at a buffet and she's taken a clean plate.
- She's already offered seconds to a guest at her table.
- Her guest takes seconds (it's nice to take a small portion at least, so her guest doesn't eat alone).

MAY 30

When to begin eating

It's proper to begin eating when everyone has been served. At the family dinner table, children wait until their parents begin. Dad sets the precedent for the children by waiting until Mom begins to eat. This eliminates reaching for a pickle or roll as soon as one is seated at the table.

Waiting to eat is a small gesture of restraint, but it sets the pace for a relaxed, enjoyable meal. It gives children an opportunity to pause and acknowledge the presence of others at the table. It symbolizes the social nature of eating—a lot more goes on at the table than filling the stomach.

When dining as a guest, your child should follow the lead of the hostess. When she picks up her spoon or fork, he may do the same. But if the group is large, it's okay to begin after three or four people have filled their plates. When this is the case, the hostess will probably tell everyone to get started so that the food doesn't get cold. Continuing to wait for the hostess when you've been urged to eat isn't a courtesy—it makes others who've already started feel awkward.

When a number of courses are served, your child should make sure others have been served at the beginning of each course. If he gets his ice cream sundae first, he doesn't dig in until others have gotten theirs.

MAY 31

Leaving the table early

Sometimes it's essential for your child to leave the table immediately. If she's suffering from a coughing fit or feels sick, she may push her chair back and go right to the bathroom. When there's an urgency but not an emergency, she says, "Excuse me, please." There's no need for her to exclaim, for example, that her bladder is about to burst. Her napkin goes on the seat of the chair while she's gone. When she returns to the table, she quietly takes her seat, puts her napkin back on her lap, and resumes eating without explanation.

Some planning ahead can make jumping up unnecessary. Before she sits down at the table, she should get rid of chewing gum, take out removable orthodontic appliances, and grab a tissue if she thinks she'll need one.

Frequently getting up from the table ruins the atmosphere of a meal. Your child shouldn't jump up to answer the telephone, get the ingredients for a peanut butter and jelly sandwich when she doesn't like what is being served, or tune in to a TV show she's had to interrupt to come to the table. Finally, she should not leave the table while her guest is still eating.

JUNE 1

Serving a meal

Your child can make it easier for his meal to be served to him by keeping the table in front of him clear of silverware, his glass, or plates. After he takes a drink, he should place his glass back at the upper right of his place setting. This looks nice, and it will prevent having the glass tipped over inadvertently. In a restaurant, his butter plate stays where it is, and if he's coloring or drawing, he should move the paper and crayons when he sees the waiter approaching with the food. Before dinner is served at home, he may sit with his hands in his lap.

At the dinner table at home, serving dishes of food are passed to the right. Serving utensils are placed to the side of the plate, with the tines of forks and the bowl of spoons turned down. Your child might like to collect coins or baseball cards, but he shouldn't collect serving utensils. They go back on the serving plate before it is passed on.

In a restaurant, individual plates are served from the left. The same is true at a formal dinner or banquet. There the first person served is a woman guest. Food is then served or passed around the table counterclockwise (to the right).

When dinner is served on individual plates filled at the table by the hostess, who is seated at the end of the table, she may let a female guest know that the first plate she fills belongs to her. The rest are then passed toward the other end of the table on the right side and then on the left until everyone has been served. The hostess serves herself last.

Drinks are served from the right because the glasses, goblets, and coffee cups are on the right side of the place setting.

Before dessert is served, all serving dishes, dinner plates, soiled utensils, salt and pepper shakers, butter plates, and condiments or relishes are removed from the table. Dinner plates are removed from the person's right.

JUNE 2

Cleansing the palate

The palate is the roof of the mouth. The word *palate* also refers to a person's sense of taste; when someone loves fine food, he is said to have a refined palate.

On rare formal occasions your child may have the opportunity to cleanse her palate just before she is served the entree. Here, *cleanse* means "refresh."

She'll be served a small scoop of fruit sorbet (a flavor such as strawberry, peach, or lemon) in a footed bowl with an underplate and a small spoon. If she's never seen it before, she may think her dream of having dessert served before dinner has come true. She should eat the tart, refreshing sorbet and begin the main course enjoying the benefit—she won't have lingering sensations from an appetizer or salad in her mouth.

When the sorbet is finished, the spoon is returned to the underplate.

JUNE 3
Using a finger bowl

Fingers bowls are brought to the table just before dessert. They're a necessity after a shellfish dinner and a nicety at a formal dinner.

After a fish course, the water in the finger bowl will be served warm. Your child may dip the fingers of both hands into the bowl and dry them on her napkin on her lap. It's fine to pat damp fingers on the mouth as well and dry the mouth with the napkin. This isn't the time for a full-fledged scrubbing—it's hardly appealing for others to see the forearms and neck being washed at the table. The waiter will clear the bowls before serving dessert.

At a formal dinner, the finger bowl may arrive resting on a doily on the dessert plate. Again, the fingers are dipped in the water and dried on the napkin. The finger bowl is then lifted, *along with the doily,* and placed to the upper left of the plate. What remains is the dessert plate. (Your child doesn't want to ruin a perfectly good dessert by trying to eat a doily with it.)

Finger bowls are so rarely seen that they often cause confusion. It's fine simply to set them aside.

JUNE 4
Finding a seat at a formal dinner

Usually there is very little guesswork in knowing where to sit at a formal dinner: From wedding receptions to White House state dinners, every detail is planned. The role of the guest is to arrive early (it takes a while for a large group to find seats in a banquet hall) and take the seat that's been assigned.

There are a number of ways for your child to find which table she's assigned to. Look around at the entrance to the dining room. There may be a table with small stand-up cards on it. Each card will have a guest's name and a table number on it. Your child takes hers and finds her table. The same system is often used with name tags. At the bottom corner of a name tag there may be a number. Your child checks for the number, then puts the tag on the right side of her outfit near the shoulder. Or there may be an easel with an alphabetical listing of all of the guests. After each name there will be a table number.

Tables are numbered, and the numbers typically run in rows across the width of the dining room. When someone's lost, she may ask an usher where her table is. He might not escort people to their tables, but will point out the table in the room or on a diagram of how the tables are numbered in the room. Table numbers are usually in the center of each table.

When your child finds her table, she needs to check to see if individual seats are assigned as well. She'll see a small card, called a place card, lying on her plate or placed above the plate. She shouldn't switch cards to sit beside someone she thinks would be more fun. This can be insulting to others at the table. If there aren't place cards, sit boy, girl, boy, girl. A woman sits to the right of a man, and a girl sits to the right of her date.

Activity

Have your child make place cards the next time you invite friends for dinner. Tent cards stand above the plate—they're a bit smaller than a credit card when folded in half. Alternatively, a flat card may be laid on the center of a folded napkin on the plate. Have your child decorate the card seasonally or simply write the person's first name on it. Be sure the names are spelled correctly.

JUNE 5

At the end of a formal meal

It's nice for everyone at the table to reach the end of the meal together. Some children appear to inhale their food, while others dawdle over every bite—they need some prompting about keeping pace with others at the table.

When your child has finished, he places his silverware at an angle on the right side of his plate. When the hostess puts her napkin on the table, he does the same. These are the only gestures that need to be made—your child shouldn't groan and exclaim, "I'm stuffed," push away his plate, tip his chair back, or casually hook his elbow over the back of it.

When others get up, he may do the same. If the adults are going to stay at the table, talking and lingering over coffee, your child may ask to be excused to go to the playroom. He should push back his chair with his feet and legs rather than putting his hands on the edge of the table and shoving himself back. His chair is then pushed in toward the table so that it isn't in the way of others passing by.

If he's dining informally at a friend's house, he should notice if others carry their plates to the kitchen, and do the same. If he's dining formally, he doesn't help clear the table.

JUNE 6
Food your child hates

When your child asks, "What's for dinner tonight?" you might cringe, knowing that you won't like his response any more than he will like what's on the menu. He might say, "Yuck! I don't like beef stew" or "I hate green beans." Everyone has food preferences, but your child should learn not to express all of his negative sentiments. It's not unreasonable to have a family rule that each person tries at least a sample of everything that is served. If your child typically eats most things but brussels sprouts make him gag, let him pass on the sprouts. But otherwise ask him to take a small portion of each item on the table.

You might ask your child to help in the meal planning. He'll probably be happy to make some recommendations and less likely to criticize what's put on the table. If his menu is mashed potatoes, macaroni and cheese, and ice cream, discuss why that isn't a well-balanced meal—he'll gain an appreciation for the effort you put into planning good meals.

At a friend's house, negative reactions to food will be completely unwelcome. That doesn't mean he has to eat everything; he just shouldn't grimace or say "yuck." If he's offered something he dislikes, he may say, "No, thank you." If he discovers that he's taken something that he really can't eat, he may just leave it on his plate. While he doesn't have to eat everything, he shouldn't stir the item with his fork to pass the time, and his only comments about the food should be positive.

Activity

Let your child help you create a week's worth of menus. Add or subtract from the list to be sure it's nutritionally balanced, and let her guess the ingredients that are needed to prepare the food. Take her along to the grocery store. Let her help with preparation.

JUNE 7

When your child is allergic to certain foods

Allergies to foods aren't preferences, and they may even be a matter of life and death. If your child has food allergies, she may avoid eating the food simply by passing it by and saying, "No, thank you." She shouldn't get into the habit of discussing her physical reactions. If someone pushes her to take just a little, she may say that her doctor has told her she isn't allowed to eat it.

If your child can't eat a number of items that are frequently used in cooking, such as milk or sugar, she needs to let her friend know before she accepts an invitation for dinner. She may offer to visit after dinner, thus giving her hostess a chance to either accept the suggestion or offer to cook something your child can eat.

Reassure your child that she doesn't need to feel any embarrassment about avoiding certain foods. It's her responsibility and right to protect her health.

JUNE 8

Afternoon tea

Sugar and spice and everything nice might be what little girls are made of, but it is also a description of afternoon tea. There's nothing more special than this centuries-old ceremony. An English duchess' afternoon hunger pangs in the 1800s sparked the tradition, and today little girls still imitate it with their teddy bears and friends.

In the 1840s in England, Anna, the seventh duchess of Bedford, began enjoying this delicate yet satisfying afternoon repast. It is said that she took an early, light lunch and a late, more substantial dinner. When she felt her stomach begin to growl in the late afternoon, she asked a servant to prepare some hot tea, a bit of toast with butter, and some cakes, which turned out to hit the spot exactly. The practice had to be repeated, of course, and soon she invited friends to join her. The rest, as they say, is history.

By the 1880s afternoon tea had become elaborate and widespread, complete with guests in fancy ruffled gowns, servants offering expensive beverages from ornate silver teapots, and musicians embellishing the atmosphere.

This all sounds too formal to be called afternoon tea, and it is sometimes mistaken for high tea. But high tea is entirely different, consisting of meats and eggs—more like a farmhouse supper. The beautiful and refined practice described here is rightly called afternoon tea.

All of the finest linens, prettiest teacups, and most decorative tiny sandwiches and cakes are served at afternoon tea. Your daughter may let her imagination run as she plans her next tea party.

Activity

Look for tea service items as you visit antique and gift shops. You'll find an infinite variety of teacups and saucers, teapots, strainers, and even locked tea chests (from the days when tea was so valuable that it was kept under lock and key). Buy different teas and sample them until you and your child have chosen your favorites, and hold a tea with your daughter and her friends on Sunday afternoon.

Setting the tea table

Setting the table for tea may be second nature to the English, but to an American who relies on tea bags, it can seem very complicated. Learning the tea ceremony can be fun for your child. Let her make it as simple or complicated as she likes.

Have your child pick her favorite teacups and saucers. (Mugs simply won't do for a tea party.) In the winter, the tea table may be a small table in front of the fireplace or in the bedroom, and in the summer, the front porch can be ideal. Choose a fresh tablecloth and linen napkins, and gather some pretty flowers. Afternoon tea calls for the prettiest, most festive table possible.

Here's a checklist of items used in a proper afternoon tea:

- *In the kitchen:* teakettle, fresh water, and loose tea (English breakfast is a not-too-strong, full-bodied tea often enjoyed by those who don't usually drink tea).
- *On the tea tray:* teapot, sugar bowl with sugar cubes, sugar tongs, cream pitcher with milk, tea strainer, waste bowl, small dish with lemon wedges, small fork for lemons.
- *On the tea table:* teacups and saucers, small plates, spoons and forks, linen napkins, several items of food such as tea sandwiches, scones, sweets, butter and jam (or Devonshire cream from a specialty shop instead of butter).

For a small group, put individual place settings out. If there are too many guests for each to be seated at the table, arrange a buffet tea table. At a buffet, place the teapot, cups and saucers, cream, sugar, and lemon at the end of the table. The other items are lined up in the following order: plates (stacked), napkins, tea sandwiches, scones, butter and jam, sweets, spoons (and forks, if needed).

Activity

There is a myriad of beautiful books about afternoon tea. Go to the library or a bookstore and let your child browse through some of these treasures. Pick up a copy of *Victoria* magazine or check out the Internet. Look for articles on afternoon tea for children—you'll be amazed at the creative materials available!

JUNE 10

Preparing the tea

Your child will need your help in preparing the tea, but she'll probably be delighted to work beside you in the kitchen. Here are the steps to brewing a fresh pot of tea:

1. Select a loose tea, such as English breakfast.
2. Bring fresh, cold tap water to boil in the teakettle.
3. Pour a bit of the hot water from the kettle (just before it boils) into the teapot, and swirl it around in the pot. This tempers the pot, warming it and allowing the water added later to boil longer and thus do a better job of opening the tea leaves. Empty the warm water from the teapot.
4. Add a teaspoon of tea leaves per cup (and one for the pot) to the teapot. (Tea balls filled with tea leaves work fine, too, and have the advantage of making strainers unnecessary.)
5. As soon as the water in the teakettle reaches a boil, pour it over the leaves. Allowing it to boil too long causes it to lose its oxygen and freshness.
6. Allow the tea to steep for three to six minutes. Give a good stir and it is ready to serve. Tea for children should be weaker and served warm, rather than very hot.

Activity

Let your child discover the delights of traditional English cucumber tea sandwiches. Here's how to make them.

Cucumber Sandwiches

1 slice thin white bread
1 tbsp cream cheese, softened
1 seedless cucumber, sliced
1 tbsp butter, softened

1. Slice the cucumber paper thin, leaving the skin on. Cut four slices per sandwich.
2. Lightly butter the bread (this seals the bread and keeps it fresh longer).
3. Spread cream cheese over the butter.
4. Place cucumber slices on the bread.
5. Cut the crusts off the sandwiches.
6. Cut sandwiches into four squares with one cucumber slice in each square.
7. Place closed sandwiches vertically on the serving plate so the green cucumber can be seen.
8. When made ahead, stack the closed sandwiches on a plate, wrap in plastic, and refrigerate.

JUNE 11

It's not a tea party without scones

If cucumber sandwiches aren't a favorite with your child, she'll love scones. The recipe might look complicated, but it is easy enough for a child to help make.

Scones

3 cups flour
1 tbsp baking powder
½ tsp baking soda
½ tsp salt
½ cup sugar
¾ cup butter

1 cup buttermilk
½ cup raisins or currants
½ cup orange juice
12 sugar cubes (one per scone)
1 tbsp milk or whipping cream

1. Preheat the oven to 400 degrees.
2. Sift the flour, baking powder, baking soda, and salt.

3. Add sugar.

4. Cut in butter using two forks or a pastry cutter.

5. Make a well in the center of the dough.

6. Pour buttermilk into the well. Mix quickly with a fork so that the buttermilk and butter don't separate.

7. Add raisins or currants and mix with hands.

8. Turn dough onto floured pastry board and press down to 3/4" thick with fingers.

9. Cut scones with floured biscuit cutter and place on greased cookie sheet.

10. Dip sugar cubes (one at a time or they'll dissolve) into the orange juice and press one cube into the top of each scone.

11. Use a pastry brush to paint the tops of the scones with milk or whipping cream.

12. Cover them with plastic wrap and refrigerate them at this point if you wish.

13. Bake 14–18 minutes (less time for small scones).

14. Serve warm with butter (or Devonshire cream) and jam.

JUNE 12

Eating scones

Here's the proper way for your child to enjoy these delectable treats. She may take a whole scone from the cake tray onto her small plate with her fingers. With a spoon, she then takes a dollop of Devonshire cream and puts it on the side of the plate. She does the same with the jam (strawberry is used most commonly).

With her knife, she cuts the scone in two horizontally. With one-half of the scone resting on the plate, she uses the knife to spread the cream rather thickly across the other. The gracious way is to cut the half scone in half again and put a bit of jam on this smaller piece, again using the knife. Then she eats this small piece with her fingers.

Remind your child to savor the moment. She should enjoy a sip of tea and chat with her friends. Then she may eat another quarter of the scone. Again, add a bit of jam and nibble. There's still half a scone left! She should eat it the same way as the first half, remembering to dab her lips with her napkin in case there are stray crumbs or jam.

The protocol of afternoon tea

The typical hour for afternoon tea is 4 P.M. The group may be any size. There is nothing cozier than two friends sharing tea, but if it's a birthday tea or a farewell tea for a friend who is moving, the more the merrier.

Tea invitations may be given by telephone or in writing, at the last minute or with advance notice, always with a specific time mentioned. Guests arrive on time. Afternoon dress is proper— nice, but not formal.

If your child is the hostess, she should greet her guests and show them immediately to the room where tea will be served. She makes introductions if there are guests who don't know each other. Guests are seated; if there is a guest of honor, she sits to the right of the hostess. The hostess pours the tea.

Tea is an afternoon pick-me-up, so restraint on your child's part is used in choosing items of food from the buffet table. Three items taken at a time is a good rule. Eat the sandwiches first. Your child should take whatever she touches and shouldn't point at the food. She may go back for seconds. Remind her to eat slowly, nibbling on small portions and taking time to talk.

When tea is finished, the cups and plates are removed, and the guests continue to visit. They don't stay longer than two hours. If there is a guest of honor, she leaves first.

A sincere thank-you at the door is adequate. Telephone calls and notes are not obligatory.

Activity

To delight the girls and take the pressure of formality off, ask each girl to bring one of her teddy bears to tea. A teddy bear tea theme is the perfect birthday party for an eight-year-old girl. Even if she is twelve years old, she'll be happy to have a favorite toy close by.

JUNE 14

Serving tea

When your child is the hostess, she is seated by the tea tray and serves the tea. If there isn't a tray, simply arrange the teapot, cups and saucers, sugar, milk, lemon, and waste bowl at the end of the table. Here's what her exchange with her guests should sound like:

Guest: May I please have a cup of tea?
Child: Yes. Would you like sugar?
Guest: Yes, please.
Child: One lump or two?
Guest: One lump, please.
Child: Would you like lemon or cream?
Guest: Cream, please.

Your child then pours a bit of fresh cold milk into the bottom of the teacup and adds a lump of sugar with the sugar tongs. She places a tea strainer over the cup to catch any tea leaves that might come through the spout, pours the hot tea over the milk and sugar, and hands it to her guest.

The tea strainer is emptied into a waste bowl that is placed to the left of the teapot. If a guest returns for a second cup of tea, any tea remaining in her cup is also poured into the waste bowl.

Milk, not cream, is served with tea, although it is called cream. The richness of cream may cause it to curdle when combined with the tannic acid of tea. The guest shouldn't combine lemon and cream, because they, too, will curdle when combined.

Activity

Visit New York City with your daughter and enjoy afternoon tea at one of the top hotels that offer a formal tea. Or try the Ritz-Carlton in Boston. Some of these hotel restaurants' linen-draped tables extend into the lobby, allowing guests to enjoy delicate afternoon sandwiches with tea while watching the fascinating bustle in a big-city hotel.

JUNE 15

What about coffee?

Few children drink coffee, though some are tempted to taste their parents' favorite brew. With so many festive and unusual coffee drinks available everywhere from grocery stores to gourmet coffee shops, children are more exposed to coffee drinking than ever. The iced versions look as good as milk shakes, the cappuccinos as rich as hot chocolate. It isn't hard to understand why some children are drawn to coffee. Some take to its taste quickly.

However popular java has become, common practice places coffee drinking squarely in the realm of adults. It's their special treat, and children shouldn't beg for a sip or ask to be served their own cup. Most times, coffee is prepared for the adults only. Discourage your child from getting hooked on coffee. It isn't the worst of addictions, but most likely it will be jarring to adults in other families if your child asks for a cup of coffee.

Activity

If your child loves the flavor of coffee, introduce a milder latte version. Fill a cup with milk; heat it in the microwave. Add a teaspoon of instant coffee and stir.

Stay Out of Sticky Situations with Food!

❧

Figuring out the proper way to eat something doesn't always involve just common sense, especially when it comes to special foods. While using the fingers might seem to be the easiest method, dining with others often calls for a better way. There will be times your child will have to overcome a natural aversion to utensils, and practice until he gets it right. You'll both be glad he did when he makes it successfully through a special meal.

JUNE 16
Removing items from your mouth

Inevitably, when your child is at the table, he'll find something in his mouth that shouldn't be there. Maybe it's an olive pit, a fish bone, or a grape seed. He shouldn't try to swallow it, but should take it out as inconspicuously as possible.

Removing something from the mouth is less noticeable if the object comes out the way it went in. When grapes are eaten with the hand, the seeds come out with the hand. The fingers cover the mouth horizontally and the seeds are removed between the thumb and fingers. An olive pit is removed the same way.

Fish is eaten with a fork, so bones are removed from the mouth with the fork. If grapes are part of a salad and are eaten with a fork, seeds that end up in the mouth come out on the fork.

Seeds and bones are placed at the side of the plate. Remind your children that only in an emergency is anything spit into the napkin.

How to handle special diets

If your child is on a special diet, he should know exactly what he is allowed to eat, what's off-limits, and the benefits of staying on the diet. When he understands and accepts the diet, it'll be easier for him to follow it when he's with his friends. If it's possible to be lenient sometimes, help him plan so that he'll be less restricted when he's a guest.

All your child needs to do is pass over a food item he can't eat, or take a bit and leave the rest untouched on his plate. Assure him that he's not obligated to discuss his diet with others. (Adults have the opposite temptation—they want to talk endlessly about their diets!) And remind him that adults who force the topic are being rude—he doesn't need to respond to prying questions. Nor does he need to give in to the adult suggestion that a little ice cream won't hurt. The simple explanation that he isn't able to eat ice cream right now is all that is needed.

If your child's friend is on a diet, it's not courteous to indulge in everything he's forbidden to eat in front of him. Try to plan a menu that accommodates his needs.

When ordering food in a restaurant, it's okay to ask for modifications of items on the menu, but try to be reasonable. For example, it's fine to ask that salad dressing or sauces be served on the side. It's not okay to ask that the sauce be made with something other than cream. It's good to order only what can be eaten—sometimes appetizers (soup and salad) are enough for a child—rather than nibbling around the edges of an entree and leaving most of it. Be sure to help your child as much as possible when making decisions about food—but try not to be too tough!

JUNE 18

How to eat difficult foods

A number of foods call for special eating techniques. Parents, here are some helpful hints you can share with your children to make mealtime a worry- (and mess-) free affair:

- *Hamburgers.* They can be messy if they're covered with fixings. To avoid catsup wings on your cheeks, cut the hamburger in half before you take a bite.
- *French fries.* Fingers are fine at a fast-food restaurant, but at any more formal table, use a fork. Put the catsup on the side and dip the fries one or two at a time.
- *Asparagus.* This cooked vegetable is properly eaten with the fingers. If that's too messy, cut it and eat it with a fork. Let your child know it's okay to discard any part that is too fibrous.
- *Lemon.* Squeeze the juice onto fish or into iced tea. Cup the left hand around the lemon to avoid squirting your neighbor. Sometimes the lemon is covered with a piece of gauze to help keep the juice from flying and the seeds out of the food.
- *Bacon.* If it is soft, eat it with a fork. Crisp bacon may be eaten with the fingers.
- *Baked potatoes.* Sweet or white, cut them in half, scoop the insides onto the plate, season, and eat with a fork. Or simply cut in half, season, and eat from the skin. Eating the skin is okay, too. The potato may be cut into small pieces or the skin may be eaten separately, the way you would eat bread and butter.

JUNE 19

How to eat an appetizer

Appetizers are small portions of food that are meant to get the digestive juices flowing. Other words for appetizers are *hors d'oeuvres* and *canapés*. They are only meant to stimulate the appetite, not satisfy it. When presented with these delectable morsels, your child shouldn't take enough to feed his third-grade class.

An appetizer may be served at the beginning of a sit-down dinner. In this case it probably won't be finger food, will be served on a small plate, and should be eaten with a fork or spoon. It could be a small portion of smoked fish, pastry stuffed with meat, or a cup of soup.

Eating an appetizer while standing is a bit trickier. If a server brings a tray of appetizers, it's fine to take one with the fingers. Since many are greasy or hot, be sure to get a napkin as well. Popping it directly into the mouth looks as if one is eating from the serving tray. Take a piece, put it on the napkin, wait a few seconds, then devour it. An appetizer on a toothpick is meant to be eaten in one bite. Put it in the mouth, close the teeth and lips over the food, and pull the toothpick out. The toothpick never goes back on the serving tray. Find a wastebasket or an ashtray, or put it in a pocket or purse.

Appetizers your child might encounter include bite-sized pieces of pizza, cheese cubes and crackers, stuffed mushrooms, and tiny quiche squares. Crudités—the fancy term for carrot and celery sticks (and other fresh vegetables) with dip—are also popular. When your child is serving himself from a buffet, three items is a reasonable amount to take. If a server comes around with a tray, taking one item is sufficient, since your child probably won't have a plate. The server will come around a number of times.

Activity

Serve kid-friendly appetizers at the next gathering of your child's friends. You might serve mini bagels with pizza sauce and melted cheese. Encourage him to use his best manners while snacking.

JUNE 20

Eating bread

Bread is passed to the right. If a basket of bread is by your child's plate, he may start it by pulling apart the napkin covering the bread, holding the basket, and offering it to the person on his left. Then he serves himself and passes it on to the person on his right. Bread may be passed after the blessing or after the appetizer has been eaten.

Bread goes on the bread plate or on the left side of the dinner plate. Butter and jelly are also placed on the plate before being spread on the bread. Rolls are torn in half at first. Bite-sized pieces are then broken off one at a time, buttered with a knife, and eaten. Your child should hold the bread on the plate as he butters it, rather than placing it in the palm of his hand.

The custom of buttering bread a piece at time began centuries ago to ensure that leftover bread had no butter on it. Servants were permitted to take the remaining bread home. Today the custom keeps busy people from eating at an uncivilized pace.

Muffins and toast are cut in half and then buttered. Again, the butter is placed on the plate first and added to the toast or muffin before it is eaten. If it is warm, though, it's fine to butter the whole thing so the butter has a chance to melt. Danish and sweet rolls are also easier to eat if they are first cut in half.

Some crusty breads, such as baguettes, leave a lot of crumbs when they're broken. Most of the crumbs should hit the plate, but those on the tablecloth can simply be picked up with the fingers and placed on the plate. At some restaurants the waiter will scrape or brush the crumbs from the tablecloth before dessert.

When bread comes on a cutting board with a knife, your child should cut only the piece that he wants for himself. If he is served pita bread, he may take the whole piece, break off a piece for himself, and leave the remainder of the torn pita in the basket. Each person after him also tears off his own piece.

Activity

Take your child to a specialty bread stand at a market and choose a couple of different breads. Practice eating them properly.

JUNE 21

Eating a salad

Most parents are satisfied if their child eats salad at all, and don't want to make too great a point about eating it properly. But for the record, here are some tips for you to pass along:

When the salad is on the dinner plate, it's eaten with a dinner fork. If it's on a separate plate, a salad fork is used. A restaurant might even provide a salad knife, which, along with the salad fork, is often smaller than the dinner fork and knife. If the greens are too big for one bite, they are cut with the knife and fork. Cut a bite or two at a time, rather than dicing the whole plate at once. Rest the knife on the edge of the salad plate while eating.

When a salad has cherry tomatoes, the larger ones are cut in half with a knife and the smaller ones may be eaten whole. Handle these juicy, exploding morsels with care.

When salad dressing is served on the side, it may be added all at once to a small salad. If it's going on a chef's salad, add it a bit at a time so that there's dressing for the greens at the bottom, too.

Small green salads are served with the entree or just before it. If a salad comes after the entree, it will probably be accompanied by cheese and crackers. The cheese is eaten with a fork and the crackers with the fingers.

JUNE 22

Eating soup

Your child's soup spoon goes into the soup and the soup is scooped away from him. Remind him that the soup comes up to the mouth; the face doesn't go down to the soup! Your child should lean forward slightly so that any drops that escape the spoon hit the bowl and not the tablecloth or his lap. He should also eat from the side of the spoon; it shouldn't disappear entirely into his mouth—nor should any slurping sound be heard.

If there's just a little soup left at the bottom of the bowl, your child should tilt the bowl away to scoop up the last spoonfuls.

When the soup is all gone, the soup spoon should be placed on the underplate if there is one. If there is only a soup bowl, place the spoon in the bowl with the handle to the right.

If the soup is too hot, your child should not blow on it to make it cool. Instead, tell him to wait a minute before eating or take a spoonful and hold it just above the surface of the soup until it cools. Don't let your child put ice in the soup or stir it repeatedly to cool it.

When soup is served in a cup, after a spoonful or two it's fine to pick up the cup and drink the remainder.

Crackers may be broken and then scattered on the soup. Croutons get spooned directly onto the soup from the serving dish, as long as your child is careful not to let the serving spoon touch the soup. Oyster crackers are placed on the bread plate and put a few at a time into the soup.

And then there's the problem of onion soup! When the soup has a cheesy crust, your child should use the soup spoon to pull the stringy cheese away from the side of the bowl and cut it (it's okay to cut it with a knife, too). That's better than getting caught with ropes of cheese hanging from his mouth.

JUNE 23

How to eat dessert

Cookies, bite-sized pastries, and small cream puffs are eaten with the fingers.

Pudding, ice cream, mousse, and other soft desserts are eaten with a spoon. Stewed fruit is also eaten with a spoon. If it needs to be cut, hold it in place with a fork, then cut it and eat it with a spoon.

Pie and cake are eaten with a fork. When either is accompanied by ice cream, use a spoon as well. If pastry is too difficult to cut with a fork (a large éclair, for example), use the edge of a spoon to do the cutting, but eat it with the fork.

When there are more dessert utensils than are needed, leave them on the table.

How to eat pasta

There are a number of ways to eat pasta. If your child is particularly adept with utensils, a fork is all that's needed. The tines of the fork should be slipped through the spaghetti and against the plate, then a small portion is twirled until the ends are wrapped around the fork. If tails unravel, your child can bite them off and let them drop to the plate. A short piece of spaghetti may be sucked (silently) into her mouth.

If your child is just learning to eat spaghetti, she'll find it easier to get the spaghetti onto the fork by twirling it against the bowl of a large spoon. Show her how to twirl until the tails are wrapped around the fork, then bring it to her mouth.

If all of this twirling is still too complicated, it's fine to cut the spaghetti into manageable pieces and eat it with a fork.

When a sauce is served on top of the pasta, a fork and spoon can be used to mix it into the spaghetti before eating it.

How to eat shish kabob

When your child is served meat and vegetables on a large skewer, he should hold the skewer in his left hand with the end of the skewer resting on the plate. With a fork in his right hand, he slides the meat and vegetables onto his plate. The best approach is to take off just a few pieces at a time so that he doesn't lose control and send the meat onto the tablecloth. After the meat and vegetables are on the plate, they're cut into bite-sized pieces and eaten with a fork.

Shish kabob served as an appetizer on a tiny skewer is held in the fingers and eaten directly from the skewer.

JUNE 26

Corn on the cob

Corn never tastes better than when it's served on the cob. It's definitely finger food and is perfect for a picnic, but it won't be served at a formal dinner.

Lots of butter is essential, but there's a way to keep from being too messy. Have your child take several pats of butter and put them on the plate. With a knife, she can then spread part of the butter on the ear, covering only several rows at a time. Nibble across the kernels, like a piano player hitting all of the keys on a keyboard. The cleaner the cob, the nicer it looks. To make it easier, she can score the rows lengthwise with a knife before beginning to eat. She should add butter as she goes.

Some people insist upon sticking handles into the ends of the ear. The handles may help your child avoid hot fingers, but they're difficult to insert and only an adult should do it.

JUNE 27

Eating lobster

Eating lobster requires some equipment—a nutcracker or shellfish cracker, a shellfish fork or pick, a large paper or plastic bib, and a waste bowl for the discarded shells. It's not a meal that every child will enjoy—many think it looks too much like a live creature! But if your child likes lobster, here's how to help him enjoy it.

Have your child get a firm hold on the lobster with one hand and take the nutcracker in the other. He can then twist the claws off the body and place them on a plate. Each claw should be cracked carefully so that juice doesn't squirt a neighbor; the meat is then removed with a pick or fork. Rarely will the nutcracker do the whole job of breaking open the shell. The fingers do the rest.

Your child should then take the meat out of one side of the tail at a time. If it comes out whole, he can cut the piece with a knife and fork into manageable pieces, then dip in melted butter and eat them. (Cold lobster is usually dipped in mayonnaise.)

The green liver (the tomalley) and the red roe (in a female lobster) are considered delicacies and are eaten with a fork. Some people combine them a bit at a time with pieces of the meat.

Put all of the empty shells in the waste bowl. There may also be a finger bowl with hot water and lemon—your child should use it to wash his fingers and then dry them on a napkin.

JUNE 28

Eating fried chicken

Meat isn't typically eaten with the fingers at formal occasions, but then fried chicken is rarely served at formal occasions. When the fried chicken comes in a bucket and is served at a picnic, it's finger food. This means your child can pick it up and eat the meat directly from the bone. Keep plenty of napkins close by so your child can use them often on both face and hands. Your child may enjoy the food, but others won't enjoy looking at his face shining with grease!

At the dinner table, some people choose to eat fried chicken with a knife and fork, but it's okay for a child to use fingers as well. If utensils are used, he should hold the piece of chicken with a fork, cut the meat away with a knife, and then eat it with the fork. Whichever way your child prefers, he should place the discarded bones on a separate plate if it's available or neatly at the side of his plate.

JUNE 29

Eating sushi

Sushi is a Japanese delicacy of raw fish or vegetables served on vinegared rice. If your child is still interested, here's how it's eaten:

The piece of sushi is picked up by hand, dipped into the soy sauce, and placed fish side down into the mouth. Usually it's eaten whole. If the piece is too big, eat part of it, dip the rest in the sauce again, then finish eating it.

When sushi is wrapped in seaweed, don't use the fingers. The Japanese use chopsticks for this.

When taking food from a serving bowl that others are using as well, use the large ends of the chopsticks. The small ends go in the mouth.

JUNE 30

Eating an artichoke

Artichokes are eaten with the fingers. They are accompanied by melted butter, hollandaise sauce, or mayonnaise.

Your child should hold the whole artichoke with one hand and pull off a leaf near the bottom with the other. At the base of the leaf there will be a fleshy part. Your child should dip this in butter or sauce, then place the leaf between his teeth and pull forward, scraping the soft portion into his mouth.

The leaves closer to the center will have larger edible parts. The inedible remainder of the leaves are returned neatly to the plate at the base of the artichoke.

When all of the leaves are gone, the fuzzy center of the artichoke (called the choke) remains. Your child should cut this part off with a knife and place it with the discarded leaves, eating the tender heart that remains with a knife and fork. This may be dipped in butter or sauce as well.

JULY 1

Eating tacos and tortillas

Hard tacos are eaten with the hands. Your child should start at the end and eat the taco lengthwise, as she would a hot dog. It's good to keep a napkin handy to clean taco sauce off her face. Inevitably, fillings will fall to the plate. These aren't picked up with the fingers—they're eaten with a fork.

A soft taco and a tortilla may be eaten with the hands as well. If your child fills the tortilla herself, she can make eating it easier by folding the ends up as she rolls the tortilla; she'll lose less of the filling. If she's really concerned about making a mess, she may cut it crosswise and eat it with a fork.

JULY 2

Fun with fondue

A fondue pot is a type of group dining experience featuring cheese, liquid, or chocolate contained in a pot kept warm by electricity or a Sterno or alcohol burner underneath. Each person has his own fondue fork as well as a dinner plate and fork.

Cheese fondue is usually accompanied by cubed French bread. When the bread is passed, your child should take a few pieces and put them on her own plate. Then she takes the fondue fork, spears one piece of bread at a time, and dips it into the melted cheese. When she pulls it out, she holds it above the pot for a second or two to allow the extra cheese to drip into the pot. With a dinner fork she pulls the cheese-covered bread onto her plate and eats it with the dinner fork. Fruit dipped in chocolate is done the same way.

When the fondue pot contains hot oil or hot broth for cooking meat, your child will put a number of pieces of raw meat on her plate and then pierce them one at a time and put them into the pot. The meat rests in the pot until it's cooked. Your child should keep her eye on the meat and make certain she pulls out her own fork (the handle is probably color-coded in some way). She should let extra liquid drip into the pot and then use her dinner fork to slide the meat off the fondue fork onto a clean plate. As soon as one piece of meat is finished cooking, she may add another to the pot. The meat is cut into bite-sized pieces, may be dipped in other sauces, and is eaten from the plate with a fork.

Activity

Enjoy a fondue night with another family. Gather several fondue pots, filling some with oil and others with cheese or chocolate sauce. Seat the children among the adults and allow plenty of time to enjoy the process as well as the food.

JULY 3

Eating watermelon

Watermelon sliced thin but still on the rind is picnic food. It's held with the hands and eaten right from the rind; this guarantees that there will be seed spitting. That's fine when the party's informal, everyone's outdoors, and everyone's spitting seeds.

When forks are available, they are used to remove most of the seeds, which are then placed on the plate. If your child still finds a seed in her mouth, she should spit it into her hand or napkin and place it on the plate. Forks also can be used to cut and eat the watermelon, making the process less messy.

Watermelon won't be served in the rind at a more formal dinner—it'll be cut up and served as fruit cup. It's eaten with a fork, or with a spoon if the fruit cup has a lot of juice.

JULY 4

Pizza

There are three ways to eat pizza. Go over these with your children:

1. It can be cut with a knife and fork and eaten with the fork.
2. It can be picked up with two hands, one hand on the edge of the crust and the other supporting the pizza underneath, and eaten from the pointed end first. This way yields pizza sauce on the cheeks and can burn the palate if the pizza is too hot.
3. The pizza can also be folded lengthwise. Imagine cutting the slice in half, then fold the pizza along the imaginary cutting line. Breaking the crust at the fold line first makes it easier to

fold the slice. This method reduces the possibility of cheese strings, pizza sauce on the face, and a burned mouth.

Your child shouldn't inhale his first piece of pizza so that he can be sure to get a second before someone else does. Nor should he grab the last piece. Compromise by cutting the last pieces in half if others want more.

And remember: The pizza delivery person gets tipped a minimum of $2.

JULY 5

Crunching ice

This is to be avoided, even by kids. It sounds terrible to anyone who is close by, and it probably isn't good for the teeth. It especially shouldn't be done if your child wears braces.

Ice is meant to cool a beverage. It shouldn't be scooped out of the glass and plopped into soup that's too hot, nor should it be picked up at a picnic table and run over the forehead on a 90-degree day. And it shouldn't be crunched!

JULY 6

Eating raw oysters, clams, or mussels

Raw oysters, clams, or mussels are served on the half shell in a bed of ice. If your child is willing to eat one of these delicious morsels, have him hold the shell on the plate with the thumb and index finger of one hand and use an oyster fork or salad fork in the other hand to take out the meat. If it doesn't all pull away at once, your child should use a fork to get the rest. Sauce can be added to the oyster on the shell; otherwise, your child can dip the oyster in the sauce after taking it out of the shell. It should be eaten from the fork in one bite.

To get every last bit of juice, have your child pick up the shell and pour it into his mouth—trying not to slurp.

Oyster crackers may be dropped a few at a time into the dipping sauce. The fork is used to get them out to eat.

JULY 7

Eating crabs

Hard-shell crabs are like lobsters—they have deliciously tender meat, but depending upon how they are served, each bite can require work. At a picnic, crabs may be steamed, seasoned, and served whole. A nutcracker is used to break open the shell, and the fingers are often needed to fully expose the meat. A tiny fork is used to pull out the meat, which is then eaten from the fork.

The process is inherently messy and fun, and requires many napkins and bowls of warm water with slices of lemon to wash the hands. At more formal meals, crabmeat is already taken from the shell when it's served.

Soft-shell crabs aren't a different species of crab—they're merely harvested at a different stage of development. Crab shells don't expand, so as a crab grows, it casts off the outgrown shell and begins to grow another. If a crab is caught just after it's shed its shell (while the exterior is still soft), it's considered a delicacy. These soft-shell crabs are cut into bite-sized pieces with a knife and fork and eaten skin and all. (Your child also may find them served in a sandwich. In this case, your child should cut the sandwich in half and eat it with the fingers.)

The skin of a soft-shell crab is usually quite tender, but if there's a bit of tough shell remaining, your child should remove it from her mouth with her fingers and place it on the side of the plate.

JULY 8

Eating fresh fruit

At mealtime, whole fruit may be served as dessert or just before the dessert course. To eat it properly, your child should quarter or halve larger fruits such as apples, peaches, or pears with a fruit knife and remove the seeds. Seeds, stems, and unwanted skins are placed to the side of the plate. Americans consider these fruits finger food, while Europeans sometimes eat them with a fork.

Smaller fruits aren't cut before eating. Cherries are popped into the mouth with the hands and the clean pit is removed with the fingers. Plums and apricots may be held as the fruit is eaten away from the pit.

Grapes are eaten with the fingers, too. When taking grapes, your child shouldn't pluck them from the bunch one at a time. A branch with several grapes on it is broken off (or cut with a scissors). If the grapes have seeds, they may be cut in half and the seeds taken out before they're eaten. If they're eaten whole, the seeds are removed with the fingers.

Blueberries are eaten with the fingers or with a spoon. Fresh fruit salad is eaten with a fork. If there's plenty of juice, a spoon is used.

Activity

Help your child practice removing pits from her mouth by serving a fruit salad that includes cherries or grapes. Rather than poking the fingers directly into the mouth, they cross in front of the mouth with the thumb underneath. The seed is caught between the thumb and the fingers and placed on the side of the plate. It's also okay to take them from the mouth with a spoon.

JULY 9

Gravies, condiments, and relishes

Gravy and sauces are spooned on top of the meat, fish, rice, or potatoes. If there is a ladle, your child should use it to take some gravy, and then replace the ladle in the gravy boat with the handle away from the spout. At a buffet, the ladle may get too hot to hold if it's left in a chafing dish. Your child should look for a plate beside the chafing dish to place the ladle on.

Condiments are served beside the cooked item that they are meant to accompany. They go onto the main plate and are eaten with a fork a bit at a time with the other food. Some common condiments are catsup, mustard, chutney, horseradish, and tart jellies.

French fries aren't drowned in catsup, but are dipped in a small portion placed beside them on the plate. Mint jelly isn't spread on top of lamb, but is placed beside it and eaten a bit at a time with each bite of meat. Horseradish isn't spooned over the roast beef; instead, a small portion is placed on a bite of meat, and they're eaten together.

Relishes such as celery and carrot sticks, olives, small pickles, or spring onions may be placed on the butter plate and eaten with the fingers.

JULY 10

Foreign matter in food

Very young children may happily put paper or dirt into their mouths but wrinkle their nose at a spoonful of peas and spit them out. When your child reaches the age where he distinguishes foreign matter from edible items, let him know that sometimes at the table it's okay to spit things out. But it should be done as subtly as possible.

When your child bites into an egg salad sandwich and discovers a piece of eggshell, he may quietly spit the shell into his fingers and place it at the side of his plate. If he discovers a piece of hair in his mouth, of course he takes it out. He may put it on his napkin or drop it to the floor.

Maybe he'll discover a small bug on his lettuce before he starts to eat or a piece of hair in his green beans. If the foreign matter doesn't ruin his appetite, he may remove it and eat the rest of the food. If he finds the remaining food inedible because of the contamination, he may leave it untouched when he's a guest in someone's home. If his host notices and asks if something was wrong, he can simply say that there was something in the salad that he couldn't eat and ask to have another serving. At a restaurant, he may ask to have it replaced.

How to hold a glass

Adults have all kinds of rules about holding stemware—a glass containing a cold drink is held by the stem rather than the bowl being touched by the hand, thus keeping the hand warm and the drink cold. And the opposite is true when the drink is supposed to stay at room temperature—the bowl of the goblet is cupped in the hand to further warm the drink.

For children, the rules aren't nearly so complicated. Most importantly, your child should drink out of *her* glass—it's to the right of the place setting. After that, the goal is simply to avoid spilling the drink and to look as graceful as possible, considering the child's age. Holding a glass with two hands might be necessary.

Tumblers are held near the base, with one hand or two. They're not held at the rim with the index finger curled over the edge into the drink. Between sips, the glass is put down. Your child shouldn't continue to hold it at chin level with elbows propped on the table.

Cups with handles and mugs are held by the handle with the index finger and middle finger wrapped through the handle and the thumb above the handle with the little finger below. It's fine to hold it with a second hand, too, if the mug feels wobbly otherwise.

Spoons used to stir a drink are taken out of the cup or glass. A teaspoon always goes back on the saucer. An iced-tea spoon may be placed on the underplate or another plate. Your child shouldn't try to drink with a spoon in the glass.

When a child holds a goblet, he may cup his fingers under the bowl, even if the drink is cold. It's held more securely that way.

If your child is passing a glass to someone else, his hands shouldn't touch the rim!

Activity

Show your child a number of pieces of drinkware—a cup, a tumbler, a goblet, and an iced-tea glass. Help her identify each one.

Then let her set the table for dinner. Remind her to hold the drinkware by the handle or at the bottom.

Eating in front of others

Eating in front of others can be an unsettling experience for some children. Visiting a friend may sound like a lot of fun, until your child realizes he has to sit down to dinner with the friend's whole family. Maybe the friend has older siblings who seem very grown-up and intimidating, or maybe the friend's family eats food your child considers "foreign."

Sometimes knowing the basic rules of table etiquette is all that's required to give your child the confidence he needs. He'll know that food gets passed to the right and that he should take modest portions, hold his utensils like a pencil rather than a shovel, eat slowly, and chew with his mouth closed.

But his stomach may feel queasy anyway. Let your child know that being in a new situation can take the appetite away. To help get rid of mealtime butterflies, tell your child not to feel pressure to eat everything that is served. He may take small portions and put his fork down occasionally, just sit quietly, and pay attention to conversation.

Activity

Talk to your child about eating in new situations. Help him think of ways to allay fears he might have.

How to use chopsticks

Learning to use chopsticks can be fun for the whole family. If your child is struggling to handle everyday utensils properly, he'll probably think it's great to be on a level playing field with his parents as you learn a new skill together. When you master it, you'll have a special way to show hospitality to Japanese or Chinese visitors.

Two chopsticks are held in the right hand, one above the other. With its narrow, rounded end forward, the bottom one rests in the crook of the hand at the base of the thumb. It's held in place by the third and fourth fingers. This chopstick stays fairly stationary while it's being used to eat.

The top chopstick is grasped between the underside of the index finger and the underside of the thumb. It's used as a lever to pick up food between the points of the two chopsticks.

Everyone is bound to drop food when they're learning this skill, so go ahead and hold the bowl under the chin to catch pieces that fall. The Japanese do the same thing.

In the same way that your child shouldn't point a knife at someone at the table, he shouldn't point chopsticks at anyone, either. When he's finished using the chopsticks, they go on the chopsticks rest.

Activity

Purchase a pair of chopsticks for each family member. Practice eating vegetables, small pieces of meat, and rice from a bowl. Find some Japanese music at the library or a music store. Play it during the meal.

Just for Boys

Let's face it: Our sons aren't born gentlemen. But learning nice ways to treat others will open doors of opportunity for them throughout life. Academic talent, musical ability, or athletic skills go much farther when accompanied by good manners. As your son develops ways to put others first, he'll also be putting his own best foot forward. His courteous habits will allow others to appreciate all of his talents.

JULY 14

Awareness of others

Help your son grow into the role of gentleman when he is in his teens by encouraging him to develop two special characteristics: awareness of others, and a sense of protection toward others who are weaker than he is. If you do this, he'll begin to focus his attention on others and become the kind of person others want to be around—a good definition for *gentleman*.

It's easy to pick out the young man who has no awareness of others. He appears self-centered or immature. He may say hurtful things, even though he does so inadvertently, or he may neglect to say nice things that ought to be said. How much more others want to be around the young man who takes into account the feelings of others when he speaks and acts. He has developed self-control that expresses his consideration for others.

How is this awareness of others manifested in a young man?

- He lets others go first in a buffet line.
- He slows his pace and walks with his sister or mother (or lets them go ahead) as he enters a movie theater.
- He makes sure everyone in a group is included in the conversation.
- He steps back in a group to make the circle larger to include everyone and won't turn his back to someone who wants to be part of the group.
- He keeps his voice low when he is inside.
- He won't turn music up so loud that everyone else hears it, too.
- He looks for ways to include the new child at school or on the soccer team.
- He puts his dog in the garage if a visiting child is afraid of dogs.
- He takes a portion of food that shows he knows he's not the only one at the table.

Activity

Create a Thumbs-Up Award. Work with your son to come up with a list of nice things to do for others. Take a three-by-five card and write: "Thumbs up for demonstrating awareness of others." Add a line for your signature and the date. When you see him demonstrating the behaviors on the list he has helped create, fill out a Thumbs-Up card. When he has five Thumbs-Up cards, take him out for a treat.

JULY 15

Protecting others

The popular movie *Titanic* reminds us of men who gave their lives to save women and children. As the ship was sinking, men refused to climb aboard life rafts until they were certain there were no more women and children left behind. In the days of horses and carriages, men protected women by walking closer to the street than women, thus taking any water or mud that sprayed up from the road as a horse and carriage passed by.

Although your young son probably won't often have to protect anyone from physical harm, he can begin to develop an attitude of protection toward others. It is still a mark of courtesy to give a girl or woman the sidewalk closest to a building. Other ways to show protection are:

- Finding an umbrella for his mother when it begins to rain.
- Treating animals with kindness.
- Offering to carry heavy items if he is able.
- Guarding against coarse speech and behavior. The young man who avoids profanity will never be accused of harassment (or worse) when he is an adult.

JULY 16
Young men: marks of distinction

Are you raising a gentleman? Here's a checklist. A gentleman doesn't need to be reminded about:

- Holding the door for others.
- Letting girls go first.
- Helping others to carry heavy items.
- Taking off his hat at appropriate times.
- Speaking to the parents of his friends.
- Not cursing.
- Allowing others to leave an elevator first.
- Helping another woman take off her coat.
- Offering his hand to shake when he is introduced.

Activity
Give your son practice in focusing his attention on others by taking Grandma out for lunch on her birthday. Have your son

accompany you and prompt him ahead of time to let Grandma go first, hold the door for her, and pull out her chair.

Sitting and standing tall

Your son should wait to be invited to take a seat when he visits a friend, takes his place at a relative's table, or enters someone's office. If no one says anything, he's free to sit after others do.

He should sit tall, with his back against the back of his chair, and keep both feet on the floor. Slouching communicates inattentiveness and lack of regard for those he's with. In a casual setting, it's fine for him to cross his legs by placing one ankle on the other knee. Remind him, though, not to get so comfortable that he props his feet up on a table.

When he stands and walks, urge your son to keep his back straight, his shoulders square, and his chin parallel to the floor. His appearance will appear respectful and confident. Raising the chin higher makes him appear self-centered. Dropping the chin and hunching over shows a lack of confidence. Encourage him to lift his feet when he walks to avoid shuffling.

Activity

Watch the news on television with your son and notice the posture of different men. Talk about why the way a man carries himself communicates something about his job or other roles in life.

JULY 18

Asking for a date

There are some courtesies everyone appreciates. The first one is being asked early. Your child may wait until the last minute because of nerves, but asking early gives the other child a chance to get permission from parents and to look forward to the date.

- Have a plan for the date: "Do you want to do something this weekend?" isn't enough. Be specific: "I have tickets to the championship basketball game on Saturday. Will you go with me?"
- Give as many details as possible—your child's date will be impressed (and so will the parents): "I'll pick you up at five-thirty if that's okay. I'll come in and say hi to your parents before we leave. We'll be going with Stacey and Sam, and we'll get something to eat after the game. Do you have a curfew?"
- Express pleasure: "That's great you can go! I'll look forward to it."
- Be on time. A few minutes early is even better.

TIP

Your child should ask for the date in person or on the phone. This isn't a friend's job.

JULY 19

When to wear a hat

Parents can't seem to win with hats these days. When your son is young, you won't be able to get him to keep his hat on, and when he's a teen, he won't want to take it off. Wearing a hat used to be a mark of a gentleman. If he was going out, a hat was a necessary part of his attire—and there were strict rules about when to remove it. Today, few men see a hat as a necessity.

It's a different story with kids. Kids are buying hats at high prices from fashion designers, but unfortunately they don't seem to have a clue about when to doff them. Caps are okay and they're fun to wear, but there are times when boys must take them off for no other reason than to reveal their faces. It's hard for Grandpa or Uncle Willis to feel that he is connecting with Junior if he can only see the child's nose and chin. Your son should remove his cap:

- At the table.
- During prayer.
- Indoors at home and at school.

- Formal indoor events, such as graduation.
- In a restaurant.
- During the playing of any national anthem.
- During the Pledge of Allegiance.

These rules help your child communicate respect for others. While your child might not see a practical reason for taking off his cap, he'll quickly lower himself in the estimation of many adults if he wears it nonstop.

Activity

Round up some old hats or caps out of the closet. Notice how styles have changed, and talk about what Grandpa and Great-grandpa wore. How does that differ from Dad and his uncles?

Just for Girls

~

Many young girls today face opportunities their mothers could only dream about. It can be exciting to look ahead to the possibilities with your daughter, but don't hesitate to look back for some time-honored courtesies as well. Showing consideration for others will never go out of style, and achieving a dignified and self-controlled manner will put your daughter ahead of the rest.

JULY 20

Sitting gracefully

When your child visits someone's home or if she goes with you to an office for an appointment, she waits to be given permission to sit. She shouldn't just plunk herself down anywhere; the hostess may indicate a seat. If nothing is said, she should take the seat of her choice after her hostess sits down.

Choosing a chair that isn't too big makes it easier to sit comfortably and get out of the chair gracefully. She should approach the chair, walking tall with good posture, and pivot when she reaches it. Her calf will feel the edge of the chair. As she sits, she keeps her back straight and her head up. Her knees relax and she leans forward slightly from the hips, with her arms extended straight toward her knees. Her thighs do the work. (She shouldn't lean back and brace herself with her hand or plop into the chair!)

In someone's home, for a photograph, or on a stage, she should cross her legs at the ankle, keeping them on one side or the other, with the toe of one foot placed at the instep of the other. Knees are always together. Her back stays straight as she sits and she places one hand loosely on top of the other, to the side of her lap. She should keep her hands still. When she gets up, her thighs do the work again; she doesn't push herself out of the seat with her arms.

Activity

Have your child practice choosing the right chair, approaching it, and sitting gracefully. It's not easy to do at first! Take a photo of her when she's mastered it.

JULY 21

Accepting a date

A date should be accepted with enthusiasm. Your child shouldn't be afraid to show happiness at being asked. She should make sure all necessary information has been given, including where to be picked up, when the date is over, what they will be doing, what everybody's wearing, and who's paying (if it's Dutch—each person paying his or her own way—that should be made clear up front).

It should go without saying, but . . . when your child says yes, the date is kept. If your child is hoping someone else will ask, she should say no.

JULY 22

Declining a date

It's okay for your daughter to say no if she doesn't want to go out with someone. There's no need to be rude about it, though. "With you? No way!" isn't okay.

Saying no kindly is a nice skill to learn. Just because she doesn't want to go out on a date doesn't mean she doesn't want to be friends. She may just say, "I'm sorry, but I have other plans." (Her plans might end up being a quiet evening with her family.) If the person persists in asking about another time, she might say, "I'm flattered that you ask, but I don't want a dating relationship for us right now."

She should keep it to herself when she's said no. She especially shouldn't tell the next person he asks who does say yes.

Young women: marks of distinction

Is your daughter growing into a gracious young woman? Here are some ways to tell. You'll notice when she:

- Converses openly and warmly with the parents of her friends.
- Volunteers at her church, at her school, or in her community.
- Dresses appropriately for the occasion.
- Speaks clearly.
- Shows kindness toward younger siblings and other children.
- Keeps the engagements she makes with her friends.
- Expresses interest in the activities of her grandparents and other adult relatives.
- Helps serve guests in her home, whether they are her friends or those of her parents.

Invitations: Giving and Receiving

~

Help your child shine socially by encouraging her to learn how to be creative in extending invitations and how to be punctual in responding. Each invitation's style gives a hint of what the event will be like. Whether formal or informal, it deserves a prompt response, though none comes with an absolute obligation to accept.

JULY 24

The nicest way to issue a verbal invitation

Children often have occasions to verbally invite friends to join them for a movie or a sleep-over. Although simple invitations issued not too far in advance don't need to be written, they do need to be expressed with courtesy to the child being invited.

The right way: The nicest way to pose the invitation is to do so *directly*. It would go like this: "I'm having a sleep-over on Friday night. We'll have pizza and play games. Can you come?" This kind of invitation makes it easy for the other child to respond. He can either say, "Yes, that sounds great! What time shall I come?" or reply, "No, I'm sorry, I have other plans and won't be able to do that. But thanks for inviting me!"

The wrong way: A much less thoughtful way for your child to issue an invitation starts out like this: "Are you busy on Friday night?" or "Do you have any plans for vacation tomorrow?" There is hardly a tactful way for your child's friend to keep her plans (or lack of them) to herself when confronted with such a blunt approach. She might be tempted to respond with "None of your business, nosy!" Or she might feel obligated to reveal information she'd rather keep a secret, such as "I'm grounded and I can't leave home."

Elementary-school children aren't usually sensitive about their schedules, but when they reach adolescence a direct invitation can help spare them embarrassment or give them the freedom to say no to something they really don't want to do.

Activity

List some activities, such as a birthday party sleep-over, roller skating, going to a movie, or attending a concert, on separate index cards. Put the cards in a bag and have your child choose one at a time. Role-play with her as she asks her friend (you) to join her in the activity. Remind her to add details that the friend will want to know, such as the name of the movie, the price of the concert ticket, where you will go roller skating, and so on.

How to issue a written invitation

An invitation is a preview to an event—its style gives clues to what the party itself will be like. Written or engraved invitations are good harbingers of formal events, such as bar or bat mitzvahs or dinner dances where teens dress up.

Formal invitations are written in the third person. They should be executed in nice handwriting, be neatly organized on the page, and contain all of the information a guest will need. The format for a written invitation is just like an engraved wedding invitation. It looks like this:

Mr. and Mrs. Edward Miller
request the pleasure of your company
at a dance in honor of their niece
Miss Jillian Williams
Friday, the nineteenth of May
at nine o'clock
The Westwood Country Club
Bryn Mawr, Pennsylvania

R.s.v.p.
212 Chestnut Hill Drive
Bryn Mawr, Pennsylvania

A formal invitation is written on white or cream notepaper and is mailed four to six weeks before the event. Don't use the computer to generate a formal invitation. They're either engraved or handwritten. Fill-in invitations that follow the same formal format may also be used.

For less formal events, colorful, store-bought invitations are fine but should include all necessary information and be neatly written. Whether the event is formal or fun, let your child help in picking out and creating the invitations.

JULY 26

Responding to invitations

When your child receives an invitation, it's courteous for him to respond. Ask him to put himself in the shoes of the child who has issued the invitation. Certainly that child must be excited about his party and eagerly waiting to hear who will be able to come. A good time frame in which to respond is within a week of receiving an invitation.

Your child isn't obligated to say yes. His response depends on whether he wants to accept the invitation, if it fits into his schedule, and if you give him permission to accept. Your child should respond in the way the invitation was given. An informal telephone call asking your child to come to a birthday party can be answered then and there, or you or your child may call back at a later time to respond after he has checked if the day is free.

An invitation with an RSVP date and telephone number should be accepted or declined by telephone by the date indicated. Even if your child sees the friend who sent the invitation at school, it's better to RSVP to the phone number given. This way the parents of the child having the party know exactly who's coming and can give information about dress or directions.

Your child should respond to a formal invitation by sending back the response card provided. If you take care of such things, show your child how you filled out the card. He shouldn't call the person who invited him.

If your child has received an invitation for a time when she'll have a friend visiting from out of town, it's okay to mention that to the hostess, but it's her decision about what to do. Explain to your child that he'll have to accept the decision gracefully.

When it's okay to decline

Invitations don't come with an obligation to be accepted—at least not most of the time. Most of the time, when your child receives an invitation her only real obligation is to respond promptly.

Your child shouldn't say no lightly, however. If it's an invitation to a birthday party, your child already had her own party, and this particular friend came and brought a gift, your child should consider returning the favor. Having recently attended too many parties and not feeling like picking out another gift isn't a good enough reason to send regrets.

On the other hand, there are other reasons—your child's shyness in the face of large groups, an activity she wouldn't be comfortable with, receiving an invitation from a child who's been mean to her—that make it acceptable for your child to decline. You might also have family considerations. If it's a particularly busy time for your family, even though you don't have a direct conflict on the date of the party, your child may decline. Always discuss all invitations with your child upon receipt.

Encourage your child to express regrets by thanking the person for the invitation and giving a brief explanation. A blunt "No, I can't come" isn't acceptable. "Thank you for inviting me, but my family has plans for that day" or "I'm sorry, but I'm not able to come this time" is a kinder way for your child to say she can't accept.

When your child isn't invited

If your child hasn't received an invitation to a party, she shouldn't ask to be invited. The hostess decides on the guest list, and as disappointing as it may be, people don't volunteer to be on it! (The best way to ensure *receiving* party invitations is to *extend* them from time to time.) Remind your child that many times space considerations limit the number of children who are invited. Being passed over this time doesn't mean your child isn't liked.

Activity

Suggest your child plan a fun activity during the time of a party to which she wasn't invited. Let her include another person who wasn't invited.

Two invitations for the same day

When your child receives an invitation, it's thoughtful to respond soon (within a week). If two invitations arrive at the same time, of course he's free to choose either one, but after accepting an invitation, he's committed to attend. The exception may be when your child knows the hostess well and he explains that he's trying to decide what to do about a second invitation.

When he's already said yes to an invitation, he shouldn't change his mind except on the rare occasion that the second invitation is of much greater significance. One youngster was planning to sleep over at a friend's house when his dad was given tickets for the two of them to fly in a private plane to a college football game. His friend understood when he called to apologize and change the plans. However, it's important that your child doesn't get into the habit of changing plans or his friends will believe he's unreliable.

One of the reasons invitations to significant events such as weddings and graduation parties are sent a month to six weeks in advance is so that people don't have to send regrets because they've already accepted another invitation.

When sending regrets, it's courteous to do so right away. Your child really doesn't owe an explanation. He simply needs to say that he's sorry he won't be able to come. Thanking the other person for inviting him and wishing him a great party is enough.

Out on the Town

❧

When your children are in public, their actions affect others. There are plenty of laws that govern public behavior, but everyone needs to develop voluntary habits of good citizenship as well. In a word—manners.

JULY 30

Movie manners

Chances are your child loves to go to the movies but doesn't always understand that the code of conduct is different in the theater than it is at home on the couch with a video.

For some reason, going to a movie theater can bring out the worst in people. Noisy chewing, excessive laughing, and even shared whispers can quickly become annoying.

No one should be forced to play theater police. Help your child be a good theater companion by giving him practice—not at a movie attended mainly by grown-ups because you couldn't find a baby-sitter, but at a kiddie matinee.

• *Be on time*. Don't enter a movie theater after the film has started. But if the dog ate your wallet, you had to make a stop for cash on the way, and you got to the theater a few minutes late, let your child know he can't be choosy about his seat. Take the one closest to the aisle.

• *First things first.* Your child should go to the bathroom and buy his snack before entering the screening area. This isn't dinner theater, so your child should be pretty much finished with his food by the time the show begins.

• *Be quiet!* Your child shouldn't ask you questions, should not make comments, and certainly shouldn't reveal the ending if he's seen the film already. Save all talking until the final credits have rolled. (Go ahead and laugh or cry, of course!)

• *Sit still.* Children whose feet don't yet touch the floor have an extra challenge. Have them cross their legs at the ankles or even sit Indian style on the seat (if their shoes are clean, of course).

• *Neatness, please.* Carry out all trash at the end of the movie.

Activity

Have an At the Theater movie night at home. Dim the lights, make popcorn, set up chairs, and help your child pretend you're at the theater and on your best behavior.

JULY 31

Seeing a movie with a friend

When your child takes a friend to the movies, she should show consideration for her friend. This begins with choosing the movie. Family rules vary regarding which movies are okay to attend. Your child shouldn't pressure a friend to see a movie the other child's parents might not approve. Some children are extremely sensitive to tense scenes in movies—even Disney films—so your child should be understanding if her friend consults with her parents. If the children can't agree on a movie, encourage them to compromise: One gets to make the choice this time, the other chooses the next movie.

If your child isn't going to buy her friend's ticket, she should tell her right away how much it costs. Your child shouldn't assume her friend will bring money along; it would be embarrassing to discover when they're in line for tickets that her friend can't pay.

Tell your child that friends stick together. No dashing off to check out upcoming movie posters without a word of explanation. Of course, it's fine to plan to use their time efficiently—one buys the tickets while the other gets the snacks. The key is to be aware of a friend's preferences and not to disappear if the two of them haven't discussed it.

Your child should offer her friend the best seat. This is the seat with the best view (closest to the center of the theater and not behind the lady with big hair). Your child may also ask if her friend has a particular preference. Finding a good seat is easy, of course, if your child has arrived early enough to have plenty of seats from which to choose.

After the show, your child should let her friend leave the theater first. She may just step aside while her friend leaves the row of seats and moves ahead of her out of the theater. This protects her friend if people are pushing from behind. Your child takes the bumps, not her friend. Some gestures, like this one, are small but very nice.

Activity

Help your child read the movie page in the newspaper. If she is inviting a friend to go along, have her call the theater ahead of time to learn how long the movie runs so that she can give an accurate schedule to her friend. Explain to your child that when calling a movie theater, she'll probably get a tape with information about a lot of movies. She may need to be patient until there is a description of the movie she's interested in.

AUGUST 1

Take a seat

If your child is taking a seat at a public program (at a theater, church, or school assembly), the most important thing is for him to be on time and take his seat before the program begins. No amount of avoiding toes and begging to be excused can make up for the distraction and annoyance when you or your child shuffles in late. Lateness bothers the performers as well as the audience.

If your child is on time but discovers that the only seats remaining are in the middle of the row, getting there with maximum grace is the goal. In our country people typically face the stage as they pass those already seated. But it seems even nicer for your child to follow the English custom on this and face those who are seated as he gets to his seat. In this way they get his face rather than his backside and can quite easily hear his murmured *excuse me*. The people in the row will probably get as small as they can, tucking their feet under their seats or moving their knees to the side. This will help your child avoid stepping on someone's feet. That's a no-no, as is brushing the heads of those in the row in front as your child moves by.

Activity

Set up two rows of chairs at home, put some people in them, and let your child practice finding his seat in the middle of the second row.

AUGUST 2

How to applaud

Urge your child not to be the first to clap, nor the last. Improperly timed applause can be very distracting to a speaker or performer, as well as to the audience. Children shouldn't wave their hands wildly or cup them when they applaud. Wild clapping raises the risk of hitting someone; cupping makes too much noise.

Boys should clap both palms together and give a good, solid clap. (Okay, they may cup their hands at a sporting event.) Girls should clap the fingers of one hand against the palm of the other. This gentler clap is a nice mark of refinement for a young lady.

How long should applause last? It depends. If you're applauding a solo in the middle of a performance, keep it short—the program will go on. But if the program is over and it's been great, applaud as long as you like. If the performance has been particularly good, your child may stand with the rest of the audience to offer the performers the nicest compliment possible—a standing ovation.

When to applaud

Children love to clap, but they need to know when it's appropriate. If your child isn't sure, tell her to look around and listen; sometimes she'll be given directions. For example, if she's at a ceremony honoring a number of people (such as a graduation), everyone might be asked to hold their applause until each graduate's name has been called. The graduates will then receive applause as a group, which saves time and avoids competition.

If there isn't any instruction, your child can simply take her cues from others (a good practice in many confusing social situations).

There are certain times when your child should applaud:

- *At an athletic competition:* when your team does well.
- *At the theater:* when the curtain goes up on a great set, at the end of an act, and at the end of the performance.
- *At a concert:* when the conductor and soloists enter and exit, at the end of a selection of music (not after a movement), and at the program's end.
- *At a speech:* after hearing something you very much agree with and at the end (at least briefly, whether or not you liked the speech).
- *At the movies:* almost never, although sometimes the entire audience erupts in spontaneous applause.

Activity

Over a two-week period, put a piece of candy in a jar every time your child tells you about an opportunity she had to applaud. Have her describe the event and tell you any guidelines from this lesson she followed. At the end of the two weeks, present her with the candy and give her a hand!

Intermission

When a program lasts a few hours, the audience is given an intermission at the halfway point in the program. This may be at the symphony, a play, a comedy show, a vocal performance, or a program with a series of speakers. Sometimes it's hard to tell if the program has ended or if it's an intermission. Typically, the printed program mentions an intermission if there is to be one.

Speaking in a normal tone of voice is fine at intermission, either in the auditorium or in the lobby. It's a good time to socialize if your child is so inclined. He may stay in his seat, stand up where he is, or leave the auditorium. If others in his row stay in their seats, he should say "excuse me" as he passes by them, being careful not to bump them or step on their toes.

Drinks and candy may be for sale in the lobby, or there may be a buffet table with finger foods. Occasionally large auditoriums will have cup holders by the seats in the auditorium, but the general rule is that food should be eaten in the lobby before returning for the rest of the program. If your child needs to use the bathroom, encourage him to do that first. This way, he won't be carrying food into the bathroom, and he'll also give himself time to wait if there are long lines at the bathroom. When the lights are dimmed and brought up a couple of times, it signals that the program will begin again in five minutes. Your child should return to his seat immediately. Take a night out with your child and practice perfect theater manners. It'll be fun for both of you.

Audience pests

Some people cringe when they notice that children are part of an audience. But a child's good behavior also turns heads and draws admiring murmurs. Help him avoid the pitfalls. Here's how your child can quickly qualify as a bona fide audience pest:

- Throw his coat over the seat in front of him.
- Talk throughout the program.
- Kick the seat in front of him.
- Come to the program with the sniffles but no tissue.
- Tear the wrapper off candy.
- Gurgle to the bottom of a drink.
- Leave his seat repeatedly to go to the bathroom.
- Fidget.
- Clip his nails.
- Hum along.
- Sigh and groan disapproval.

Activity

Write each of the behaviors listed above on a separate slip of paper. Add several phrases describing positive behaviors at the theater, such as "Eat only at intermission," "Go to the bathroom before being seated," "Keep your limbs in your own space," and so on. Let him look through the papers and pull out those that qualify someone for the "pest" category.

AUGUST 6

At a museum

Many museums provide interactive exhibits, making them more appealing places to visit with children. For example, at a museum of colonial life, your child can learn to weave; at an air and space museum, she can use a computer to determine weather patterns.

For maximum enjoyment, keep your child's early visits to museums short and choose subjects she's interested in. If you leave before she's exhausted, her enjoyment of these visits will grow.

Remind your child before you enter the museum that she'll probably be with many people inside. She should be careful not to push ahead of others, block their view, or make distracting noises. Tell her if you tug on her sleeve, you're prompting her to move back.

When you enter the exhibit area, guide your child to her right. Typically, traffic moves to the right from exhibit to exhibit, and if there is a developing theme, this is the direction in which it progresses.

Choose guided tours with your child's attention span in mind. If a tour is primarily planned for adults, make the tour with your child shorter and self-guided. Most exhibits provide information sheets that can be helpful in guiding your child's tour. If she can read, encourage her to read some of the labels beside exhibits.

Don't let your child get too hungry or tired. Most museums offer a place for refreshment, which can make all the difference in how much your child can take in.

Activity

Children love to get things in the mail. Buy a membership for a local museum that offers special programs for children. She'll get notices about new exhibits she may find appealing. Let her know her membership supports a nonprofit organization.

AUGUST 7

Museum tips

When you're headed for a museum tour, make sure your child is dressed in casual, comfortable clothes. If he becomes too restless inside, call it a day and go on a picnic. While in a museum, your child should:

- Keep his voice low, even if he is talking about the exhibit.
- Check his coat (and camera, if no pictures are allowed). He'll be more comfortable.
- Walk at all times. Pay extra attention to some exhibits, rather than flitting from one to another.
- Stay with the family.

- Listen to the guide. He can ask questions, but he should give others a chance to ask questions as well.
- Touch *only* if a sign says he may. Some exhibits for children are very hands-on, but in some cases, items are historic, fragile, and irreplaceable. If items are roped off, he should not reach or walk beyond the space available for the public.
- Thank the tour guide for the tour. No tip is necessary.

Activity

Museum gift shops offer fascinating and educational items for children. Let him choose a souvenir to take home (possibly something to add to a collection). Take a brochure home as well and start a scrapbook.

AUGUST 8

Reading a restaurant menu

Restaurants often make things easy for your child by providing a children's menu. Portions are smaller, and the items are more pleasing to a child's palate—chicken fingers rather than duck à la orange. Children's menu portions are just right for a child's appetite, so food isn't wasted, but they can become dull after a while because there are usually only three or four items and most restaurants offer the same choices. As soon as your child can read, you may begin to familiarize her with the adult menu. Even if she splits an entree with a sibling or just orders an appetizer, she'll learn to order (and enjoy eating) more than a hamburger or macaroni and cheese.

The parts of the menu are:

1. *Appetizers* (also called "starters" or "beginnings"). These are small portions of foods such as shrimp cocktail, onion soup, smoked salmon, and so on.
2. *Entrees* (or main course). This takes up the most space on the menu. Since the names can be confusing, there is often a description of the food under the name. If your child still has

questions, it's okay to ask the server what it is or how it's prepared.

3. *Cheese or salad course.* In fine restaurants, you may find that a selection of cheeses follows the main dinner.
4. *Desserts.* These are listed at the end of the menu or are discussed by your server at the end of the meal. Samples may be brought on a tray or cart when you have finished the main course.

Ordering from a menu

The first priority for your child after being seated at a restaurant table is to decide what to order and then to place the order. Remind him that his first priority is *not:*

- Going to the bathroom (do that *before* being seated or *after* ordering).
- Coloring on the children's menu.
- Making houses out of sugar packets.

Your child shows respect for others at the table by not holding up the ordering process. Asking the server for a few extra minutes could turn into quite some time while everyone waits with stomachs growling.

Should your child consider price when he makes his selection? Yes, some items might be too expensive, but if Grandpa is paying, your child shouldn't find out the acceptable price range by blurting, "I like lobster tail. Is it too expensive?" He may consult you, or he may ask Grandpa what he recommends.

Explain to your child the sequence of ordering:

1. *Beverages.* The server will take this order first, then give you time to study the menu while he gets the drinks.
2. *Appetizers and entrees.* These are ordered at the same time. Child-sized appetites rarely make it necessary to order both.

Your child may also need to make a decision on vegetables or salad dressing.

3. *Desserts.* Wait until the meal is finished. What sounds fabulous when your child first sits down may be unappealing after he's eaten spaghetti and meatballs. The server will take this order when the dinner plates are cleared.

Your child should look at the waiter and speak clearly when he orders. Adding *please* to his order will make him a welcome guest at any restaurant.

Activity

When you're in a restaurant, ask your child to notice how the menu is organized. What words might be used in place of *appetizers*? In place of *entrees*? How does he know the cost of each item? What are the side dishes? Let him try ordering for himself, practicing what he's learned at home.

AUGUST 10

Confusing menu terms

Since not every word is in English, reading a menu can feel like trying to crack a code. Help your child realize that foreign words can be fun rather than frustrating by describing what some of the most commonly used foreign words mean.

There are two terms that explain how the menu is set up. *Table d'hôte* or *prix fixe* indicates that the complete meal is offered for a set price. This may include everything from beverage to dessert or may be limited to an entree, vegetables, and a salad. Though it isn't necessary to take all of the food offered, don't ask for substitutions and don't ask to have the price reduced. Such menus may constitute a specialty of the chef that can be prepared in quantity and offered at a more reasonable price than separately priced items.

An *à la carte* menu is for the person who wants to eat less or have the opportunity to choose each item of food separately. On this type of menu, each item of food is listed separately and priced separately as well. The price can add up to quite a sum if you don't pay attention. To keep the cost in line, make small concessions such as taking the vegetable du jour rather than choosing a special side dish. *Du jour* means "of the day." That's the particular soup, vegetable, or dessert that is offered that day, but it may change from time to time.

AUGUST 11

Foreign words commonly found on menus

Some foreign words are so commonly used in our language that we don't think of them as foreign, such as *quiche*. We wouldn't even think of describing it as a tart of eggs and cheese—we know what it is. But other words, not as common in daily use, may often be found on menus. It is never a problem to ask a waiter to explain something on the menu that your child doesn't understand.

Here are several with their meanings:

Au jus (oh-jhoo): in its own juice (as in prime rib au jus)
Béarnaise sauce (bear-nez): butter, egg, and vinegar sauce
Crêpe (krayp): thin pancake served as dessert or an entree
Demitasse (dem-i-tahs): literally, "half cup"; a small cup in
  which strong black coffee is served
En croute (ahn croot): baked in a pastry crust
Escargots (es-car-go): snails
Filet mignon (fi-lay meen-yon): beef tenderloin
Flambé (flahm-bay): served flaming
Hollandaise sauce (hahl-en-dayz): butter, egg, and lemon sauce
Hors d'oeuvres (or-dervs): appetizers
Lait (lay): milk, as in café au lait (coffee with milk)
Mornay (mor-nay): white cheese sauce
Mousse (moos): light dessert of flavored cream and eggs
Sorbet (sor-bay): fruit sherbet (has a tart taste that freshens the
  mouth)

Activity

Review the list above and add other foreign words that you know. If you are dining at a fine restaurant with your child, ask him to point out foreign phrases on the menu. Let him order a crème brûlée, for example, if he knows what it is.

AUGUST 12

Restaurant protocol

The old adage "Children should be seen and not heard" may not be practiced anymore in the home, but it still may be beneficial in restaurants. Help your child plan for ways to be entertained during the inevitable wait. You need only to observe a parent desperately trying to keep a young child in a chair while feeding him packs of crackers to understand the importance of such entertainment.

Encourage your child to take along a few items that will engage his attention. A book, tablet and pencil, or coloring book and crayons are good choices. A small, *quiet* handheld game is also acceptable.

Upon entering the restaurant, ask your child to hang up his coat if there is a place available. Less clutter at the table means a smoother meal and fewer spills.

When being shown to the table by the hostess, children should follow adults (or at least walk between Mom, who goes first, and Dad).

The best seat at the table goes to the guest of honor. This is the one that has the best view of the restaurant, since no one prefers to face a wall or the kitchen door. If it's Grandma's birthday, of course she gets it. It there isn't a guest of honor, an adult gets the best seat. Remind your child that this is not a time for children to beg for preferential treatment.

Activity

Ask your child which seat he thinks is the best at your dining table at home. Discuss why. Do your family members always choose the same seat at mealtimes? Why does your child think each person chooses a certain seat?

AUGUST 13

More restaurant protocol

An enjoyable restaurant experience requires cooperation from everyone at the table. Your child should learn not to squawk that she is starving, and everyone should stay at the table until all of the orders have been placed. Closed menus signal to the server that your table is ready to order.

After orders have been taken, your child should occupy herself quietly at the table, either with crayons and coloring book or conversation. Voices should be low enough that other tables aren't forced to listen in. She shouldn't play with items such as utensils, straws, or condiments.

Your child should clear her area of crayons and papers when she sees the food arriving. Food will be served from the left, drinks will be served from the right, and empty plates will be cleared from the right. Encourage your child not to dig in until everyone has what they've ordered. If some at the table ordered appetizers and others did not, they may get started ahead of the rest.

Whatever the style of the restaurant (even fast food), good table manners are a must. With practice they become second nature.

While it is all right to ask to have food redone if it isn't to your liking, let your child know that this should be the exception rather than the rule. Spoiled food, seriously underdone food, or the wrong order may be sent back, but other things should be overlooked. Dining out is meant to be a happy social occasion, and the atmosphere shouldn't be ruined by minor complaints about the food.

AUGUST 14

Handling problems in restaurants

As much as we'd all like to avoid them, "most embarrassing moments" happen. Here's how to solve common dining-out problems:

When your child drops a utensil. Your child shouldn't go searching for a dropped utensil, but the other utensils he has left are probably for other courses. When a utensil slips to the floor, ask the waiter for another one.

When your child doesn't have a napkin. If it fell to the floor, he should handle it the way he did with the dropped utensil. But if your child discovers that someone else has taken his napkin, there's no need to embarrass the culprit and announce it to the other diners. Again, simply ask to have it replaced.

When your child spills food on the tablecloth. A small amount of food that ends up on the tablecloth may be scraped off gently with a knife and returned to an edge of the dinner plate. If it is a big spill of food or beverage, ask the server for help. He'll bring extra napkins to do the job and will leave a clean, dry one to cover the soiled spot. Rely on the server to take the soiled napkins away—don't go dashing through the restaurant carrying a pile of dirty napkins in search of a wastebasket.

When food hits your child's clothing. Scrape it off with a knife or clean it up with the tip of a napkin that has been dipped in a water glass. It's okay to ask for a bit of seltzer so that the stain doesn't set.

If you've given the server a good bit of extra work, be sure your tip reflects your gratitude for his help.

Activity

As you read the daily newspaper, clip stories or pictures of people who have had "most embarrassing moments." Discuss with your child how they were resolved.

AUGUST 15

Keeping your area neat at a restaurant

Eating in a restaurant doesn't give your child license to make a mess. A table strewn with litter, bones, crumbs, shredded napkins, and sticky utensils can kill another diner's appetite. Of course, each meal will have some refuse. Encourage your child to show respect for others at his table as well as for the restaurant staff by disposing of it properly. Here's how:

1. Put all paper waste on the corner of an extra plate, such as the bread plate. If there are no extra plates, tuck the paper under the rim of the dinner plate. Tear sugar packets open only three-quarters of the way so that you don't have two pieces of trash.
2. Bones or shells go on the side of the plate, not the tablecloth.
3. Food on the plate should be left intact if it isn't eaten. Nothing looks worse than a plate where food has been stirred and pushed around. Take portions of the food from the edge, not from the center. The plate will stay neat-looking.
4. Keep all used utensils on a plate (or propped on another utensil if there isn't a plate). At a gourmet restaurant, this keeps the tablecloth clean; at a fast-food restaurant, it keeps your utensils or food off a table surface that is touched by many people.
5. Don't write on the tablecloth.
6. At a nice restaurant, don't stack dishes or help to clear them. The servers are very good at doing this, and helping them makes it more likely there will be a spill. You *do* help them by placing your utensils in the center of your plate when you're finished, rather than keeping them on the edge of the plate, which is okay while eating.
7. If it's fast food you've been enjoying, clear the table down to the last straw paper.
8. When you leave the table, push in your chair. You want to return your table as closely as possible to how it looked when you arrived.

AUGUST 16

The people who work in a restaurant

Your child will feel more confident and at ease if she understands the various roles of the people who work in a restaurant. She should understand that they *work* at the restaurant and are there to *serve,* but they always deserve the respect and courtesy of the customers who come to dine.

One of the first people your child will meet is the host or hostess, or in fine restaurants, the maître d'. It is this person's role to welcome you and show you to your table. If you have reservations, he will confirm that. Your child's conversation with this person should consist of no more than a polite hello.

After being seated, your child will notice the server (waiter or waitress) for your table. He or she will take your order, bring your food, and deliver your check when you are finished eating. Any request your child makes of the server should be preceded by "May I please . . ." Upon receiving food, "Thank you" is in order.

Restaurant staff are not to be ordered around. They are people who are trained to serve, and although everyone occasionally has a bad day, they generally want to give good service to diners.

Other employees include busboys and -girls. Their job is to clear tables after diners have left and put down fresh place settings for the next diners. They may also assist a busy waiter by refilling water glasses, bringing a fresh basket of bread, or clearing salad plates before an entree arrives. If your table has a request regarding the food, it's better directed toward the waiter than the busboy.

In some fancy restaurants, there is also a sommelier. This person's job is to take wine orders and to serve wine. Children will have no occasion to interact with the wine steward, but they will probably be fascinated by his expertise as he talks with you.

As if that weren't enough of a group, the table might also be visited by another person as the entree is being finished. The owner or chef (or both) may come by the table to be sure guests are happy and the food was to their liking. No matter how informal the restaurant, families have their favorite places to return to again and again, and often it's because they have come to know and developed a fondness for the owner.

What about tipping?

Tipping is something your child should not do with his chair in a restaurant. It's something a gentleman should do with his hat when he meets a lady. But what about tipping after dining out? The word *tip* is an acronym for "to insure promptness." While tipping is meant to be a reward for prompt service, it's not an optional part of dining out.

Your child won't pay the bill or be asked to tip after a meal in a restaurant, but he should understand that tipping is not simply the icing on the cake for the servers. It constitutes most of the servers' wages, and servers count on this income. Because of this, tipping has become standardized. Typically it's 15 percent to 20 percent of the bill. In the United States, a tip (or gratuity) is not usually included in the bill but is added on by the customer.

Of course, if service is poor, the tip may be reduced, but only on the rarest occasion should it be completely eliminated. If the server hasn't been overtly rude but service hasn't been up to par, give the server the benefit of the doubt. Reduce the tip, but remember that anyone can have a bad day. Maybe she just wrecked her car or his steady date broke up with him. Never chastise the server in front of your children, or they may be prompted to do so as well.

Activity

As soon as your child shows some proficiency in math, let him help figure out what the size of the tip should be. Tell him to calculate ten cents for every dollar and then add to it five cents for every dollar (or half of his first calculation). He'll have figured out a 15 percent tip.

AUGUST 18

Things not to do in a restaurant

Parents risk putting ideas into the heads of their children when they study lists like this, so if you already have a little angel, move on to another page. But if not, this might help. In a restaurant, your child should never:

- Blow through a straw—not to blow bubbles in the beverage and not to blow off the straw wrapper
- Crawl under the table even if a piece of chocolate has fallen
- Talk or laugh so loudly that people at another table cannot avoid hearing
- Entertain himself by mixing the contents of salt and pepper shakers or sugar dispensers
- Play practical jokes such as loosening caps on catsup, salt, pepper, or other dispensers on the table
- Change his mind about his order after the waiter has taken it and left the table

AUGUST 19

Salespeople

It's amazing how many children are adept shoppers—but they must be taught to show respect to the people who work in stores. Social skills not only make your child a more pleasant person for others to be around, but help put her above suspicion for crimes like shoplifting. When your child makes eye contact with the salesperson and says hello, she establishes trust. And she makes the salesperson feel the way everyone wants to feel—like a person! She should feel free to ask a clerk for help but should not monopolize the clerk's time, especially if she's really not planning to buy anything.

AUGUST 20

In a store

Help your child be a nice shopper. She should wait patiently if there is a line at a dressing room. She won't want to feel rushed when it's her turn to try something on. Once in the dressing room, she should be clean if she tries on clothing—no touching clothing with sticky fingers and then hanging it back on the rack. She should put things back on hangers after trying them on.

Your child should leave the merchandise display intact. Whatever comes off a shelf should go back on. She shouldn't create a play area in an aisle and then leave it.

If she breaks something, she should let a clerk know. She may simply be forgiven, or she may have to pay for the item. Either way, it will be a character builder for her.

Activity

Ask your child to make a list of what she wants to buy before you go shopping with her. Go over the list and help her eliminate items you don't feel are necessary or that you won't have time to look for. Agreeing on the list before you go to the store will help you avoid disagreements at the store.

AUGUST 21

Saving a place in line

Saving a place in line usually isn't a good idea. Doing a favor for one person inconveniences another.

It's discourteous to others in line to save a place for someone who needs to make a time-consuming transaction. Your child shouldn't save a place when she's waiting to pay for an item at a cash register. Her friend shouldn't do extra shopping, then jump into the line when it's your child's turn to pay. The same is true at a movie ticket counter. It's a bad idea to save a place for a group of friends in the line for a movie showing that is likely to sell out.

Getting their money ahead of time and buying their tickets is okay, but letting them jump in at the counter risks starting a riot.

Stress to your child that saving a place in line for a friend at an amusement park ride is a good way to make people angry.

Occasionally it's okay to save a place. Maybe Dad was parking the car and he joins his daughter and all her friends in line. It's much better for one person to join a group than for a group to join one person.

AUGUST 22

Butting into a line

Butting in is joining the middle of a line when no one has saved a place for that person. It's fundamentally unfair and rude, and it makes people angry. Some bad manners, such as chewing like a pig, turn people off but don't really inconvenience them. Butting into a line does both.

Remind your son that if someone pretends not to know that he has butted into the line in front of him, it's okay for him to say, "Excuse me. Maybe you didn't notice that the end of the line is over there."

AUGUST 23

When you bump into someone

Encourage your child to move carefully through crowds. Walking is mandatory; running is annoying to others and almost guarantees a disaster. When your child is in a public place such as a department store, a church, an airport, a fair, or a theater lobby, he should be careful not to bump into others. Elderly people especially, who may be insecure on their feet, find running threatening and disrespectful.

Being boisterous is never the preferred way for a child to stand out in a crowd. Tell your child that the more self-control he displays in public, the more compliments he'll receive on his behavior.

If your child does bump into someone, he should apologize with "I'm sorry. I didn't mean to bump into you." If he causes someone to drop something or if he knocks something from a counter, he should pick it up.

On an escalator

Escalators require manners *and* safety guidelines for kids. Of course, sometimes manners and safety rules are one and the same—as in the prohibition against licking your knife. For children, there's some danger in riding an escalator, especially if they decide to sit down for the ride or don't pay attention as they approach the end.

Here's how to make it a safe and mannerly ride. Stand to the right and don't take up the whole step. Someone might need to pass, which is okay to do as long as the person isn't running. If your child wants to pass but can't get by the people in front of him, he should just stop behind them. It's rude to make them feel as though they're holding him up, and he shouldn't try to brush by, making them fear he'll knock their packages out of their hands.

On an elevator

Years ago there were elevator attendants who would press the button for your floor, announce when you arrived, and hold the door until you disembarked. Today you're on your own. Kids love to press the buttons, so if your child is by the control panel, let him do it. And he should keep the "door open" button pressed until everyone's gotten on or off.

Step onto an elevator, move to the back, and do an about-face. Stay to the side near the front if you're getting off soon.

When an elevator is crowded and people need to get off, those closest to the door step off and hold the door, even if they haven't reached their floor. They get back on after others have gotten off.

Silence is golden on an elevator. Conversation can't possibly be private, and while a congenial soul might be able to entertain everyone comfortably with light remarks, generally it's fine not to talk. There's no obligation to get to know perfect strangers in such a short period of time.

Elevators are close quarters, so remind your child not to stare unless he stares at the door. Fellow riders can't help but feel someone's eyes on them.

AUGUST 26

Giving up your seat

Your child won't see many people jumping up to give someone else their seat these days. In crowded restaurant lobbies, on public transportation, on benches at the mall, and in waiting rooms of any kind, it often seems that it's every man for himself. But it's still a great kindness, however uncommon, to give up your seat to someone who needs it.

Prompt your child to be aware of the elderly, someone who is on crutches, a woman who is pregnant or has small children, or anyone who doesn't appear strong enough to stand for a period of time. He'll amaze anyone watching by his thoughtfulness if he stands up and says, "Please take my seat."

AUGUST 27

Stay to the right, please

Making your way down the hall at school or through the aisles of a department store can feel like negotiating an obstacle course. Only an artful dodger can keep from being bumped and brushed by people who are walking in every direction. How much easier it would be for everyone to get where they're going if they followed a time-honored convention—stay to your right when you're walking.

Whenever your child is approaching others—on the stairs, on the sidewalk, in an aisle, at a crosswalk, in a hallway, at double doors, in a lobby—it's always courteous for her to stay to her right to avoid plowing headlong into someone.

Appointments

When your child sets an appointment (or when you set it for her), she's made a commitment. She needs to keep it or else cancel it in a timely fashion. Help your child understand that appointments aren't made only for her benefit; not showing up affects others as well.

When she decides to take music lessons, her teacher assumes that she'll be there on a weekly basis. Make sure your child understands from the outset what her obligation will be. Decide if there is anything that will take priority over music and would necessitate canceling or rescheduling the lesson. Ask the teacher if she reschedules when you must cancel your child's lesson and whether or not she charges for the lesson that was missed. Your child may be happy to skip a lesson, but her feelings aren't the only ones that need to be taken into account. The teacher may depend on her lesson as part of her livelihood.

Being on time is important. Your child robs others of their time if she arrives late for an appointment that is scheduled back-to-back with others. Your child may have to wait for the orthodontist, but that doesn't justify arriving late the next time.

Your child should also respect the appointments she makes with friends. If she agrees to go to a friend's house to play at 2 P.M., arriving at 3 P.M. isn't okay. Even though nothing special is planned, her friend will be looking for her. If this happens repeatedly, her friends will know they can't rely on her word.

Help your child understand how important it is to think carefully about his schedule before agreeing to an appointment. It's better to say no right away than to cancel at the last minute. Everyone experiences illness or an emergency at some point, but if your child has been unreliable, no one will believe her when she really is sick.

Activity

In a place where the whole family will see it, hang up a calendar with large blocks for each day. Write in family members' activities, using a different color for each person.

AUGUST 29

Forgetting an appointment

Since your child relies on you to take her to a friend's house, a doctor's appointment, a church activity, or a party, the burden of paying attention to her schedule often falls on you. But by the time she's in fourth or fifth grade, she should be familiar enough with her commitments to know what each day's schedule holds, to remind you about her activities, and to get ready on time.

If she misses an appointment at the doctor or dentist, unless she's well into her teens you'll want to call to reschedule. (Such phone calls are intimidating to kids, and there may be a fee involved for the missed appointment.)

When your child forgets an engagement with a friend, she needs to apologize. She should call the friend immediately to say she's sorry. It shows extra sensitivity to send a note of apology, especially if she missed something special, such as a birthday party or dance recital.

Activity

Buy your child a small pocket calendar and encourage her to keep track of appointments, just as you do.

At Church
or Religious Services

೭

In a country as wonderfully diverse as ours, your children may have an opportunity to attend unfamiliar religious services. Your children will enjoy it more if they know what to expect, and others will appreciate their interest. Of course, your children won't need to participate in sacred creeds and rituals different from their own, but they'll want to sit, stand, and listen along with the rest of the group. This section describes a number of religious services your child might encounter.

AUGUST 30

Basic Protestant weddings

Protestant wedding services may be simple or elaborate, but your child will find certain rituals common to most. Before she attends the wedding, explain to your child each of the following rituals and the behavior expected of her.

• *A processional.* While the organ plays a wedding march, the bridal party proceeds from the vestibule to the altar. There they meet the clergyman and the groom. The bride, holding her father's right arm, is last in the procession. During the processional, your child may turn to get a better view but should stay seated and remain quiet. When the mother of the bride gives the cue for guests to stand as the bride enters the sanctuary, your child should stand as well and stay standing through the next ritual.

• *A betrothal.* The clergyman asks, "Who gives this woman in marriage?" and the bride's father replies, "I do," or "Her mother and I do." When he takes his seat by his wife, your child takes her seat with the rest of the guests.

• *Vows and a blessing.* The bride and groom, and maid of honor and best man, move closer to the altar. The bride and groom say their vows; rings are given to the clergyman to be blessed and are then returned to the couple, who place them on each other's hands. The clergyman concludes the ceremony and congratulates the couple; if the church permits, the new husband and wife kiss. Your child should remain a quiet observer during this time.

• *A recessional.* The entire bridal party, this time with the bride and groom leading the way, moves briskly out of the sanctuary. Your child stays seated during the recessional and waits for an usher to dismiss her pew. Let her know that she is allowed to talk in a low voice at this time.

AUGUST 31

Quaker weddings

Your child will find that a Quaker wedding reflects the religion's emphasis on simplicity and equality among believers. Quakers believe that each person receives messages from God, so ministers are not part of Quaker services. At a traditional Quaker wedding, the couple believes that God, not a minister, marries them.

When your child attends a Quaker wedding, he may enter the meetinghouse and sit where he chooses. Assure him that most likely he will feel warmly welcomed. When everyone is seated, including the bride and groom, someone will stand up to explain what will take place. Then he'll sit down. There may be short or long periods of silence while the meeting (people who are there) meditate or listen for God to speak to them. Tell your child he should stay seated and remain quiet during this time.

After a while the bride and groom will rise and exchange their wedding vows. This, too, may be followed by a period of silence. Sometime after the vows have been said, those attending the wedding stand up and give blessings to the couple. Anyone at the service may say a blessing.

The service is over when the leader of the service for that day rises and shakes someone else's hand. After the service, everyone present at the wedding ceremony signs the marriage certificate. Then there is a reception—simpler than many Christian wedding receptions, perhaps, but every bit as happy. Remind your child that however simple the reception, self-control and respect for the solemnity of the occasion are in order.

While the above rituals are traditional for Quaker weddings, some Quaker services are much like other Christian services. Your child shouldn't be surprised if a Quaker wedding includes a pastor and is similar to other Christian weddings.

SEPTEMBER 1

Mormon weddings

If your child is invited to a Mormon wedding, here's what to expect:

Mormons are married either in a temple ceremony or in a civil ceremony. At a civil ceremony, a bishop of the Church presides, and the vows are taken "until death do us part." The civil service will be less formal than a religious ceremony, but remind your child to sit quietly and attentively.

At a later time, upon meeting the requirements of the Church, the couple may also have a temple marriage. A temple marriage is performed by a member of the Mormon priesthood. These vows not only are until death, but include the afterlife as well, "for time and all eternity." It is believed that children born to parents who have had a temple marriage will belong to the parents in eternity. At this formal ceremony, the bride wears a white gown and veil, even though she's been married before. Your child should dress up, too.

After a temple or civil marriage, a reception is held for the couple's family and guests in a cultural hall associated with the church or in the bride's home. This may be a large affair, so your child should be prepared to exercise patience as well as use her best table manners.

Roman Catholic weddings

Traditional Roman Catholic weddings include many aspects of Protestant weddings, but they also have unique rituals that your child may want to understand.

The service is held in the church; when it includes a nuptial mass, it takes place in the morning. Let your child know that the service could last up to an hour, but it isn't the time to read or draw. Your child should quietly observe the proceedings.

During the mass the bride and groom, Catholic members of the bridal party, and parents will take holy communion. The mass may be a low mass, lasting a half hour; a high mass, lasting forty minutes; or a solemn high mass, lasting an hour, with three priests officiating. At a large Catholic wedding, mass books containing the wedding service will be provided to the guests so that non-Catholics are familiar with the proper way of doing things. Help your child follow along in the book.

Remind your child that non-Catholics do not have to genuflect (bend the knee halfway), cross themselves (touch the forehead and both shoulders in the shape of a cross), or repeat a creed, but they should sit and stand when the rest of the congregation does so.

Orthodox Jewish weddings

Let your child know what to expect when she is invited to a Jewish wedding. She'll want to conform to the customs of the group. For your daughter, this could mean dressing conservatively, with shoulders and arms covered. She should also be ready to sit sep-arately from the men. She'll be given instructions when she enters the synagogue. Your son may be given a black or white skullcap (yarmulke) to wear when he enters the synagogue. He should be willing to comply, as this is the tradition for all males at such a ceremony, even though they are not Jewish. Here's what your child can expect at an orthodox ceremony:

Before the wedding ceremony, the bride, along with her atten-dants, receives guests in a room apart from the sanctuary where she will be married. She does not see the groom until the cere-mony.

The bridal party enters the synagogue in a processional that includes both of the bride's parents and both of the groom's par-ents, who walk on either side of their children. They proceed to the holy ark at the front and stand under a canopy called a *hup-pah,* symbolizing the home. They are joined by the rabbi, their closest attendants, and by their parents if there is room.

The service includes prayers, drinking of ritual wine, and a ring ceremony. The groom places a round gold band on the bride's right index finger (the special finger that's used to mark the spot as one reads the Torah). After this, the marriage contract, called the *ketubah,* is read. Then the rabbi speaks about the sacredness of marriage and encourages the couple in their com-mitment to one another.

Following the rabbi's meditation, seven blessings are recited, a second glass of wine is drunk by the bride and groom, and the groom crushes a glass underfoot. The broken glass is meant to temper the joy of the festivities by causing the people to remem-ber the destruction of the Temple in Jerusalem as well as other calamities that befell the children of Israel.

A typical wedding reception follows the service. Your child should anticipate two special blessings for the meal, one before and one after. She should sit silently during both and be certain not to leave before the final blessing has been said.

Eastern Orthodox weddings

If your child is invited to an Eastern Orthodox wedding ceremony, she should prepare for a lengthy service, lasting an hour, and should be willing to stand throughout, as not all churches have pews.

Explain to your child some of the unique traditions of such a service. She'll probably find it quite beautiful and interesting. She should participate as much as possible, joining in the singing and watching the ceremony attentively.

Here are some of the customs she can expect. The pageantlike ceremony begins, much like any other Christian service, with a processional, after which the bride is given away by her father. The service takes place at a table near the front of the church. Some churches permit only vocal music, while in others, choirs are accompanied by an organ. The bride and groom hold candles to symbolize the light of the Lord and have wreaths of flowers or gold crowns placed upon their heads by the priest.

The significance of the Trinity is emphasized when rituals are performed three times. The rings are blessed three times by the priest and then each ring is placed on both the bride's and groom's finger. The best man then exchanges the rings three times on the bride's and groom's fingers. Before they say their final vows, the bride and groom have their hands bound together by the priest. Along with their wedding party, they are led three times around the table.

Accepting the religions of others

Religious influences are felt in art, literature, music, and education. While there may be strong religious sentiment in the United States, there is also religious freedom. Each one of us wants others to respect our religion; parents need to help children develop respect for the religious preferences of others.

Respecting another's religion doesn't mean it's necessary to participate in the ceremonies of that religion, although it can be an honor to a friend to do so if those religious practices don't conflict with your own. Sometimes children are completely in the dark about the religions of others. Helping your child learn about his friends' religious practices can open doors of understanding.

Sometimes there are religious differences among the different generations in a family. If you're raising your children in a faith different from that of your parents, your children will have opportunities to show respect for the choice of their grandparents. They shouldn't take opportunities to argue with their grandparents about the merits of one religion over another, but they should be willing to talk about religious celebrations in both faiths if the subject isn't too sensitive. Explain to your child that religious convictions are very deeply held, and encourage only positive remarks about a relative's religious preference.

When your child is relating to people of other religions, he should follow a good principle found in the holy books of most of the world's major religions. It is the Golden Rule: Treat others as you would like them to treat you.

Activity

Make a trip to the library or go online to learn about other religions. Help your child make a card or gift to celebrate a relative's or friend's religious holiday.

SEPTEMBER 6

At religious ceremonies

Your child may not feel a sense of reverence when she attends a religious ceremony, but she can be sure that many others who are there feel deeply about what is taking place. For this reason, disruptive behavior on the part of your child can be particularly offensive.

By about the second grade, children can begin to understand the parts of the service. If your child is old enough to join the adults in the service, she should try to sit quietly. Many churches provide nursery care, so very young children aren't expected to do the impossible and sit perfectly still for an hour or more.

Encourage your child to stand or kneel with the adults. If she is able to read, she should hold the hymnal or prayer book and follow along. At first it will help if you guide her attention with your index finger, marking the spot on the page. She can even put a portion of her allowance in the offering plate. Encourage her to participate in any way that she can.

Your child may take along items to entertain herself if she is unable to understand the ceremony, but she should keep the entertainment to a few crayons or a pencil and some paper. Don't bring candy with a wrapper that crackles when it is removed, and don't invite one of your child's friends to sit with her to help pass the time.

Activity

Get your child a small notebook that is used only during a religious service. When your child understands a concept during the service, she can draw a picture to remember it or write a few words from it to practice her letters. If her focus is directed toward the service from a young age, when she's older she won't be tempted to catch up on homework in church by slipping a social studies book under her Bible.

SEPTEMBER 7

Jewish religious services

There are different branches of Judaism—Orthodox, Conservative, Reform, and Reconstructionist—and their practices and beliefs differ. Orthodox and Conservative congregations typically have weekday prayer services held early in the morning and lasting a half hour to forty-five minutes. To hold such a service, ten Jewish males over age thirteen (called a minyan) is needed.

A Sabbath service, the main service of the week, is observed by all branches of Judaism and is an appropriate service for a visitor to attend. It's held on either Friday evening or Saturday morning.

Dress for women and girls attending an Orthodox service may be colorful but very modest: Hats are worn, arms are covered, and skirts are long. Pants are not acceptable. Female visitors should dress in the same modest way, wearing a scarf or hat. Orthodox men wear dark suits and skullcaps (yarmulkes). Males who visit where yarmulkes are mandatory show their respect by wearing one of the caps available in a container outside the sanctuary.

Reform congregations have fewer requirements for dress at services. Men don't have to wear yarmulkes, although many do, and women wear anything that is appropriate, including pants.

If your child visits a Jewish service, he will notice that worshipers sit and stand to pray. In the Orthodox and Conservative services, men may rock back and forth in prayer and may beat their chests to indicate sorrow for breaking God's law.

Men and women sit separately in an Orthodox service, and the men of the congregation will be primarily responsible for leading the service. In other branches, the rabbi plays a more central role, and there may be female rabbis.

Taking out the Torah is a significant part of the service. It's carried in a procession through the sanctuary, and members reach out to touch it with their prayer shawl (*tallith*), fingers, or prayer book. They then bring their shawl or fingers to their lips, symbolically bringing the Torah to themselves.

Appropriate passages from the Torah are read according to the Jewish calendar, together with chanting or responsive reading and much singing.

Be sure your child knows what to expect when visiting a synagogue for the first time.

SEPTEMBER 8

Protestant religious services

The main service for Protestant churches is held on Sunday morning and lasts an hour. A traditional service includes formal organ and choral music and is led by a minister in black clerical robes. At a less formal service, there may be contemporary music and participation from members of the congregation, and the minister will wear a suit or something less formal. Men and women sit together, and the formality of dress varies. Typically, men and women wear their Sunday best for traditional services and dress more casually for contemporary services.

At Protestant services, worshipers sit for most of the service. They may also stand to sing and when bowing their heads to pray. Some congregations provide a time for members to greet each other during the service. They stand, shake hands with those around them, and introduce themselves.

An offering is taken by ushers, who hand plates or baskets to the person at the end of the aisle; this person then passes it down the pew. Visitors are not obligated to give money. The ushers then present the offering at the altar, and a doxology is sung in praise to God for his blessings.

When coffee is served afterward in a fellowship hall, visitors are welcome to attend.

SEPTEMBER 9

Quaker religious services

The Quaker religion is one of simplicity and holds that each person has a guiding inward light or inner voice. Quakers believe that because every person has an element of God's spirit within, this enables each one to understand the Word of God. Quakers believe that individuals have direct access to God.

Initially, Quakers thought of themselves as friends of Jesus and so called themselves Friends of Truth; later they became known simply as Friends. The name "Quaker" was originally an insult. When a Quaker elder stood before a judge and suggested that the judge "tremble at the word of the Lord," the judge mocked the leader, calling him a "quaker."

Quakers emphasized a simple lifestyle with plain dress, concern for the poor, and a quiet religious meeting where people sat for long periods in silence as they inwardly sought God. They would not go to war, nor would they pay taxes to the state church. They opposed slavery and often aided runaway slaves.

Quakers give no place to what they call "empty forms"— churches with steeples, ceremonies, rituals, robes, and creeds. At Quaker meetings, the congregation sits in a square or circle, so that each one faces the others and no one has an elevated position. In some areas, meetings are held in silence until someone is moved to speak. Other congregations include readings from the Bible, the Book of Discipline, prayers, and singing, along with silent waiting.

SEPTEMBER 10

Catholic religious services

Religious services are made up of rituals, procedures that are faithfully and regularly followed. Christian services have some rituals in common, but there are also rituals unique to Catholics and to Protestants.

The weekly religious service of the Catholic Church is a mass. A priest officiates at this service. Mass is open to men, women, and children, and dress for worshipers is typically conservative, although different parishes may range from informal to formal. Women may attend with their heads covered or uncovered; either practice is acceptable. Past generations of women faithfully covered their heads, and there are still women who feel it is proper to wear a scarf or hat to mass as a sign of reverence. It is never proper for a man to wear a hat at mass.

An usher shows worshipers to their seats. He leads the way, then steps aside while adults file into the pew, followed by children. It is courteous to move to the center so that others who arrive later do not have to pass in front of you.

Upon approaching the pew, Catholic worshipers genuflect (bend the knee halfway) and make the sign of the cross on their chest with the right hand while facing the altar. Then they take their seat. If this is new to your child and he is visiting a Catholic service with a friend, remind him to prepare for this by slowing down at the pew so he doesn't plow right into his friend when he stops to genuflect. A non-Catholic does not need to genuflect.

During the service, an offering plate is passed down the pew from one worshiper to another. This is used to collect money to support the work of the church. While it isn't necessary for a child who is visiting the church to put money into the plate, it's a nice gesture if he does. Giving an offering is more commonly done by adults.

Your child should follow along with the service as well as he can. He will feel less out of place if he stands when others stand or kneels when others kneel. If some part of the service goes against his own religious conviction or if he isn't certain how to participate, he may just sit quietly in his seat. To get clues about proper behavior, he may look around at other worshipers.

SEPTEMBER 11

Taking communion (if your child isn't a member)

Your child may need to make a decision about taking communion when she visits a church with a friend. Protestant churches offer communion monthly or quarterly; Roman Catholic churches offer communion at each mass. If your child is a member of another congregation in the same denomination, she may participate as she would in her own church.

At most religious services, guidelines determine who is qualified to take communion. This part of the service is considered by the congregation to be very important and sacred, so anyone who isn't certain about participating should refrain from doing so. A visitor may simply stay seated when others go to the front of the church, or may pass the bread and grape juice on to the next person without taking any.

It's important to sit quietly during communion—slightly bowing the head will show respect for the occasion. It's not a time to gaze at others in the pews.

SEPTEMBER 12

Christenings

Attending the christening or baptism of an infant can be a delightful experience for your child. If she's invited to one, let her know what to expect ahead of time. She'll find the infant adorable and the family celebration joyful. Remind her that it's a solemn occasion as well, and she should sit quietly during the service.

Catholic and most Protestant infants are christened (baptized) between two and six weeks of age. (In the Unitarian Church, the service is called a dedication.) Special arrangements are made with the priest or minister, and the ceremony takes place at the church or in the child's home. Family and close friends are invited to the ceremony.

If godparents are present at a Catholic ceremony, the godmother or godfather holds the baby. The priest or minister conducts the ceremony at the baptismal font (a basin on a pedestal containing water). The baby's baptismal certificate is signed; for Catholic infants, it is an important document for his first holy communion, confirmation, and marriage.

Many families mark this happy occasion by having a reception or luncheon after the service. It may be simple, with cake and punch, or more elaborate if the family chooses. Your child should be more quiet than usual, since the tired infant will probably need a nap while others eat. If the infant is awake, your child shouldn't insist on holding her. That is better left to the adults.

Activity

Discuss with your child religious celebrations that surrounded her birth. Also, let her look forward to the christening by helping you pick the baby's gift. For example, you could get the first book for the baby's collection, letting your child choose one that she has enjoyed.

Jewish birth ceremonies

Jewish families mark birth ceremonies differently for their sons and daughters. These ceremonies are small, involving only the family and closest relatives. On a rare occasion, your child might be invited to such a ceremony. Encourage her to be quiet and respectful, because the occasion is a very special one for the family. Your child's behavior shouldn't become a distraction for the family, who is probably still adjusting to the thrill and fatigue that accompany a baby's birth.

On the eighth day after the birth of a son, the family celebrates Brith Milah. This circumcision ceremony takes place at a hospital, at a synagogue, or, most often, in the home. During the ceremony, the child is given his name and may also be given godparents; a small breakfast or luncheon may follow. If your child is invited to a Brith, you should buy a gift for her to take along for the baby (anything appropriate for a newborn).

Girls are given a naming ceremony, a simple ceremony in the synagogue, often on the first Sabbath after birth (or up to several weeks after the birth). The child's father recites a prayer at the altar and repeats his daughter's name; the rabbi then offers a blessing. As is customary for a Brith Milah, there may be a small luncheon afterward, and baby gifts are brought.

Catholic traditions: godparents

Before an infant in a Catholic family is christened, godparents are chosen as the spiritual overseers of the child. Only those who are close friends of the family and members of the Catholic faith are asked to be godparents. It's a great honor to be chosen and thus difficult to decline, and it also comes with obligations that only a friend would be expected to meet. As your child grows, help him develop an attitude of respect and appreciation for his godparents.

Godparents take the initiative in befriending the child, just as a favorite aunt or uncle might do. They remember the child's birthday and Christmas with gifts and celebrate other special occasions for the child. Encourage your child to thank his godparents for their gifts and kindness, and when he is old enough to write, he should send a thank-you note. It's thoughtful to ask the godparents how they would like to be addressed. Some prefer being addressed by their surname, but others ask to be called "aunt" or "uncle" or a nickname.

Most importantly, godparents take responsibility for part of the child's spiritual development by ensuring that he receives religious instruction and is confirmed at the appropriate age. Your child's friendship with his godparents may continue into adulthood, but it's okay if this isn't the case. The vital role of the godparent is fulfilled at the child's confirmation.

Activity

If your child has godparents who live at a distance, encourage the relationship to flourish by having your child periodically send letters, cassette tapes, or videotapes to his godparents, telling about his activities such as family events, school, sports, and hobbies.

SEPTEMBER 15

Jewish confirmation: bar and bat mitzvah

The coming-of-age ceremonies for Jewish children can be quite elaborate and are very significant occasions for the children. They invite many of their friends to celebrate with them, Jewish and non-Jewish alike. If your child receives an invitation, she should respond promptly and honor the occasion with the extra attention it deserves. Accepting the invitation will mean dressing appropriately, choosing a gift, and attending the lengthy and diverse parts of the celebration.

On the first Sabbath after a Jewish boy turns thirteen (later in some congregations), the bar mitzvah is celebrated. The term "bar mitzvah" means "son of the commandment." Having reached the age of thirteen, he is now obligated to observe the commandments. Before the special day, the young man attends Hebrew school and spends a great deal of time in preparation; after the ceremony, he will participate as an adult member of the congregation.

Girls celebrate bat mitzvah in much the same way, although there are congregations who wait until the girl's sixteenth birthday. As with boys, the celebration of a Jewish girl's coming of age is an exceedingly joyous occasion in the life of her family. She has become a "daughter of the commandment," and the gladness is compared to that of her wedding day. While her parents may have encouraged her to obey the commandments as much as she could as a child, she is now obligated to do so as an adult. If your child is unfamiliar with bar and bat mitzvah preparations, reinforce for her the great significance it holds for the child involved.

The religious part of the bar mitzvah or bat mitzvah ceremony takes place in the synagogue and is a very reverent and meaningful service. Non-Jewish friends are welcomed into the synagogue along with members of the congregation and should wear something dressy, not casual. After the Sabbath worship service, there is usually a reception in the social hall of the synagogue, where the young person and his family greet friends. Encourage your child to attend all of the events rather than choosing those that sound most fun; her Jewish friend will appreciate her presence at all of them.

Finally, the party may move to another location for what may be a quite formal event. Many Jewish families save for a long time to be able to host a black-tie party. Your child will need to change into formal party attire for such a celebration, which could go on until midnight.

Gifts are welcome, but your child should not bring the gift to the synagogue. It should be presented at the party afterward or sent to the child's home. For girls, jewelry is an appropriate gift, as is cash.

SEPTEMBER 16

Catholic traditions: first communion and confirmation

A child's first holy communion is a very significant occasion for him and takes place around the second grade. He is instructed in the teachings of the Church; when he has learned about the ceremony and its meaning, he participates in a special mass along with a group of children his age.

At this mass, the homily is directed toward the children, and they are served communion before the adults. Close non-Catholic friends who attend don't take communion because of the very sacred nature of the ceremony.

If your child is invited to attend the first communion of a friend, he should dress up because the children taking communion will be very nicely dressed. The girls wear white dresses and the boys wear dark suits with white shirts and ties. He should also get his friend a small gift. Something religious in nature is nice, such as a Bible, prayer book, or gold cross.

Confirmation is a service that occurs when a child becomes a member of the Catholic church. It takes place around seventh or eighth grade and is celebrated more quietly than first communion. This is the occasion when he confirms the vows that his godparents made for him at his christening. He has gone through a period of instruction in the beliefs of his church and is now old enough to take those beliefs as his own. Thus while it is a happy occasion, there is also a serious tone to it.

As at first communion, the children dress up in white dresses for the girls and dark suits for the boys, and gifts of a religious nature are appropriate.

General audience with the pope

Many people who find themselves in Rome hope to visit Vatican City and would be thrilled to meet the pope, the head of the Roman Catholic Church.

The privilege of an audience with the pope is open to both Catholics and non-Catholics and requires that a reservation be obtained before arriving in Rome. This is done by having a priest place the request in writing on your family's behalf to the official American liaison to the Vatican at the Office of the Papal Audience, Casa S. Maria dell'Umilita, Via dell'Umilta 30, Rome 00187.

A general audience takes place in the Papal Audience Hall at St. Peter's Basilica on Wednesday morning. The audience is very animated in its greeting of the pope. They all rise when he arrives on his portable throne, carried by Swiss Guards. He then takes his seat on a permanent throne, and the audience sits while he addresses them in several languages and blesses them. People in the audience may also carry items in their hands to be blessed at the end of the ceremony. When the pope says the benediction, the audience kneels.

If you and your child are content to be part of a large group who see the pope but don't meet him personally, you may join other visitors to Rome in the square at St. Peter's Basilica. Here on Sunday at noon, if the pope is in residence, he appears at the window of his private apartments and addresses the thousands gathered in the square.

The noisy nature of the crowd may be surprising, but it is a sign of respect and affection for the pope and is said to be music to his ears. He delivers a short meditation, presenting it in several languages, and then blesses the crowd. When being blessed, Catholics in the audience cross themselves and may kneel. Individuals of other faiths are not obligated to do so in the square.

For an audience in St. Peter's Square, tourist clothing will do. For a general audience, dark, conservative clothing is expected. No jewelry is appropriate.

Semiprivate and private audiences with the pope

A semiprivate or private audience with the pope is much more difficult to obtain than a general audience. These audiences are usually reserved for people of rank, either in the Catholic Church, the government, or other positions of leadership. A semiprivate group includes fifty to two hundred people, and a private group is twelve or fewer. These audiences are often reserved for dignitaries and special groups, and the help of a bishop is needed in arranging such an audience.

Rules regarding dress for these audiences are not as restrictive as they once were; however, conservative clothing is expected. This means Sunday best for children. Women dress modestly, with no bare arms or legs; and while it isn't required, many women do cover their heads. Men wear dark suits. It's not appropriate to wear jewelry.

When making reservations for an audience inside St. Peter's, the visitor is also making a commitment to participate in standing and kneeling and, at the personal meeting, to kiss the pope's ring. If you aren't a Catholic and these gestures violate your religious convictions, sometimes changes in the procedure can be made. Rather than force the issue, however, it's better not to attend.

What your child should expect at a funeral

Very young children are not obligated to attend funerals, even if they are children of the deceased. If they do attend, explain what they're likely to encounter.

Most Christian funerals will be held in a church. Friends enter the church quietly and take a seat. The front pews are reserved for family members of the deceased, while close friends sit behind them. Acquaintances of the deceased sit in the middle and to the back.

A processional may take place after the audience is seated. The minister will lead, followed by the pallbearers and the casket, and then family members of the deceased.

The funeral service may include choir and organ music, a message from the minister, and possibly a eulogy (a tribute to the deceased, given by a family member or friend).

Some services are open to the public, while others are private and may be attended by invitation only. If it's a private service, the newspaper will state this, and invitations will be given by phone.

After the service, the casket is placed in the hearse and taken to the burial site. Those who want to attend the service at the grave follow the hearse in a procession of cars.

It isn't necessary to wear black to a funeral unless you plan to sit with the family or have been asked to be a pallbearer. However, nice clothing in subdued colors shows respect for the occasion. Girls wear their nicest dresses and shoes, and boys wear dark blazers with gray slacks (or something similar), and clean shoes.

SEPTEMBER 20

At a funeral home

When someone dies, the body is held at a funeral home until the day of the funeral. The death notice in the newspaper will state the time when relatives and friends may visit the family of the deceased at the funeral home. If your child wants to attend the viewing at the funeral home, you should allow him to do so.

The atmosphere at the funeral home should remain quiet and solemn. Visitors wear dress clothes in conservative colors. When your child meets the family, he should keep conversation brief. It's fine simply to say, "I'm very sorry," and gently shake the hand of the person who has lost a loved one. Your child shouldn't talk at length about how tragic the situation is, but should be willing to listen if the bereaved wants to talk.

If the casket is open, your child may pass by and pause a few moments by the casket to show his respect.

After greeting the family, your child may meet and chat with other people he knows who are also visiting. The conversation should be kept low but doesn't need to focus only on the person's death. He should not laugh, carry on, or run around the funeral home. A visit to a funeral home may last only ten to fifteen minutes.

SEPTEMBER 21

Sitting shiva

A Jewish funeral and burial take place as soon as possible after the death. Since Jews believe that the soul has returned to God, it's a matter of shame to have the body linger with the living. For this reason, there is no embalming or viewing of the body.

Sitting shiva is the Jewish period of mourning that lasts for seven days after the funeral (the term *shiva* comes from the Hebrew word *shevah,* meaning "seven"). Shiva is observed by immediate family members, including mother and father, son and daughter, brother and sister, and husband and wife.

Friends and family members (both Jewish and non-Jewish) come to the home to comfort the mourners. They bring kosher foods, such as whole fruit or baked goods from a kosher bakery. It's not appropriate to bring other gifts or flowers that might be associated with celebrations.

Silence is observed while sitting shiva. Jews are reminded of Job's friends who came to sit on the ground with him for seven days and nights, not saying a word, after he had lost his family. If there will be conversation during sitting shiva, it's begun by the family in mourning. Visitors should not stay long, and when they leave, the traditional farewell is "May God comfort you among the mourners for Zion and Jerusalem."

Birthdays, Weddings, Receptions, and Other Special Occasions

❧

By their very nature, special occasions come along only once in a while—so prompting your child ahead of time on what is expected, and role-playing courteous behavior, will help make your child a welcome participant in the special events of others.

SEPTEMBER 22

At your child's own birthday party

One of the most compelling reasons for learning manners is that they help us control ourselves in emotionally charged situations. A child's birthday party is certainly one such occasion. Naturally, your child is going to be very excited about his party. Although being the star of the show seems wonderful to your child in anticipation, in reality it can produce less-than-desirable behavior.

This is why it's not a good idea to have a surprise party for a young child; the nice part about letting your elementary-school child in on his party planning is that you can coach him beforehand on how he can be kind to his friends at the party. Establish the foundation for a good party by following the very wise rule of not inviting more children than the age of your child. There are some ways to help your child to be nice to his guests. He can:

1. Greet each of his guests by name at the door.
2. Let the friend offer the gift—no snatching it out of the child's hands.
3. Spend some time talking with each guest at the party. Introduce friends who might not know each other.
4. Stand by the door as friends are leaving so he can say goodbye to each one and thank them for coming.

Activity

Let your child help plan the theme and activities of his party. If you check out children's birthday parties on the Internet, you will find complete party plans with coordinated decorations, activities, and food.

SEPTEMBER 23

Attending a birthday party

It's a privilege to be invited to a birthday party. Your child's behavior should reflect that from the minute she receives the invitation. She should RSVP to the invitation right away. It's especially important to RSVP early if your child can't come. Disappointing news received late is worse than prompt regrets.

Get a gift the child will like, and allow your child to help choose it. Consider the child's preferences, interests, and hobbies, and ask the child's parent for suggestions if necessary, but don't ask the birthday child. It isn't your job to shop at her bidding.

Your child should understand that even though the birthday child may be her best friend, at the party she won't be able to give your child exclusive attention. It's a group affair; your child should use the time to make new friends and avoid monopolizing the birthday child's attention.

Make sure your child gets to the party on time, but don't come early, either. Your child's presence will distract the hosts. Your child should remember to say "happy birthday" to the birthday child when she meets her at the door. She should offer the gift to the child or ask where she can put it.

Encourage your child to be willing to take part in the activities at the party.

When your child leaves, she should say goodbye and offer thanks to the birthday child and her parents.

Activity

On the ride home from the next birthday party your child attends, have her tell you about what took place. Compliment her on all the things she did right.

SEPTEMBER 24

Receiving lines

Receiving lines require patience on the part of children, but sometimes they must be endured. Very large parties make it difficult for the guest of honor to talk with each guest, so the receiving line makes it possible for him to have a short connection with each person who came to the party. If your child can imagine how disappointing it would be to go to a birthday party that is so big he can't get a chance to talk with his friend, he'll probably see the purpose of receiving lines.

Your child could encounter a receiving line at a wedding reception, a political event, or an anniversary party. Here are some guidelines for your child:

- *Don't try to escape.* Going through the line might be the only way he has of letting the host or guest of honor know he's attended.
- *Have clean hands.* Eat *after* going through the receiving line, and never carry food or drink through a line. Getting hugged while holding a drink is a guaranteed disaster.
- *Keep comments short and positive.* "Congratulations. You look beautiful. This is such a nice party. Thank you for inviting me." Chat only briefly and keep moving. The purpose of the receiving line is for the guest of honor to meet many people in a short time.

- *Shake hands with people in the line.* Your child should be ready to get hugged if he knows people well.
- *Introduce yourself.* If there are strangers in the receiving line, say: "Hello. I am Tom Ryan, Mr. Gold's nephew."

Activity

Role-play a receiving line with family members or stuffed animals. Have four people in the line for your child to meet. Describe the situation and let your child know that the guest of honor will probably be the second or third person. The first person is often able to make introductions.

SEPTEMBER 25

Taking a child to a wedding

A wedding may be one of the first important social events your child attends where his behavior will be noticed and where his actions really make a difference. The bride and groom hope their once-in-a-lifetime event will go smoothly. They have enough to worry about with guests who don't RSVP and family members who don't get along; they shouldn't have to add rambunctious or thoughtless children to their concerns.

Not every child is ready to attend a wedding. Since weddings can be lengthy affairs, children whose attention span and ability to sit are still developing may be happier at home with a sitter. If your child has demonstrated a measure of self-control, *and he's been invited,* take him along. He's invited if his name appears on the inner envelope of the invitation. He isn't automatically included because his parents are, even if they are relatives of the bride and groom.

SEPTEMBER 26

What to do at a wedding

Your child has been invited to attend a wedding with you—so be sure to rehearse everything she can expect. Your child will be a welcome guest at a wedding if she:

- *Arrives on time.* At a wedding this means twenty to thirty minutes before the time on the invitation. The time listed on the invitation is when the bride will walk down the aisle. Your child doesn't want to get caught in that parade.
- *Waits quietly while her parents sign the guest book.* Explain that guest books will probably be kept for a lifetime and are not places for children to practice penmanship.
- *Walks down the aisle with her parents.* Parents are seated according to whether they are friends of the bride or groom. The mother takes the usher's arm, and the child and father follow them to their designated seat.
- *Sits quietly during the organ prelude and processional.* Your child may read the program but should not crinkle it up or shape it into an airplane. She may turn to see each of the bridesmaids walk down the aisle, but she should not speak out.
- *Stands when the bride's mother stands* to acknowledge that the bride is walking down the aisle.
- *Is attentive during the ceremony.* This isn't a time for coloring books and games. If a child is too young to sit through the ceremony, she should spend the time in the nursery.
- *Stays with her parents after the ceremony.* There may be a time for taking pictures of the bridal party.
- *Goes through the buffet line with his parents.* She should never run around.
- *Uses her best table manners at the reception.* Again, she stays with her parents or sits where she has been assigned. She doesn't beg to have the seating arranged so that she can sit with friends.
- *Says goodbye to the bride and groom before leaving.*

SEPTEMBER 27

When your child is a junior bridesmaid

Members of a wedding party are esteemed friends or close relatives of the bride or groom, and it is an honor to be asked to participate in a wedding. A junior bridesmaid is between eight and sixteen years of age and carries out some but not all of the obligations of the bridesmaids.

If your child is chosen as a junior bridesmaid, you will need to buy the dress the bride wants the child to wear; usually it matches the bridesmaids' gowns. Your child will be invited to attend a bridal shower but probably won't have responsibilities to help plan it, as the bridesmaids do. She should attend the rehearsal and rehearsal dinner and should dress up for the occasion.

On the day of the wedding, she will dress with the other bridesmaids before the wedding. At the wedding ceremony, she will participate in the processional and recessional. At the reception, she will be expected to join in the celebration, socializing with other guests, dancing with the ushers, and participating in the bouquet toss.

It's an honor to be asked to serve in a bridal party. Young girls usually love weddings and all of the frilly trappings associated with them. And of course the icing on the cake is receiving a gift from the bride, possibly jewelry to be worn at the wedding, and getting to keep the bridesmaid dress.

If your child doesn't want to be in the wedding, either because she is too young or feels shy about it, it's okay to decline the invitation. This will spare you and the bride the dilemma of having the child back out of her role just before the ceremony or participate with a stricken look on her face throughout the event.

If your child is a flower girl

A flower girl is usually between the ages of four and eight. If your daughter is asked to do this, her primary responsibilities will be walking down the aisle ahead of the bride, scattering flower petals along the way or simply carrying a bouquet, and looking as cute as can be! She may have a partner as well, since having two flower girls is acceptable.

The flower girl probably will dress in white organdy or cotton in warmer months and in velvet or taffeta in cooler months; her dress may be from the same fabric as the bridesmaids'. Often a flower girl will wear a wreath of flowers in her hair.

A flower girl will participate in the rehearsal so that she will know what to expect during the wedding ceremony. As her parent, you may be invited to accompany her to the rehearsal dinner if she is quite young. You will also be responsible for buying her dress and shoes and making sure that she gets to the rehearsal and the wedding.

There is no need for you to be concerned that she might not perform her role perfectly. She'll be adorable to look at, and that's enough. Do take time to answer questions she has about what being in a wedding will be like, but don't create unnecessary anxiety by discussing the "big day" too much.

When your child is a ring bearer

The ring bearer at a wedding is traditionally a young boy who carries the rings on a satin pillow in the processional. The rings are lightly sewn to the pillow or tied to it with small satin ribbons so that there can't be any accidents! Sometimes the best man and maid of honor have the real rings and those on the pillow are just for effect.

The ring bearer walks just in front of the flower girl, if there is one, or in front of the bride and her father. If he is quite young and isn't carrying the actual rings to be exchanged in the ceremony, he may take a seat in the bride's mother's pew during the ceremony. If he has the actual rings, he must remain at the front of the church with the wedding party.

A ring bearer usually wears a suit in white or a dark color, with either long or short pants. He does not dress like a miniature groomsman.

The ring bearer attends rehearsal so that he knows what is expected of him and he can become familiar with the groomsmen. Some of his anxiety may be eased if he is introduced to a buddy—a groomsman whom he can stand beside during the ceremony and turn to if he is uncertain.

Boys don't seem to have the fascination with dressing up and being in weddings that girls have. In fact, they might be outright opposed to the idea, so be sure to discuss his duties with him. If that's the case, it's better to tell the bride than insist that your son plow ahead with a responsibility he can't handle. If he is willing but not terribly excited, he should say yes, since it is an honor to be included. But if he strongly resists a couple of months before the wedding, and you insist that he participate, you might find yourself with a child on the day of the wedding who is completely unwilling to join the processional.

SEPTEMBER 30

Self-control at a reception

Your child may be invited to a variety of receptions—at Grandpa and Grandma's fiftieth wedding anniversary, at your business open house, in a church fellowship hall, or after a piano recital. Food will be displayed on a buffet table, and it will look absolutely tempting. These are occasions that require much self-control on your child's part. You don't want to see him dash across the room to the buffet, run headlong into someone, and send a plate of food flying into the air. That's funny only in the movies!

Prompt your child ahead of time on making the reception a success. Here's what he should do:

- Stay with you. He's less likely to get into trouble, and he has a model to follow if he's not sure what to do.
- Greet people with whom you are talking: "Hello, Mrs. Adams" is the respectful way for your child to address your friends.
- Refrain from interrupting conversation to demand to be fed or taken home.
- Walk—never run.
- Stand still, or better yet find a seat at a table when eating. Never move about a room nibbling on hors d'oeuvres or sipping a drink.
- Find a tray or wastebasket to get rid of used plates, utensils, or napkins. They aren't returned to the serving table. If it's a fancy party, look for a waiter who will take these things.
- Pay attention during a presentation, and don't eat.
- Before leaving, if the size of the event makes it at all possible, find the host to say thank you and goodbye.

Activity

Rent an old slapstick movie that includes a food disaster. Watch it and laugh about it with your children. Discuss how they would feel if that happened to them in real life.

OCTOBER 1

Serving yourself from a buffet table

Buffet tables can quickly become unappetizing. You can bet your child will see some poor role models at his next buffet—the double dippers, the slowpokes, the sloppies, and the overeaters. But that's how it's going to be. While you won't browbeat rude adults who park themselves at the buffet, you can help your child know just how to behave.

Of utmost importance at the buffet is a preference for others. Your child should stifle the urge to hurry to be first in line. Encourage him to stay with you and let older guests go first.

Have your child take a plate and proceed through the line, taking small portions. He should remember that there are more people following him. He shouldn't pause and study the food endlessly, and he shouldn't take ten pieces of shrimp. A small serving of three or four items is fine—the size of the plate will give your child a clue as to how much is too much.

Of course, there is no tasting along the way, either from the serving dishes or from the child's own plate. Following this rule will eliminate the appalling practice of double dipping. No stick of celery should ever dive back into the dip after your child has munched on it! Nor should he dip a finger in a sauce or dressing to see if he likes the taste.

Although you should generally prompt your child ahead of time about what's expected, in the buffet line you might need to intervene. Certainly you would do this instinctively when you notice your child pick up an item of food, study it closely, and move to put it back on the serving dish. Also remind him there is no need for him to touch each cookie on a tray as he considers which will be the tastiest. He should know that whatever he touches, he takes.

As soon as he has served himself, your child should move away from the table. It might feel nice to be close to the table in the event he wants seconds, but this is *not* the place to visit with others.

Activity

Go over these tips before your child's next buffet. After the buffet, discuss everything he did correctly. Praise him for his courtesy.

OCTOBER 2

Hang on to your plate at a reception

Eating while standing can be an accident waiting to happen for children and adults alike. The first step in avoiding disaster is to show your child how to hold the plate, napkin, and cup properly *in one hand.* In this way, she can accomplish the essential—keep one hand free to eat. Your child's second hand is also free to shake hands with someone to whom she is introduced. Don't teach your child to initiate a handshake while she's eating finger food, however. It's an invitation to spread germs, and to many people it isn't appealing.

In the left hand, put the partly opened napkin between the pinkie and ring fingers. Put the small hors d'oeuvres plate between the index finger and the middle finger. Place the cup on the edge of the plate with the index finger and thumb curled around it to steady it. The pinkie, ring, and middle fingers are balancing the plate underneath. With a cup on an already small plate, your child may wonder how she can get any food on it. Let her know that at a reception, she takes a modest amount of food—it isn't intended to be a full meal. She may go back for seconds after others have served themselves if she must have more.

Activity

Getting this right takes practice. Put out a few items of finger food, such as crackers and cheese, grapes, and brownies. Have your child hold a small plate, napkin, and cup with juice in it and practice eating standing up. Don't expect a child who is five or younger to do this. A child this age should serve herself, take her cup in her left hand, and find a seat before eating.

OCTOBER 3

Wearing flowers

Wearing flowers has its place—at festive occasions such as weddings and dances, but rarely at funerals. On occasion, a white carnation may be worn by a pallbearer.

Boys wear boutonnieres. This is a French word that means "buttonhole" and indicates where the flower is worn. It is tucked into the buttonhole on the left lapel or pinned to the lapel. These flowers are either white or dark red and should be real. It's better not to wear a flower than to wear an imitation.

Girls wear corsages. They have a great deal of freedom regarding where to put the flowers—on either shoulder (make sure the flowers aren't too far down, drawing attention away from the face), on the wrist, pinned to a purse, fastened at the waist, or tucked into the hair.

Girls love getting any kind of flower, but it's kind of the giver to check ahead about the color of the girl's dress. It's also courteous of the girl to wear the flowers even if they don't match perfectly (she might attach them to her purse).

The language of flowers

Young people in the Victorian era were familiar with an extensive language of flowers. Friends communicated with each other through "talking bouquets" called tussie-mussies. Each flower had a message to convey, and there were dictionaries to consult to understand a bouquet's meaning. Not only was it fun to receive one of these tiny bouquets (they weren't much larger than a fist), it was also exciting to decipher its message. Tussie-mussies were given by lovers, friends, family members, and guests.

Children today can learn the most rudimentary floral language—red roses declare "I love you" and yellow roses mean friendship. But they may also discover in tussie-mussies a new (old) way of communicating with friends. If you find a book about the language of flowers in the library or bookstore, you can help your child create a meaningful gift of flowers to express congratulations, birthday wishes, thanks, a wish for good luck, love, or sympathy.

Activity

Help your child make a tussie-mussie for her grandmother or a friend. Choose a variety of flowers at a flower shop, consulting with a book on their meanings. Wrap the ends of the flowers with floral tape and decorate the bouquet with lace or ribbons.

Your child might want to pass along a flower dictionary with the gift. Maybe it will be returned with a floral message!

Getting an autograph

There are times when it's fine to ask a celebrity or author for an autograph. If a celebrity has made an appearance at an event or an author is at a bookstore promoting a book, your child may ask for an autograph. He should purchase the book and ask to have it signed. He may ask a celebrity to sign a program from the event.

People who are willing to give autographs make themselves available to do the signing. They will remain in the audience for a period of time after the program just for that purpose.

On the other hand, it isn't considerate to let your child go up to someone who is going about his regular business and ask for an autograph. Celebrities need their privacy, too. It's not fun to be interrupted many times during a meal or a private walk to sign an autograph. Nor is it thoughtful to put a book or picture in the mail and ask that it be autographed. It isn't the celebrity's obligation to return items in the mail, and there is no guarantee that the item will be returned.

Teach your child the importance of respecting the privacy of celebrities you might happen to meet as well as that of locally well-known people. One local elected official had to give up her swimming pool membership in her neighborhood and travel across town to relax by another pool because people who knew her insisted upon discussing business with her while she was taking a much-needed break from work.

Receiving an award

Hearing your child's name called to receive an award or be honored in some way and watching her make her way to the front of the room can be enough to make a parent's heart stop. You feel a queasy mixture of anxiety and pride and hope she doesn't trip on the steps to the stage or call out, "Hi, Mom!"

It can be unnerving for your child as well. While one child can think only of getting to the stage and back to her seat alive, the situation brings out the ham in the next. A few tips before the event will help ensure that it isn't embarrassing to your child or to those watching.

Your child should walk with her best posture, hands out of her pockets. "Best posture" means back straight, no shuffling, and chin parallel to the floor. If she needs to look at the floor (which she should if she doesn't want to fall), she should cast her eyes down, not her head. This stance gives her an air of confidence and communicates her personal respect for the event.

She should not be chewing gum or fiddling with her clothes— and she should be wearing a smile.

When she gets to center stage, she should not wave at Mom or Dad or do a little jig. This is a time for others to focus attention on her, not for her to draw attention to herself. She accepts the award with a low "thank you" and either takes her seat or stands at the appointed place if others are to be honored as well. If her coach, teacher, or club leader feels particularly affectionate toward her and gives her a hug, she should return the hug rather than stand there with limp arms.

While waiting for others, she doesn't open her certificate, but holds it by her side. When she takes her seat, she may look at the certificate, but only if it can be done in a way that isn't distracting to others. She doesn't bend it or deface it in any way.

Activity

Help your child practice receiving a certificate. Encourage her to offer her right hand to shake and to reach underneath to accept the certificate with her left hand from your left hand. Remind her to look at you when she says thank you.

At a school dance

School dances are supposed to be fun, but sometimes they're nerve-racking. The same positive, friendly attitude that gets your child through the school day will help her at a dance. Most kids find it easier to go with a couple of friends, and there's no reason to worry about pairing off, especially at middle-school dances.

A dance doesn't have to be threatening. It's not a contest to see who dances the best. It's an opportunity to enjoy the music and have fun with friends. During the fast dances everyone dances together.

If someone asks your child to dance but she's uncertain about her dance skills, she should go ahead and admit it. Her partner will probably be thrilled to teach her a few steps. At the end of the dance, she should thank the boy for asking her to dance.

Tell your daughter that if she's being followed around by someone she really doesn't like, she can get something to eat with her friends, take a bathroom break, or ask a friend to dance with her. It's good to give others the benefit of the doubt, though. If she waits for Prince Charming to come along, she might wait all evening.

When she helps herself to cookies and punch, she shouldn't stand by the buffet table nibbling on food as she picks it up. It's better to take a few items and go to her table to eat. If she's getting herself a drink, it's nice to get one for a friend as well.

When your child is behind the camera

Cameras can make special moments last a lifetime, and it may be fun for kids to take pictures, but they can also ruin solemn occasions. Adults and kids need to get permission to take pictures at religious services—sometimes it's strictly forbidden. If permission is granted to photograph a baptism, for example, only one person should have a camera. At weddings, guests take photos only after the service. They should be careful not to shoot at the same time as the wedding photographer.

Photos shouldn't be taken during performances by an orchestra, a vocal artist, or an acting company. Flashing lights are distracting to performers and audience alike.

At occasions where photos are allowed, remind your junior photographer to:

- Be conscious of the feelings of others.
- Not block someone's view with a whirring video camera.
- Know how to operate the camera, so that people don't have to hold a pose indefinitely.
- Not train a camera on people who clearly don't want to be photographed.

OCTOBER 9

When your child is in front of the camera

When the camera is on your child, it isn't the time to be a ham. One person making faces and sprouting fingers up behind someone's head ruins the picture and makes everyone wait while the photographer gets a better shot. It's even worse if no one notices the antics until the worthless photo is developed.

If your child is lucky enough to get his picture taken with one of his sports or entertainment heroes, he should step right up beside the celebrity, face the camera, and smile. He may briefly thank the celebrity but shouldn't get into a long conversation. There are probably many others waiting in line for their picture.

Some tips to get the best photo:

- Look at the camera.
- Stand tall.
- Lower your chin a bit.
- Button your suit jacket.
- Keep your hands by your sides, thumbs at the side seams.

- One hand in a pocket is okay, but never two.
- Place your feet not more than a couple of inches apart.
- Smile.

Activity

Take a series of pictures of your child, encouraging him to stand tall in some and allowing him to break the rules in others. Compare the pictures and talk about why some look so much better than others. Use a Polaroid camera for instant gratification.

Gifts—Giving and Getting

❧

Adults may know that it's better to give than to receive, but children will probably need to be reminded. It's easy for children to count the days long in advance of their birthdays, anticipating the gifts they'll receive, but sometimes they find it difficult to be content when it's a friend's special day. Helping your child learn to give and to receive graciously provides a valuable social skill.

OCTOBER 10

Birthstones

If your child wants to give a birthday gift with personal significance, a birthstone necklace or ring is a good choice. The gift will feel special to the one receiving it, and there'll be instant recognition: "You picked my birthstone!"

MONTH	BIRTHSTONE
January	Garnet
February	Amethyst
March	Bloodstone or aquamarine
April	Diamond
May	Emerald
June	Pearl, moonstone, or alexandrite

July	Ruby
August	Sardonyx or peridot
September	Sapphire
October	Opal or tourmaline
November	Topaz
December	Turquoise or zircon

OCTOBER 11

Gifts

Children love to get gifts—so much so that they may break a fundamental rule of good manners and *ask* for them. Their early gift giving (birthday gifts to friends) is sometimes done with a hint of reluctance. How they wish they could just keep the gift themselves! Or you might find yourself buying duplicate items—one for your child to give away and one for him to keep.

As your child gets older, getting and giving gifts will take on more meaning. He'll begin to realize that he should give gifts in a similar price range as his friends; he shouldn't outspend others. Nor should he ever feel obligated to buy a gift that hurts your family's budget. It's more thoughtful to buy a gift that reflects the interests of the other person than to spend a lot of money.

Gifts are given to mark special occasions—birthdays, anniversaries, graduations, Valentine's Day—or they may be given just as a token of friendship and love. A girl may bring her friend some beautiful shells when she returns home from a beach vacation. A boy can offer his buddy an enlarged and framed snapshot of the two of them. These gifts should always be given out of sincere affection and regard for the other person.

Your child should never use a gift to try to influence another person. For example, one elementary-school girl craved the friendship of another girl in her class and repeatedly gave many gifts—money, candy, desserts—trying to bribe the other girl into friendship. She didn't understand that you can't buy friendship. The child who received the gifts felt torn inside. Of course she liked getting gifts, but she didn't like the obligation she began to feel. Help your child understand that it isn't truly a gift if the other person doesn't feel good about it.

OCTOBER 12

Choosing a gift

Gift giving is a ritual for some occasions, such as birthdays or weddings. In an attempt to make the job easier, gift givers ask either the child or the parent for suggestions. Some children know so explicitly what they want that they turn you into their personal shopper: "I want the classroom wardrobe for my Molly doll, the latest Britney Spears CD, and a black tattoo necklace."

If your child is asked for suggestions, that is exactly what he should give—general suggestions, not a shopping list: "I always like things for my dolls, music, or jewelry. But anything is fine— being surprised is fun."

Your child should take the other person's interests, preferences, and sensibilities into account when giving a gift. He should never give a gift in hopes of reforming the other person. If your child loves to read and his friend loves to fish but can't be bothered with books, your child shouldn't choose a book. Your child's gift should reflect the preferences of his friend, not his own.

OCTOBER 13

Giving gifts at home

Choosing the right gift is a wonderful expression of affection or appreciation, but it's a skill that can take time to develop. Children can learn by watching your example or by getting practice at home.

Gift giving doesn't come without its pitfalls—sometimes the wrong gift is chosen, too many gifts are given that aren't reciprocated, or appreciation isn't shown when a gift is received.

Don't let your child miss the birthdays of family members. Elementary-school children will need to be reminded of approaching birthdays. But just because they don't remember them doesn't mean they don't want to give a gift. One fourth-grader woke up on her mother's birthday and had no idea what special day it was. Typically she would have decorated a special card or helped her dad pick out some flowers. She felt sad to have missed the birthday, but it wasn't her fault, because no one had reminded her.

Let your child see you giving gifts to your spouse. Some married couples do not give gifts even at holidays and birthdays. Not only do they neglect to give their relationship a boost, they miss an opportunity to model gift giving for their children. The husband who picks up a book by his wife's favorite author when he's traveling or the wife who gets her husband a recording of his favorite vocalist are showing their children how to be generous and thoughtful.

Children can gain confidence in choosing gifts by giving gifts to their siblings at holidays or birthdays. These gifts don't need to be bought; a gift that has been handcrafted can be just as thoughtful.

OCTOBER 14

Gifts for the host

When your child visits a friend for dinner or stays overnight, it's very nice to take a small gift for his friend's parents. If your child has dinner at the friend's home once a week—after a soccer game, for example—a gift isn't necessary. But when it's a special occasion, a gift is a nice way to express appreciation for the invitation.

Your child might take some flowers, a small candle, gourmet coffee beans, or a box of chocolates. The gift should not add work for his host, so he shouldn't give fresh flowers without a vase. If he takes chocolate chip cookies, he shouldn't expect that they be served with the meal. Dessert will already have been planned. He should tell his friend's parents the cookies are for them.

If your child is staying overnight with a friend while you travel for a couple of days, a tray of brownies or a video for the family's collection would be a thoughtful gift. Or you might give his host something upon your return home. Some suggestions might be a candle, a coffee table book, a basket filled with bath and body products, an art print, or a basket of fresh fruit.

Whatever your child gives, help him wrap it nicely or put it in a gift bag with pretty tissue paper. It'll be a beautiful, tangible expression of his appreciation and respect for his friend's family.

Activity

Create a gift drawer in your home. Fill it with different kinds of gift wrap, ribbons, tape, and a few small gifts. Give your children access to the drawer. Replenish the supply when you see items on sale.

OCTOBER 15

"No gifts"

When an invitation says "no gifts," guests should honor the request. On occasion a child will be invited to a "no gifts" birthday party, although children do love to get gifts, so this is rare. Such a party may be planned if a child has birthday parties several years in a row, while his friends have them less frequently. His parents may want to entertain his friends but don't want them to feel obligated to purchase a gift every year. As with parties for adults, children should take the recommendation at face value. They don't have an obligation to take a gift. However, if your child's best friend is having such a party and your child has already picked out the perfect gift, have her give it to her friend when they are alone.

"No gifts" should not be understood to mean "give money."

Occasions to give a gift

There are many occasions when giving a gift is a kind, thoughtful gesture. Keeping the gifts small helps this social ritual not to become overwhelming. Handmade gifts can be the perfect thing for a child to give. Help your child attach a note or card to the gift. Practically, it identifies the giver, but a handwritten message from the heart also adds immeasurable value to the gift. It might be the only part of the gift that is saved through the years.

Here are a few occasions when your child should be reminded of this social duty, and some suggestions for gifts:

- *Teacher's birthday or end-of-year gift:* coffee cake, flowers, notecards.
- *Friend's birthday:* art supplies, model car, compact disc, hair clips and fun makeup, bicycle accessories, fishing lure, stuffed animal, board game.
- *Bar or bat mitzvah:* jewelry, pen, book, journal, money (take the gift to the reception, not the synagogue, or deliver it to the child's home).
- *Thank-you to a nurse* (when your child has an extended stay at the hospital): basket of fruit, chocolates to share with coworkers, flowers.
- *Athletic coach at the end of season:* restaurant or sports store gift certificate, ball for the sport autographed by each team member.
- *Good friend on no particular occasion:* handmade jewelry, framed snapshot of special time together, souvenir from your child's travels, small item for the friend's collection (stamps, coins, rocks, stuffed animal).

Activity

Brainstorm with your child about gifts that are made in your area. Suggest that your child let the person know about the special connection when she gives the gift. The person will be reminded of your family when she uses it.

OCTOBER 17

Opening gifts at a party

One of the biggest potential pitfalls of a birthday party is how the gift giving is handled. First of all, remind your child that he shouldn't grab the gift from the guest as she comes through the door. Make sure she allows the guest to offer the present.

Pile the gifts off to one side until you're ready to open them. You should plan to have your child open gifts at the party rather than waiting until later. Your child's friends want to see her face as she unveils the treasures they probably spent a good deal of time choosing.

When gift-opening time arrives, don't allow your child to dive into the pile, ripping off wrappings and tossing the gift aside without any acknowledgment. Practice with her the strategy of gift opening before the first guest arrives:

1. Your child should open the gifts slowly. This prolongs the joy of anticipation, and it also gives her the time she needs to say thank you to each guest.
2. When opening gifts, your child should look at the card first. If there isn't one, check the gift tag so she knows who gave the gift before she opens it.
3. She should look at the giver and smile before opening the gift.
4. Have your child respond positively to the gift and say thank you to the giver. Encourage her to look at the giver when she says thank you.
5. You may want to station an adult by your child's side to write down the gift and who gave it as a backup for thank-you notes later.

OCTOBER 18

When your child doesn't like the gift

Not liking a gift isn't an excuse to escape writing a thank-you note. This happens to everyone at some time or another. Maybe the sweater isn't your child's style, the video is one he already has, or the seashell clock is simply ugly. Unless the giver lets your child know the sweater or video can be returned or exchanged (and even then caution is urged), the best response is a sincere "thank you."

Tell your child to focus on the giver, not the gift. The giver put time and thought into its selection, and certainly meant to please your child.

There is no need for your child to lie when writing the note by saying, for instance, that the dancing chihuahua was just what he wanted. It would be better to say, "Thank you for remembering my birthday. You have a talent for finding one-and-only gifts. I will always think of you when I see the dancing chihuahua."

Encourage your child to be creative and sincere and have fun with difficult thank-you notes.

OCTOBER 19

When your child receives duplicate gifts

If your child receives duplicate gifts, he may:

- Keep them both.
- Return one of them.
- Keep them both and give one as a gift to someone else.

Each of the givers put effort into the gift's selection, so it's courteous to express pleasure and gratitude for both gifts. Your child may say something lighthearted upon opening the second gift, such as, "This gift shows you know me well—I can't get enough Winnie the Pooh." Your child shouldn't ask where he got the gift so that he can return it. It's better to leave it up to the giver to recommend returning the gift.

If your child is going to give the gift to someone else, he should be sure that it's done with a different group of friends. He doesn't want to be obvious about doing that, but he shouldn't hide it, either. If the giver asks him about it later, he may admit that he returned it or that he loved it and knew that another friend would love it, too.

Great Holiday Etiquette

❧

Many families find it enriching to teach their children the meaning of holidays, both those they celebrate and those commemorated by others. To help you get started, this section covers a diverse group of holidays, from Easter to Yom Kippur to Kwanzaa. Help your child understand that holidays reflect the deeply held beliefs of a community. It's okay if your child asks a friend about family get-togethers, gift giving, or service to others that accompany a holiday. Taking the time to learn the traditions of a friend makes the other person feel special.

OCTOBER 20

Christian holidays

Many Christian religious holidays, with Christmas as an exception, are celebrated according to the lunar calendar. Easter, for example, falls on the first Sunday after a full moon occurs on or within twenty-eight days of March 21. This explains why the specific dates of celebration change from year to year. The calendar used by Christians is now in the twenty-first century, having begun approximately at the birth of Christ two thousand years ago. Years are marked by the letters A.D., which stands for *anno*

Domini, "in the year of the Lord." These are some significant Christian holidays:

> *Easter (the resurrection of Christ):* March or April
> *Good Friday (the day Christ died):* the Friday before Easter
> *Palm Sunday (Christ's entry into Jerusalem):* the Sunday before Easter
> *Lent (a time of penitence):* forty days leading up to Easter
> *Ash Wednesday (first day of Lent, when ashes are placed on the forehead as a token of penitence)*
> *Pentecost (the coming of the Holy Spirit):* May or June
> *Ascension Day (Christ returns to heaven): forty days after Easter, ten days before Pentecost*
> *All Saints' Day:* November 1
> *First Sunday of Advent:* November or December
> *Christmas (birth of Christ):* December 25
> *Epiphany (day the Three Kings arrived):* January 6
> *Twelfth Night (eve of Epiphany)*

Activity

Have your child create and decorate a calendar with all major Christian holidays, and involve everyone in planning celebrations.

OCTOBER 21

Easter

The most significant Christian celebration is Easter, commemorating the sacrifice of Christ. This holiday can occur as early as March 22 or as late as April 25 because it takes place on the first Sunday following the first full moon on or after March 21. Holy Week, the week leading up to Easter, begins with Palm Sunday, named after Jesus' triumphal entry into Jerusalem when adoring crowds laid palm branches at his feet.

Holy Thursday commemorates the Last Supper. This was Jesus' last meal with his disciples before the Crucifixion, where he washed their feet and served them bread and wine, asking them to continue the practice. To remember this event, Christian churches hold solemn services, partake of bread and wine in the sacrament of communion, and look ahead with sober gratitude to the sacrifice of Christ, to be commemorated the following day. Your child will be welcome at these services but should be prepared to be a quiet observer. She should follow the church's guidelines about when to begin taking part in communion.

Friday of Holy Week is the commemoration of the Crucifixion, when Jesus Christ gave his life on a Roman cross.

Easter Sunday is a day of triumph as Christians celebrate their Redeemer's resurrection from the dead. Celebrations may begin at sunrise, as Christ's tomb was discovered to be empty early in the day. Church services are filled with rejoicing, the music is exultant, and worshipers dress in spring finery.

The word *Easter* is derived from a Scandinavian term, *Ostra,* and a Teutonic term, *Oetern* or *Eastere,* both referring to mythological goddesses symbolizing spring and fertility. The Easter rabbit is also a symbol of fertility, and the bright colors of Easter eggs represent the sunlight and bright colors of spring. Christians also believe that eggs represent the new life that the risen Christ brings to mankind.

Children often celebrate Easter by searching for hidden eggs and candy. Remind your child to be conscious of younger children, take only her share of candy, and thank the adult who arranged the egg hunt. If your family is invited to a friend or relative's home for a meal, let her pick out some spring flowers—lilies, daffodils, or hyacinths—to take as a gift for the hostess.

Activity

If you're looking for ways to celebrate this holiday with youngsters, help your child decorate an outdoor tree by hanging brightly colored plastic eggs on it. Then hide candy eggs around the lawn and invite the children of neighbors or relatives to come for an egg hunt.

OCTOBER 22

Lent

Lent is the season of penitence preceding Easter. It begins on Ash Wednesday, forty-six days before Easter. The Lenten season lasts only forty days, however, because Sundays are not considered part of the observance. Explain to your child that families who observe Lent do so seriously, and she shouldn't tease a friend who is giving something up, or purposefully indulge in it in front of the friend.

Lent is a time for feeling and expressing remorse for sins. Christians may observe the season with acts of self-denial, such as giving up a favorite food or certain entertainments.

OCTOBER 23

Christmas

Christmas is the yearly Christian holiday that celebrates the birth of Jesus Christ. It is commemorated on December 25, and while it may be second in significance among Christian holidays (Easter being first), it is the one celebrated most elaborately. It has also become a major secular holiday.

The Bible does not provide guidelines for the observance of Christmas, but religious tradition begins the sacred season of Advent on the fourth Sunday before Christmas and continues to Christmas Day. Advent candles are lit on each of the Sundays and prayers are said as believers focus on different aspects of Christ. The Twelve Days of Christmas begin with Christmas and continue until January 6, Epiphany. Epiphany commemorates the arrival of the Magi, or wise men from the East, who brought gifts to the Christ child.

Religious services are usually held in churches on Christmas Eve. Catholics hold midnight mass, and Protestants hold special services.

The tradition of Santa Claus was brought to New York in the eighteenth century by Dutch settlers. The Dutch term was "Sinter

Klaas," and it described a tall religious man who rode a white horse through the air. In Germany, he was known as Saint Nicholas, also a religious figure, and was accompanied by an elf who punished disobedient children. In America, the poem "A Visit from Saint Nicholas," by Clement Clark Moore, with drawings by Thomas Nast, helped created the legend of a roly-poly, kindly old man who came from the North Pole in a sleigh pulled by reindeer to bring gifts to good children.

Christmas trees, originally a symbol of fertility, became a Christian symbol of rebirth. Brought into homes and decorated with ornaments, angels, fruits, and lights, the festive Christmas tree became a focal point during the Christmas season.

As time went by and the industrial economy grew, families had access to a greater amount of material things and began to place a special emphasis on home life. Gift giving within families replaced public celebrations.

Encourage your child to show courtesy to family members during holiday preparations and celebrations. Each child should allow others a turn opening a door on the Advent calendar. They should work together choosing and decorating the tree, so that no one feels left out and no one has all the work to do. When gifts are received, they should be acknowledged with gratitude.

Activity

Take a family shopping trip to the mall during the Christmas season. Prompt your child to notice the manners of others and to think about how she can be a courteous shopper (not grabbing items, waiting patiently in line, avoiding bumping into others). After you've returned home, make hot chocolate and have a family discussion about your own manners and what you noticed in others.

OCTOBER 24

Kwanzaa

The African-American celebration Kwanzaa (the word means "first fruits of the harvest") began in 1966, with the goal of focusing on traditional African values. It is observed for seven days, from December 26 to January 1, and is neither religious nor political in nature. Kwanzaa emphasizes seven guiding principles for African-American people, their culture, and ancestors. Each principle—unity, self-determination, collective work and responsibility, cooperative economics, purpose, creativity, and faith—emphasizes the importance of doing what is good for the community.

Kwanzaa celebrations take place in homes, community centers, and churches. The colors of Kwanzaa—black, red, and green—are dominant in decorations. Families gather symbolic items to place in the home. The centerpiece is a candleholder with seven candles, reflecting the seven principles of Kwanzaa. The candles (one black, three red, and three green) are set on a straw place mat along with fruits and vegetables, a unity cup, an ear of corn for each child (reflecting the African concept of social parenthood), and gifts of an educational or artistic nature.

On December 31, it is traditional to hold the Kwanzaa feast. The feast is a cooperative effort, held in a community center decorated with an African motif in black, red, and green and a large Kwanzaa setting with candles, unity cup, and other symbolic items in a prominent place. The food is attractively displayed for each person to serve himself. There is also an informative and entertaining program, including songs; music; group dancing; reflections by a man, woman, and child; and a speech by a distinguished guest.

On the last day of Kwanzaa, parents and children exchange gifts of creativity and personal value. Gifts are to be affordable and may be handmade.

Explain to your child that good manners make activities with others more enjoyable for everyone. Using good table manners during the feast is a practical way to illustrate some of the Kwanzaa principles, such as self-determination, responsibility, and purpose. Help him avoid boredom and be a well-mannered participant in the celebrations by giving him a role to play. He might perform a song and dance with other children, tell something he appreciates about his community during the program, or make a gift for a family member.

Activity

During one of the evenings of Kwanzaa, make a large place mat for the table. Give each member of the family a chance to participate using paints, needlework, or another favorite medium. Illustrate the seven principles of the celebration and use the colors black, red, and green. Use the place mat for the feast and save it to use in future years.

OCTOBER 25

Jewish holidays

Observance of Jewish holidays begins the evening of the day before the holiday, about two hours before sundown. The normal activities of daily life at one's school or business cease. Special prayers and services are held in the synagogue.

The calendar used by those of the Jewish faith is now in the fifty-eighth century. Some of the most significant Jewish holidays include:

Rosh Hashanah (New Year): September or October

Yom Kippur (Day of Atonement, a day of fasting): September or October

Sukkoth (Feast of Tabernacles, which commemorates wanderings in the desert): September or October

Hanukkah (Festival of Lights, which celebrates the rededication of the Second Temple in Jerusalem): a week in December

Purim (Feast of Lots, which commemorates the rescue of the Jewish people in ancient Persia with feasts, special prayers, reading of the Book of Esther, gifts): February or March

Passover (commemorates the exodus of the Jewish people from ancient Egypt with a special family meal called a seder): March or April

Shavuot (Feast of Weeks, celebrating the giving of the Torah and Ten Commandments to the Jews at Mt. Sinai): May

Rosh Hashanah

Rosh Hashanah is the Jewish New Year, celebrated for two days in late September or early October. It's a holiday of rejoicing and reverence. Not only do Jewish people rejoice as they remember the anniversary of the creation of the world and the beginning of the Kingdom of God, they also recognize with reverence that the day represents judgment as God decides their fate for the coming year. Thus it is a holiday of intense prayer.

The Torah commands that a shofar (horn) be sounded on Rosh Hashanah. The shofar is often made from a ram's horn, which commemorates the ram that God provided Abraham for a sacrifice when he was about to offer his son Isaac on the altar. It is to encourage them to be willing to make sacrifices as they live for God. The sound of the horn is also meant to call the people to repent, to acknowledge God as their king, and to strengthen their commitment to the Torah.

Special foods are eaten, accompanied by short prayers, as an expression of hopes for the coming year. An apple may be dipped in honey, followed by a prayer for a sweet year ahead. Or a pomegranate may be eaten and a prayer said requesting that a person's merits increase as the seeds of the pomegranate. Typically, sweet rather than bitter foods are eaten.

Activity

Create a family journal, giving each person a page on which to write a resolution for the new year. Make it a tradition to bring out the journal each year and discuss the progress each person made.

Yom Kippur

Yom Kippur (Day of Atonement) is the holiest Jewish holiday. It is a day of fasting, prayer, looking inside oneself, and considering how one can change. No work is done, nor are there any light-hearted activities.

Preparation for the day of fasting is made the day ahead by participating in two festive meals, one at noon and one in the afternoon. People are careful not to overeat and to remember the significance of the coming day.

Just before Yom Kippur, there is also the custom of taking a chicken or money and circling it over your head while saying a prayer. The prayer indicates that the chicken goes to its death (or the money goes to charity) and the one praying goes on to a good long life. It is a way of expressing that without forgiveness, the person would be worthy only of death.

The fast of Yom Kippur is very strict. For more than twenty-four hours there is no eating, drinking, or washing (except for the fingers only, after using the bathroom). Men may wear a white tunic, called a kittel, to symbolize purity. The day is committed to prayer and concentrating on the significance of the prayers.

Only Jewish adults are required to fast for this holiday. Children show their respect for their family's traditions by being attentive to blessings that are said and participating in services that welcome children at the synagogue. They may also look forward to the feast that takes place at sundown, and should participate with their family in welcoming relatives and guests who join them.

OCTOBER 28

Hanukkah

Hanukkah lasts for eight days and is also called the Feast of Lights. This holiday celebrates a religious victory for the Jews—the triumph of a Jewish rebellion against Greek suppression of Judaism. The Jewish revolt drove the Greeks out of Jerusalem and made it possible to resume the Temple service. The word *Hanukkah* means "dedication ceremony," because of the rededication of the Temple.

Hanukkah rituals commemorate a miracle that took place during the Temple service. Pure olive oil was required to keep the lamp lit, but because of the abuse of the Temple under the Greeks, there was only one small container of oil left, which couldn't last longer than a day. The Jews used the only oil they had and, miraculously, it lasted for the full eight days. To commemorate this miracle, Hanukkah celebrants light a candelabra called a menorah.

Jewish law requires that Jewish men and women light the menorah on the days of Hanukkah to spread knowledge of the miracle. Members of a family take turns lighting a menorah at nightfall. A menorah has eight lamps in a row, with a ninth separated from the others. On the first day one lamp is lit, two on the second day, and so forth. Olive oil is the preferred oil, and enough is used so that the lamp burns at least a half hour past nightfall. Candles may also be used. The light from the menorah is not used for any practical purpose such as reading.

Fasting is prohibited during Hanukkah, and work is allowed. Meals are more festive, and it's customary to give extra gifts to charity. Playing with a four-sided top called a dreidel is a traditional children's activity during Hanukkah. The letters on the dreidel stand for "a great miracle happened here." Some traditional foods are the potato latke (pancake) and the sugfania (donut).

Children participate in the many activities of this holiday. They join their family in lighting a menorah candle each day. They develop habits that lead to family unity by playing dreidel with a younger sibling or helping a parent prepare traditional food.

OCTOBER 29

Knowing what to expect: Ramadan

In the Islamic religion, adults commemorate the first revelation of their holy book, the Koran, to the Prophet Muhammad by observing the fast of Ramadan. This observance is one of the five essential duties of a Muslim. (The others include acknowledging that there is one God, Allah, and one prophet, Muhammad; praying facing Mecca five times daily; giving generously to the poor; and making a pilgrimage to Mecca once in a lifetime if possible.)

Ramadan is observed in the ninth month of the Muslim year. Because it's based on the lunar calendar, it's observed in different seasons.

Ramadan is a period of fasting, required of all Muslim adults the world over. The purpose is for the Muslim to increase his consciousness of God and obtain forgiveness of sins. Adults may not eat any food or drink liquid between dawn and sunset for the entire month. The Koran tells participants that their attitude and behavior must be good as well; it's not enough just to give up food and drink.

Muslims must be very careful to follow the regulations of the fast exactly. If they mistakenly take a drink, believing that it's not yet dawn, they must make up the missed day at a later time. People who are sick or who are traveling may be excused from the fast or make up the missed days later.

Muslim children don't fast, but they can be encouraged to learn the meaning of their family rituals. Since generosity toward the poor is encouraged during this season, children might collect coins in a jar and give them to an organization that helps needy people.

OCTOBER 30

Quinceañera

In the Spanish-speaking community, girls begin to take on the status and responsibilities of women at their fifteenth birthday. This very happy occasion is observed with a quinceañera celebration. The word *quinceañera*, which means both the celebration and the girl who is the focus of the celebration, comes from two Spanish words: *quince,* meaning "fifteen," and *años,* meaning "years."

The celebration may begin the evening before the girl's birthday, with a mariachi band serenading her at her home, or it may start with a special *misa* (mass) in the church. There the priest reads from the Bible and gives the girl a special blessing as she stands at the altar. He reminds her that up to this point in her life, she has received much from her community, and now it is time for her to give to God and to society. A girl may have her own ceremony at church, or a priest may bless a number of quinceañeras at one time.

After the religious ceremony, there is a fiesta. It may be at her home or at a dance hall. At the fiesta, there is music and dancing and lots of food. Traditionally, the girl chooses fourteen couples who will dance and celebrate with her, along with other family and friends. The couples, who represent the first fourteen years of her life, gather before the event to rehearse a special waltz. The quinceañera dances the first dance with her father. After that she is asked for many more dances, by her escort and others.

A girl's parents provide for her dress, invitations, and celebration, and her godparents contribute as well. They often provide the cake, gifts for her, and her last "child" gift—a doll, which may be used as a table centerpiece. The doll's skirt is made of bows with the girl's name and birthday printed on them. Each guest receives a bow as a memento.

Quinceañeras wear beautiful formal dresses, often in white as a sign of purity. If your child is a guest at a quinceañera, she would give the guest of honor a gift of jewelry, fresh flowers to offer to the Virgin Mary, a rosary, or a Bible. Families differ in how elaborately they celebrate this birthday, but it is an exceedingly joyous occasion for everyone, and especially for the girl, who enjoys the warm spotlight of everyone's attention.

Vacation Time

❧

Vacation time is meant to relax and refresh, and that's exactly what it will do—as well as build memories—when family members work together. It takes some creativity and planning ahead, because on vacation the daily routines enjoyed at home won't be in place. But with many of your daily responsibilities set aside, make it your family's goal to learn new ways of being thoughtful toward each other as well as toward new people you meet.

OCTOBER 31

Traveling on an airplane

When family members live at great distances from each other, air travel becomes necessary for children if they are to keep in touch with grandparents, aunts, uncles, and cousins. Any kind of travel with children can be a task, but airplanes pose a unique challenge.

First of all, planes are *public* transportation. Unlike riding in the family car, where you alone bear the brunt of your child's unrest, in a plane everyone can be affected by it. When taking to the air, have your child travel-ready.

Let your child know that there will be limited space on the airplane. His seat will feel confined, and unlike in a car, your child will not be able to lobby for the seat of his choice. His ticket will tell him where he sits. Some airlines may allow very young children to share a seat with a parent, but the whole experience will be better for everyone if Junior has his own seat.

Sit between your child and another passenger, if you can. While you may have become immune to your toddler's constant chatter, others on the plane may have passed through that stage in child rearing and have no desire to be reminded of it ever again. Brief conversation is okay, but your child can't assume that a stranger is responsible for the flight's entertainment. Make sure your child keeps his voice low so that other travelers can sleep or simply enjoy the company of their own thoughts.

Don't rely on food alone for your child's entertainment. Gum or candy (or a bottle for an infant) is a good idea, especially during ascent and descent, to keep the ears open, but too much to eat can make the child sick.

If your child needs a car seat on the plane, make certain your seat passes Federal Aviation Administration guidelines so that the flight isn't delayed while a flight attendant finds a suitable seat.

Activity

Pack a small bag of surprises for your child for your next plane trip. This could include new crayons, a small book, a travel game, colored paper, or stickers. Get the things out one at a time through the flight.

Travel by train

Airplanes make the best time, buses provide the best fares, but trains are the most fun. Every child should enjoy the freedom that traveling in a train provides. There is spacious seating, leg room, and quite a rumble, so talking in a normal voice isn't going to disturb others. There is usually a dining car (in fact, some families like to sit in the dining car for most of the trip, since the tables allow the children to play games, do art projects, and so on). There is no fear of being at a high altitude, your child's ears won't pop, and he'll enjoy a panoramic, though fleeting, view of the countryside. And depending on the trip, he may even get to lie down comfortably and sleep.

While the same caveats apply to any kind of public travel—children shouldn't bother other passengers—train travel generally allows kids more freedom.

Be sure to discuss proper behavior before going on any train journey with your child.

NOVEMBER 2

How to tip on a trip

When your child sees you tipping, he learns an essential part of showing consideration for people who provide services. Here are guidelines for tipping at airports and nice hotels, which you should explain to your child.

- Airport staff who check your bags: 50 cents a bag (no need to tip when checking bags at a ticket counter).
- Taxi: 15 to 20 percent of the total fare, never less than 50 cents.
- Hotel doorman: $1.
- Bellman: $2 (if lots of bags, $3).
- Room service: 15 percent of the bill, not less than $1.
- Maid: $1 a day ($2 if two people are in the room).
- Bellman (for bringing something, such as an iron): 50 cents to $1.
- Restaurant: 15 to 20 percent of the bill.

Activity

Take an ample supply of one-dollar bills with you when you travel. So your child can participate, let her keep some of the ones in a purse or fanny pack. Ask her for the amount you need when it's time to tip.

Consideration of others in a hotel

If your child is fortunate enough to spend an overnight in a hotel, he should consider it a privilege and not a free-for-all. Having this experience with his family will help prepare him to be considerate of others in his teen years, when he might travel with a group of friends on a school trip or to a sports tournament.

Your child should remember that there are other guests in the building, even if he can't see them. Many a guest has disappeared into his room to get a good night's sleep, only to get angry when neighbors were inconsiderate. After 10 P.M., your child should assume there are other people behind all those closed doors. He should make as little noise as possible. Here's how your child can be a neighbor in a hotel:

- Don't run or talk loudly in the hall.
- After 10 P.M., avoid talking in the hall.
- Keep the noise low in the room—including the TV. Don't assume the hotel room is soundproofed.

With the family in a hotel

Your child should be considerate of other guests in the hotel, but she should also be considerate of her family. Be even more considerate in a hotel than you are at home!

Your child should keep things picked up. Nothing shrinks the already small space in a hotel room like a child's clothes, books, and toys strewn over the floor. Show her which drawer to use.

Even though there is maid service, your child should not act like a pig just because someone will be there to clean up. She shouldn't drop shampoo or tissues on the bathroom floor or leave clumps of toothpaste in the sink, nor should she cover the bathroom floor with water.

Pack up everything when it's time to check out. Five miles down the road, the driver doesn't care to receive news from the backseat that a favorite pillow has been left at the hotel. And don't let your child disappear when it's time to pack the car. Even young children can help with this task.

Activity

Show your child how to tip the maid when you leave. Help your child learn respect for people in the service industry by letting her know you are doing this; a dollar or two a night is a nice thank-you.

NOVEMBER 5

In the family car

The family car—the place that brings out the best in everyone! Your child's behavior in the car should be well-mannered. Children arguing in the backseat are being unkind to each other and distracting to the driver. Here are a few guidelines for behavior in the car so that you aren't compelled to make up a drastic, over-arching rule such as "No child will ever look at, touch, or talk to another child in this car again!"

Your child should:

- Fasten his seat belt right away.
- Respect others' preferences and compromise on temperature, windows, radio stations, and places to sit.
- Keep the car neat.
- Keep arms and legs from sprawling into the space of others.
- Take turns sitting in less desirable spots.
- Tell you immediately when he has left something behind.

Activity

To avoid the dreaded question "Are we almost there?" tell your child how long the trip will take and that you will let him know when half the time has passed. If he's old enough, show him a map, point out your starting point and destination, and have him use a highlighter to mark the route between the two. Let him refer to the map throughout the trip.

When your child is a guest in a car

When your child is in someone else's car, she is their guest. She can show her appreciation (and increase her chances of being given a ride again) by:

- Greeting everyone when she hops in. "Hi, Mrs. Smith. Hi, Tommy."
- Sitting where she is asked to sit. (She may ask for another seat if she gets carsick; everyone will appreciate the request!)
- Joining in the conversation, keeping her voice low, and talking about positive things.
- Saying thanks for a snack.
- Taking all of her things with her when she hops out.
- Thanking the driver for the ride. (Extra points for using the driver's name!)
- Closing her door and walking around the car where she can be seen as she leaves.

Activity

Suggest activities your child would enjoy in the car. She and her friends might brainstorm a list of homonyms (words that sound the same but have different meanings, such as *aunt/ant* and *bear/bare*). Or they might race to find every letter of the alphabet on signs and billboards.

Camping: thinking about others

Your child doesn't have to be an Eagle Scout to be a courteous camper. Of course, some rules of etiquette don't apply to the great outdoors. Spills while eating? No problem. Eating with the fingers? Go right ahead! They make great utensils for campfire foods.

When camping, your child should imagine that she is the guest of the great outdoors. She treats the woodland, streams, and beaches with the greatest of care, doing no damage to nature and leaving little trace of her visit when she leaves.

Help your child show respect for others on campgrounds:

1. Understand that walls of tents and campers are quite thin. Even low voices at night can often be overheard. Follow the campground rules for quiet hours.
2. Keep the campsite clean. All trash should go in designated containers, and food should be stored where animals aren't attracted to it. For those camping in bear country, this is a matter of safety.
3. Say hello to neighbors, but don't assume they came to the park to spend time with you. If your child does strike up a friendship with other children, be sure she gives the other family some time alone.
4. Leave the campsite in the same or better condition than you found it.

Activity

Take sleeping bags and a snack out under the stars and have a family "camp-out" at home. Remind children to keep their voices low so that you won't offend neighbors. Give everyone a cleanup job in the morning.

Camping: courtesy toward your family

When you go camping, your child can show respect for members of his own family:

- Look for ways to enjoy being with his family. If everyone wants to take a hike, he shouldn't insist upon going fishing.
- Help with the chores. Camping is fun, but only if the burden of work is shared by everyone.
- Keep things in order. There won't be room for personal items to be strewn around the campground.
- Leave the radio, cassette player, or CD player at home.
- Don't dig in the campfire until smoke and sparks billow out.
- Let a parent know where he will be if he leaves the group.

Activity

Make a memory book of your camping trip. It might just be a diary with a drawing or a few words for each day, or a collection of postcards from the spots that you visited. If you're traveling for a number of weeks, stop regularly and get film developed. In the evening by your kerosene lamp, let your child help you fill an album with your pictures. By the time you get home, your photo diary will be complete.

NOVEMBER 9

At the beach

Some people are lucky enough to have a summer home on a private beach, but most of us need to get along with others on crowded public beaches and help our children do the same.

Choose a spot on the beach for your family and keep your beach bags, toys, chairs, and blankets together. If you have young children who will do a lot of running from the water's edge to their sand castle, select a spot close to the water. Talk to your child about not running through the sand or snapping his towel in the air—flying sand stings and sticks to sunbathers covered with lotion, and cold water from the suit of a child who has just been in the surf is jolting when it hits someone nearby.

Your child should play with his own toys. He shouldn't borrow the toys of others—nor should he be expected to generously hand out his sand shovel and pail to perfect strangers. If he does strike up a friendship with a child nearby, sharing is okay. Just keep the toys in one spot and be sure your child returns anything he's used.

Don't let the low standards of others set a precedent for your family. You might find candy wrappers and empty lemonade cups marking the carelessness of previous visitors. Dispose of all of your trash (and a few pieces more if you're very public-spirited) and leave your spot cleaner than when you arrived.

Follow posted guidelines for swimming suits. For children this primarily means that they should wear them. The sun might feel fine on your young child's bottom, but others on the beach may not find it quite so amusing to see children running around in the buff.

If your child plays music, he should keep the volume low so that only your family can hear it. If your neighbors had wanted a disc jockey, they would have gone to a club. The same is true with conversation. Of course, during the day there's going to be a higher noise level on the beach. In the late afternoon and evening hours, take extra care to show respect for older people who are hoping for quiet.

Activity

Play a game in the sand. You might dig holes and level out a "bowling lane" for a game of beach ball bowling. Or make up your own game. Invite children who gather to watch to join you in the game.

NOVEMBER 10

Boating

Being a guest on someone's boat is not like visiting a beach house. Space can be cramped, and there is always the risk of danger if safety procedures aren't followed. Because it's difficult for a first-time boater to anticipate situations that could arise, the guest on a boat should immediately comply with the suggestions of the captain without asking questions.

If your child is going boating, make sure he takes along the necessary clothing and not one stitch more. That will include a sweatshirt, soft-soled shoes, his own towel, and a bathing suit.

When he arrives at the dock, he should get into the boat after the captain and not attempt to get out onto the dock without permission. He should never get aboard when everyone else is out of the boat. Most of the time he should stay seated when the boat is moving (unless he's lucky enough to be on a yacht) and avoid blocking the view of the driver.

He should help to keep his eyes on any other member of the group who is engaged in water sports. If he's the designated spotter for a water skier, for example, he must take the responsibility with utmost seriousness.

Your child shouldn't ask to take more turns than everyone else in water sports, nor should he suggest activities if he isn't asked for suggestions.

He has no obligation to do anything that feels dangerous to him just because everyone else thinks it's fun. If he is uncomfortable with a certain water activity, he should simply say he doesn't care to go tubing or jump off the rope swing. At the end of the outing, he should thank his host for inviting him along.

Be a Great Guest (and Host)

❦

If you've ever hesitated to let your child invite a friend to your home a second time, you'll understand the importance of this section. Your child might want to learn these manners, if only out of self-interest. It's no secret that well-mannered children get more invitations—they're a pleasure to be with, both for adults and for other children. And when your child masters being a good host, he'll give you one more reason to let him fill the house with his friends.

NOVEMBER 11

A good attitude for a good guest

Your child may be a guest for a very short time—just an hour to play at the home of a neighbor—or he may be invited to stay for a day or two and sleep over at someone's house. The longer he stays, the more his presence will wear on his host's family if he doesn't make every effort to be a good guest.

The first thing a good guest should do is *pretend he's the host!* That might sound odd, but it doesn't mean he should go around acting like the host—it means he should *think* like the host. He should put himself in the shoes of the other person and imagine what the host might be feeling. Your child should treat the host the way he would like to be treated when he is a host himself.

That means your child should be agreeable and easy to get along with. Tell your child to:

- Refrain from making unreasonable requests. ("Why can't we drink our hot chocolate in the TV room?")
- Offer help if he can. ("I'll help you put the paints away")
- Be open to suggestions. ("Sure, I'll play Monopoly")
- Avoid negative comments. ("I've already seen that video ten times")

Every effort your child makes to fit in will be appreciated by his host. If he is an agreeable guest, he'll probably get a chance to suggest some of his own favorite activities. And he's likely to get invited to play again.

Help your child develop a good guest attitude by letting him know that different families have different ways of doing things. As long as he isn't violating a moral rule of his own family, your child should go along with the practices of his host. He should fit into the schedule of the host family—when to eat, when to go to bed, how much television to watch, or how much time is allowed on the computer, even if it's vastly different from his own family's habits. And he should emulate habits of the family, such as carrying his plate from the table to the dishwasher or not wearing shoes in the house.

Activity

Ask your child to name the two children he most enjoys inviting to your home to play. What characteristics make these friends good guests?

What a guest should pack

When your child is a guest, she should pack everything she needs and not a bit more. If she's old enough to stay overnight at a friend's house just for fun, she's old enough to help with her packing.

Encourage her to think about what she'll need. What activities does she anticipate? How long will she stay? She should pack just enough so that she:

- Won't have to borrow clothing from her friend.
- Won't have to ask the host family for a toothbrush and tooth-paste.
- Will have clean clothing each day.
- Won't take up too much space with her clothes.

Unless asked, she shouldn't take things such as a CD player, CD collection, videos, and computer games. Not only do these take up lots of space, they communicate that your child doesn't believe she will be entertained by what her friend has. The host parents may limit their child's time with videos or computer games. If your child brings along everything she owns, this may put pressure on the host child's parents to stretch the household rules.

Activity

If your child is going to a sleep-over, help her write a list of the things she'll need to pack. Encourage her to cross out things she won't need. When she has packed, go over the list with her to be sure essentials such as a toothbrush made it into the bag.

Nice things for a guest to say

Help your child express himself with courtesy as a guest by giving him a few nice phrases to use when he visits a friend.

• "Hello, Mrs. Green." Your child should greet his friend's parents as soon as he arrives by smiling and looking into their eyes as he says hello. If your child is too shy to initiate more conversation, that's okay. But before rushing off to play, he should be willing to take a few minutes to respond to conversation or questions if his friend's parent wants to chat.

• "I'd like chocolate ice cream, please." It's courteous to express a preference when asked. If your child is given the choice between vanilla and chocolate ice cream, for example, he shouldn't say, "I don't care" or "It doesn't matter." Making a choice gives the host the satisfaction of pleasing your child.

• "I had a nice time at your house." These words make your child's friend feel very good. He shouldn't have to guess whether or not your child had fun.

• "Thank you for inviting me." Words of gratitude are a must for any guest. Your child might also mention how much he liked the tacos at dinner or the fun he had shaping and baking clay.

• "Goodbye, Mrs. Green." Before dashing off to the car when you arrive to pick up your child, a brief word of farewell is in order to the parents of your child's friend. It's the perfect ending to the visit.

Activity

Make an I Spy Good Manners calendar chart with your child. When you notice your child saying or doing something nice, write it in the box for that day of the week: "Thanked Mrs. Green for the ride. Chatted with Grandma when she came to visit. Put his napkin on his lap at dinner." Your child will notice your unspoken compliments. After a month, take the chart down and keep it. A couple of years from now, it will be fascinating to see how much your child has improved.

How to become a guest who is invited again

A return invitation is almost guaranteed for the child who:

- Calls the host if she's going to be late.
- Respects the property of others (doesn't run or jump in the house, track dirt in from outdoors, or play roughly with a friend's toys).
- Doesn't go snooping, open closed doors, or read personal papers that may be lying on a desk or table.
- Leaves the bathroom neat, puts her toothbrush back in her overnight bag, and gathers any clothing she has taken off and puts it in her bag.
- Keeps her voice low.
- Is friendly to everyone at the house and relates to her friend's siblings and parents, however briefly.
- Uses her best table manners: chews with her mouth closed, keeps her fingers and face clean with her napkin, and says thank you for the meal.
- Goes along with the host family's plans and schedule for meals, sleeping, and so on.
- Thanks her hosts when she leaves; if she really wants to knock their socks off, she writes them a thank-you note when she gets home.

Say goodbye and leave promptly

Saying goodbye and leaving promptly are valuable social skills your child should practice as soon as she is invited to a friend's house. Leaving promptly shows as much respect for others as arriving on time does.

Children often find it difficult to separate from their friends when a parent arrives to take them home, and they may beg to stay and play longer. Set a good example for your child by keeping your own goodbyes short. Chat briefly with the parents of your child's friend, have your child thank the hosts for the invitation, and then leave promptly. Your child will get involved in play again if she knows you will take twenty minutes to say goodbye when you come to pick her up. No one endears herself to others by standing at the door, coat on, hand on the doorknob, bringing up one subject after another. The host may still be participating in the conversation, but it's probably because he can think of no polite way to boot his visitor out the door.

Activity

Coach your child at home about the importance of leaving promptly when you arrive to pick her up. Encourage her to discuss with you privately, future plans to be with her friend. Reward her for leaving promptly by allowing her to discuss plans for another play date with her friend when you're in the car on the way home.

NOVEMBER 16

Being a good host

Your child should remember that her home and family schedule may feel new and strange to a child who visits. Everything should be done to make her guest feel comfortable. This may involve some planning and work—responsibilities your child can share. The more your child learns at an early age about showing others a nice time, the more confidence she'll have as she enters her teen years.

Before the friend arrives, your child can prepare by making sure her toys are in order and by having an idea of what she wants to do. She shouldn't merely ask her friend, "What do you feel like doing?" Even though suggesting activities is the host's responsibility, she should be open to her friend's ideas as well.

Sometimes compromise is necessary. Your child's goal should be for her friend to have fun, not to communicate that "this is my house, and we do things my way."

Help your child make her guest feel welcome:

- Focus on the guest.
- Say, "I'm glad you could come."
- Stop what she was doing before her friend arrived (don't finish a TV show or continue playing a computer game).
- Start an activity that allows her friend to fully participate.
- Anticipate the needs of her guest.

Activity

Provide your child and her friend with a large sheet of newsprint and colored markers. Suggest that they draw a picture together. Your child should let her friend go first, drawing a few lines with one color. Then your child chooses another color and adds to the drawing. Her friend follows with another color, and so on. The end result will be a surprise to both, and they'll learn a lesson in cooperation.

NOVEMBER 17

For first-time guests

There are a number of things your child should do if it is the friend's first time at your home. Remind your child that his tone of voice should be kind when he is communicating this information—he shouldn't sound bossy. These include:

- Showing his friend where the bathroom is.
- Telling him if there are any rooms that are off-limits: "This is my dad's home office, and we aren't allowed to go in—he's working now, so we should keep our music down."
- Letting the friend know what time you eat dinner.
- Telling him about family rules: "We're allowed to watch one show on television, and we aren't allowed to eat snacks before dinner."

Activity

Children enjoy making lists as soon as they can write. Help your child make a to-do list of things that need to be done to prepare for a friend coming to visit. It could include making a snack, planning an activity, putting his room in order, and renting a video. Go over the list with your child and let him cross things off as they are completed. Let him know you will help him with the tasks.

NOVEMBER 18

Serving food to your friends

By the time your child is in third or fourth grade, she can begin taking some responsibility at home for serving snacks to her friends. Keep the food simple at first—cookies and milk or cheese, crackers, and juice. This is a training ground for your child in taking initiative, focusing on others, and anticipating their needs.

If parents take complete responsibility for serving food, children can reach the teen years and be clueless about how to do anything but grab a soda from the refrigerator for themselves. One teenage girl I know invited a group of friends over to watch a video. She never got around to offering them anything to eat, even though there were chips, veggies and dip, and sodas in the kitchen. "No one asked for anything to eat!" she explained to her mother later.

When your child invites a friend to visit, she needs to take the initiative. She shouldn't wait for a friend to say she's hungry; right away, she should get out snacks and serve them in a special container. Line a basket with napkins and put chips in it. Put cookies on a plate. Put ice cubes in cups rather than just handing out soda cans. Food should always be served in something other than its container. Even microwave popcorn tastes better in a bowl.

Your child should make sure each guest has a napkin or small plate. Germs can be spread if everyone eats right out of the popcorn bowl.

Remind your child that she's in charge. She should ask if anyone would like more to drink, and she should initiate cleaning up. When everyone is finished, everyone should help clean up. Your child may ask her friends to help throw away paper supplies, and she can put leftover food away.

Activity

If your child likes to help in the kitchen, let her make party mix for her friends. Many cereal boxes have a recipe on the back.

NOVEMBER 19
The right guest list

There is an art to inviting just the right group of people for a social occasion to ensure that everyone has a good time. The president of the United States has a social secretary who labors full time to plan events and create guest lists.

Planning a birthday party or a sleep-over for your child doesn't require a social secretary, but inviting just the right children requires sensitivity to different personalities. Children seem to know intuitively how to plan a guest list. Because they are immature in their abilities as a host, they want friends to be together who get along naturally, and often they have a good sense of who that is. Your child might suggest inviting only friends from the swim team or only friends from church. Or she may really like both Kelly and Laura, but she knows that when they're together, they get into arguments. Be receptive to your child's concerns, even though as a parent you'd like to have one big party and pay back all of your child's social obligations. The party will be more fun for everyone if there is a common bond, especially if it's small enough that each one will need to relate to the others who are there.

Activity

Suggest your child make a list of friends she'd like to invite to a party, along with their phone numbers. She can make a note of their response on the list: *Y* and *N* for *yes* and *no* or, if she wants to be more formal, *A* and *R* for *accept* and *regret*.

Inviting friends over again

A child who will be permitted to invite friends over again:

1. Gives his parents advance notice.
2. Is willing to compromise on some of the details: "Okay, we won't stay up all night, and we'll rent one movie instead of three."
3. Helps his parents prepare for his guest by cleaning his room and making sure games and toys are in order.
4. Communicates the details of the invitation clearly to his friend, and doesn't embarrass his parents and his friend by telling his friend he has to go home at an earlier time because that's what he and his parents agreed upon.
5. Introduces his friend to his parents.
6. Spends some time with his family while his friend is visiting and doesn't disappear with his friend.
7. Doesn't ask his parents in front of his friend for permission to do things if he thinks his parents will object.
8. Is restrained in his noise and activity level inside the house.
9. Cleans up after his friend leaves.
10. Sticks with the length of visit he initially agreed upon with his parents.

Activity

Pick two or three items from the list where you believe your child could improve. Ask him to do the same. Compare your choices. Compliment your child in areas where he's doing well.

NOVEMBER 21

Sleep-overs: bathroom etiquette

When the host says, "Make yourself at home," it shouldn't be taken as an invitation to spread toiletries on the bathroom counter, linger in the shower for ten minutes, or toss your towel in the corner. It's good to ask a few questions to figure out the host family's schedule.

Your child shouldn't be so shy she won't even use the bathroom, but she should pretend she's taking a cold shower—get in and get out. If she prefers privacy, she shouldn't feel pressured to share bathroom time with anyone else. She may simply ask for a few minutes alone, then go in and lock the door.

It's good to bring along everything she needs, but if she's forgotten something essential, it's better to ask the host for it than to start pulling drawers and cupboards open. Guests usually bring their own toothpaste and may feel free to use the host's soap and shampoo.

When she's finished, she cleans up and does the following:

1. Rinses the sink.
2. Wipes the counter with a washcloth or tissue.
3. Flushes the toilet.
4. Pushes back the shower curtain and cleans any hair from the drain.

All of her toiletries go back in her bag and are put in her bedroom. Be efficient with bathroom time by using the bathroom only for the essentials. She can dry her hair, put on lotion, and get dressed in the bedroom.

NOVEMBER 22

Sleep-overs: bedtime etiquette

Your child should make a sleep-over worthy of the name—he should get some sleep. Of course, a certain amount of bedtime talking and laughing is fine, but it shouldn't go on endlessly. Getting quiet within a reasonable amount of time is in your child's best interest, since loss of sleep makes adults grumpy, and they're the ones to decide if there will be more sleep-overs.

Your child should go to bed and get up with his friend. If your child is an incurable night owl and his friend's habits are more like Rip van Winkle's, it's okay if he asks permission to stay up a bit longer to read a book. Whatever he does, it must be done quietly. This isn't the time to raid the refrigerator or play noisy computer games.

When he crawls out of bed in the morning, he makes the bed or asks if it should be stripped. And he should remember the proverb "A loud greeting in the morning is worse than a curse." More adventures with his friend don't begin until the entire household has gotten up.

Activity

Have your child create her own sleep-over pillowcase. Give her a plain pillowcase and fabric paints or fabric markers in different colors. Suggest she ask her friends to sign it whenever she goes to a sleep-over. Ask her to tell you about new friends whose names appear on the pillow.

NOVEMBER 23

Sleep-overs: mealtime etiquette

Kids should fit in with their host family's schedule when it comes to eating. Here are a few dos and don'ts:

Do

- Ask what time your friend's family usually eats if no one has told you.
- Be willing to help your friend set the table.

- Be ready to come to the table when everyone else is (hands washed, bathroom needs taken care of).
- Ask for a piece of fruit if you're feeling very hungry and mealtime is a long way off (remember to say please).
- Eat a bit of everything unless you're allergic to it or it would make you sick in the stomach.
- Use good table manners.
- Participate in table conversation.
- Say thanks at the end of the meal.
- Help clean up.

Don't

- Open a friend's refrigerator, unless you have been given specific permission to do so.
- Assume that because your friend opens the refrigerator, you have permission to do so.
- Ask for permission to open the refrigerator.
- Mention that you were served the same food the last time you visited.
- Take a lot more than you can eat and leave it on your plate.
- Take such big portions that everyone else only gets a small amount.

NOVEMBER 24

Guests go first

Guests should get preferential treatment. Your child would know something was wrong if he stayed at a hotel and realized that the staff took care of themselves first, butting in front of guests in line at the buffet, diving into the pool in front of guests, and running through doors and letting them fly back in a guest's face.

The example is an exaggeration, but when your child is a host, he should put others first. Remind your child of two simple words that show preference to his guest: "After you!"

Here are a few ways to make guests feel welcome:

Guests go first

- At the table, food is offered first to the guest—even snacks.
- When only one person at a time can play a video game, the guest plays first.
- If there's a more comfortable chair for TV watching, it goes to the guest.
- When there's one bathroom available, the guest uses it first.
- Getting into the car, the guest goes first.

Be a Good Sport

❧

At the end of a sports season, the child who is most loved and respected by peers and parents is likely the one who encouraged teammates, didn't demand the limelight, worked hard, and didn't get too serious. School-age athletes should enjoy the experience and work hard, but not participate as though winning is everything. Most kids won't go on to play professional sports; the legacy they're building should be one of fond memories and fun experiences with the team.

NOVEMBER 25

Enjoy the game

Being involved in sports gives your child an opportunity to exercise, learn new skills, develop friendships, work on a team, and pursue her personal best. But athletics can also expose her to stressful competition, unreasonable expectations, physical injury, and the negative shouts of players and parents alike. While children have more athletic opportunities than ever before, they also face more demands than any previous generation. Sports are played year-round, indoors and out—and college scholarship money may often hang in the balance. In light of these changes, more than ever children (and parents) need to be fortified with a commitment to good sportsmanship.

Encourage your child to focus on giving her best, developing the discipline that all sports require, and enjoying the game. Help her not to give up if she isn't the best person on the team. Being the star is a goal that is bound to disappoint—there are so few athletes who can truly be at the top. Make sure your child knows the efforts of many are needed for a successful team.

Your child's skills will improve over time, but she should understand that skill must be multiplied by effort. It's rare that anything worth achieving happens overnight. Your child may return to a team to find that one player's skills have improved since last season because she has spent her time practicing.

Help your child understand that winning is not everything. Rather, learning about herself and her own unique gifts can take the pressure off athletic competition in the early years. And above all, if there isn't a lot of fun involved, talk to your child about another sport she might want to pursue.

Activity

Gather mementos of your child's sports season and help her make a scrapbook to remember the good times. Include a team picture along with candid shots taken during the season, the team's schedule, statistics about your child, ribbons, and certificates.

NOVEMBER 26

Rituals at athletic events

Athletic events can be packed with emotion. Rituals help provide self-control for both athletes and spectators and bring order to the event.

Rituals are more important than ever before. Your child faces a different sports world than you did. He starts competing earlier, he practices longer, and the stakes are probably higher. He faces the growing perception that he's worth something only if he's on the starting team. He's also exposed to sports figures who are tops in their field and spotlighted by the media but whose lives off the court or the field are daily displays of rudeness. The pressure your child faces, as well as the mixed messages in the media, may make it doubly difficult for him to be courteous in the game.

Explain to your child that rituals set a standard. They aren't practiced just to fill in time. Their purpose is to remind everyone involved to be civilized, to show respect for others, and to participate in the game with dignity. Intense competition is okay, and teams may not feel friendly toward each other, but rituals remind everyone to keep negative emotions from flaring. Here are a few rituals your child will observe at athletic events, and what they should remember:

- *National anthem.* Always show respect while the national anthem (or the anthem of other countries) is played. Stand during the music, do not talk or giggle, and remove hats.
- *Introductions.* When introduced, players should shake the hand of the opposing team's coach; captains also shake.
- *Respect the ref.* The referee's decisions stand, even if everyone doesn't agree with them.
- *Afterward.* No matter who wins, players line up as a team and walk by the opposing team to give a sports shake and say, "Good game."

NOVEMBER 27

Good sportsmanship

An attitude of gratitude on your child's part is a good start in sportsmanship. Help your child understand that participating in a sport is a privilege. Sports require the selfless dedication of many people and cooperation among parents, players, and coaches. It's the rare parent or coach who is adequately compensated financially, and the thanks of the players can more than make up for this. A sincere "Thank you for all you do so that we can play basketball" is all that needs to be said.

Your child should also have an appreciative attitude toward the other players on his team. He should recognize their contributions to the team and encourage them, always realizing that the more he does to contribute to team morale, the better the team will be. Encourage your child to tell the other players the positive things he's thinking: "That was a great play!" or "You were awesome today."

Your child should win and lose graciously and be willing to congratulate the other player immediately after the game, no matter who won. When he wins, your child shouldn't be arrogant toward others; compliment the opponent on a good game. Win or lose, your child should leave the field or court with a pleasant look.

Activity

If you have a room that is suitable, let your child and his friends play balloon volleyball indoors. They should make their own net out of a rope with ribbons hanging from it and make boundary lines with masking tape on the floor. The group may make up their own rules, and everyone should practice good sportsmanship by playing by the rules.

NOVEMBER 28

Realistic attitude on the court or field

Your child's teammates probably have a realistic attitude about her, and so should she. She should expect a lot from herself and know that she'll have to work hard. She shouldn't think she's better than she is, nor should she think she is better than everyone else on the team. Even if her skills are at the top, she should realize that she couldn't win a game by herself—it requires the whole team.

She should always speak realistically about her skills and not say she's a terrible player before a game when she is bound to win by a long shot. Others will think she's fishing for compliments.

Encourage her to give her best effort consistently. This is especially important in team sports, where it can be demoralizing for everyone when a talented teammate doesn't seem committed to giving the game her all.

She shouldn't believe she alone is qualified to make the most important plays. And when she blows it, she needs to be able to forgive herself. If she expects too much of herself, she may also demand too much of others and be angry with them when they don't play a perfect game.

Every sport requires skill, but just as important are athletes who bring a positive attitude to the game. When the trophies are handed out at the end of the season, the athlete who respected others takes first place in everyone's mind.

Activity

After his next game, talk to your child about how he feels about it. If his attitude is right, compliment him on his good sportsmanship.

NOVEMBER 29

The valued teammate

The child who cultivates the following habits will be a player who is valued by teammates, coaches, and parents alike:

- *Learns the rules.* He doesn't frustrate the others by drawing penalties for the team.
- *Controls his temper.* He doesn't yell at the ref or other players, nor does he angrily toss a ball or racquet to show his disgust with himself or others. When a child on a team loses his temper, it reflects poorly on the whole team.
- *Respects everyone.* He doesn't trash other players and avoids swearing; he doesn't taunt other players.
- *Refuses to place blame.* If a poor play is your child's fault, he should resolve to do better the next time. If a teammate makes the mistake, he holds his tongue or responds positively.

- *Learns from his mistakes.* Help him learn that everyone blows it at one time or another.
- *Plays an honest game.* Your child should never pretend to have been hurt by a player from the other team in order to gain an advantage.
- *Fulfills his basic obligations.* He goes to practices, maintains his uniform, helps out with fund-raisers, and alerts the coach if he has to miss practice.
- *Keep supplies on hand.* He doesn't regularly depend on teammates for water bottles, socks, towels, tape, and so on.

Activity

Your child might add to team unity by getting ribbons in the school colors for all of the girls to wear in their hair. Your son or daughter might invite the team to your home for spaghetti.

Be a Model American

❧

When your children stand tall and quiet during the national anthem, they are honoring their country, but they are also making it clear to others that they have an appreciation for the sacrifice others have made for freedom. While it's difficult for children to fully appreciate a veteran's valor or the worth of the Constitution, it's important that they go through the motions of good citizenship. Eventually they will realize the value of their heritage.

NOVEMBER 30

The national anthem

Help your child understand the rudimentary obligations of patriotism and remind her of how grateful she can be that previous generations have given their lives to achieve the freedom she now enjoys. A child can begin by showing respect during the singing of "The Star-Spangled Banner," our official national anthem. She should stand with her attention fixed on the flag throughout the song. If others sing, she should sing along as well as she can. Otherwise, she remains quiet and still. Males should remove their hat; it's a nice touch to place the palm of the right hand over the heart.

If the anthem begins while your child is making her way toward her seat, she stops where she is and faces the flag until the anthem is completed. If she is eating, she stops.

If your child is at an international event based in the United States that calls for several national anthems to be played, the other countries' anthems are played before "The Star-Spangled Banner." In expression of respect for foreign guests, your child may salute during all anthems (although she never pledges allegiance to another flag).

Activity

Sing the national anthem with your child. It's not an easy song, but practicing can help. Show her how to put her right hand on her heart. Help her learn the proper words and discuss with her the meaning of words that aren't clear.

DECEMBER 1

Pledge of Allegiance

I pledge allegiance to the flag of the United States of America and to the Republic for which it stands, one nation under God, indivisible, with liberty and justice for all.

These words, repeated daily by schoolchildren, describe the profound significance of that red, white, and blue banner with its fifty stars and thirteen stripes that we know as the U.S. flag. The flag is *the* symbol of our country, and it's flown at many public buildings and on American ships at sea. On buildings it salutes our democracy; on the ships it's an identification.

Not all children know that our government has set strict limitations on how and where a flag is displayed and how it is cared for. In fact, there is a lengthy federal law pertaining to its use; the United States Army has its own Institute of Heraldry that interprets the law and answers questions the federal government and ordinary citizens have about the flag.

Whenever your child is pledging allegiance to the flag, he should stand, look at the flag, and place his hand over his heart (although it's okay to stand quietly with attention on the flag without saluting). Boys should *always* remove their hats. The only exception to the hat rule is for military personnel.

DECEMBER 2

Care of the U.S. flag

A U.S. flag that is displayed outdoors is raised on a flagpole with a flourish in the morning and is slowly lowered at sunset. Only if the flag is illuminated is it proper to allow it to fly through the night. (The sun must never set on Old Glory.)

A flag may cover a casket, but it is never used in a practical way, such as to cover a table.

A flag may be displayed only if it is clean—never if it has become soiled or tattered. If it shows signs of wear, it should be disposed of respectfully. Government guidelines recommend burning the flag as a preferred method of disposal, not throwing it in the garbage with the coffee grounds and chicken bones.

Explain to your child that the *public* burning of a U.S. flag is a way that some people, in our country and in foreign countries, have chosen to express anger with America. This type of burning is a federal offense and is punishable by up to a year in prison, a fine of up to $1,000, or both.

Federal guidelines also state that the U.S. flag is never dipped (lowered when carried on a pole) in deference to anyone else. For example, at an international parade during the Olympics held in a foreign country, our athletes should not lower the U.S. flag when passing a reviewing stand. (Although lowering it would represent a disregard for our government's guidelines and a long-standing tradition of our country, it is not an offense that is punishable.)

Explain to your child other meanings of the flag: When first raised to the top of the pole and then lowered and flown at half mast, it indicates mourning. When flown upside down, it indicates an emergency situation. At no other time is the flag flown at half mast or upside down.

Activity

Watch the Olympics on television with your child and point out the role of a country's flag and national anthem when the medals are awarded. The sight of one's own flag and sound of the music of the homeland bring tears to the eyes of many athletes. It is a tremendous privilege for that athlete to bring honor to his flag and thus his country.

DECEMBER 3

Appreciating ideals and learning patriotism

Kids hear criticism of their country's leaders in the press and maybe even at the dinner table. However well-founded the disgruntlement may be about specific leaders, help your child develop an unshakable appreciation for her country and its Constitution, the freedoms and opportunities she has in the United States, and the responsibilities she should happily accept as a citizen.

As a young child, she should know her country's heroes. This means not that she won't hear about flawed characters who dot the pages of history, but that rather than developing cynicism, she learns to love her country. She should look to our heroes and learn the virtues that those heroes cultivated as habits. Your child might want to start with George Washington, who as a teenager copied 110 rules of etiquette into a notebook and tried to follow them.

Activity

Here are some more activities to encourage patriotism in your children:

- Fly the flag.
- Go to a July Fourth parade.

- Show respect during the national anthem.
- Visit the nation's capital.
- Talk regularly about why it's great to live in this country.
- Read biographies of famous Americans.

DECEMBER 4

When in another country

If your child is visiting another country, he should learn as much as he can about the customs of his host country. Something that seems harmless at home (showing the soles of one's shoes, for example) may be quite offensive abroad. Traveling with a curious, friendly, and accepting attitude makes him a welcome visitor. Too often Americans are demanding travelers, expecting everything to be as convenient abroad as it is at home. Libraries, bookstores, the Internet, tourist agencies, and international airline ticket offices can be helpful sources of information on a foreign country. Here are some areas to study as he prepares to pack his bags:

- Greeting (in some countries the standard greeting is a kiss on both cheeks).
- Eating (usually forks and spoons will be available, but maybe he should practice using chopsticks).
- Communication habits (loud laughter or conversation may be offensive).
- Gift-giving customs (in some countries, if you praise someone else's possession, that person will give it to you).
- Time (some countries prefer punctuality, while in others it is okay to arrive late).
- Common words (know how to ask where the bathroom is).
- Shopping practices (bartering may be okay).
- Tipping.

DECEMBER 5

Being part of a community

As your child enters her early teen years, she should be aware of her role as a community member. Political leaders sometimes describe this role as "giving something back to the community." By taking pride in her community, your child can learn about its history, attend a holiday parade, be a fan of a local sports team, or invite a student from another state or country to visit her community.

Here are some ways your child can be a valued member of her community:

- *Volunteering:* baby-sit at her church nursery, paint faces at a fair, fold and sort clothing for a clothing drive, stuff envelopes for charity, help with a political campaign.
- *Following community guidelines:* keep her radio low in public, clean up after her dog during a walk, throw away litter.

DECEMBER 6

Environmental manners

Taking care of the environment is everybody's responsibility—even kids can do their part. Your child might have to get over the hurdle of thinking that what one person does doesn't really make a difference.

Help your child think about her responsibility to the environment by asking herself a question: "What if everyone did what I am doing?" If she drops a napkin at a picnic, she can imagine what the park would look like if her entire group left napkins on the grass. If she's hiking and wants to gather some beautiful wildflowers, have her consider what would happen if everyone who passed by that spot picked a bunch. If she wants to play music at the swimming pool, ask her to think about what it would be like if everyone played music equally loudly.

Encourage your child when you see her doing something positive, and let your child know about your own activities to protect the environment. Learning about this increases your child's awareness of ways to care for the environment.

Activity

Spend a summer morning at the beach with gloves and trash bags, removing debris. Explain how trash that gets into the sea can harm sea animals. Enjoy the afternoon hours splashing in the water.

Being Considerate to People with Special Needs

∾

Help your child understand that people with special needs have feelings, too. If your child can imagine the other person's point of view—maybe by imagining what life is like for him—your child can begin to develop the important trait of empathy.

DECEMBER 7

Visiting someone who is sick

Your child's best friend breaks her leg and has to be in a cast for the next six weeks . . . a cousin was in a car accident and is in the hospital suffering from broken ribs . . . Grandpa had open-heart surgery and won't be out of the hospital for weeks. How can your child help cheer up those who are special to him?

First, he should find out how the patient is feeling and whether or not a visit would be welcomed. Ask a family member, or check with the nursing staff at the hospital. If the patient is at home, always call before dropping in.

Your child should keep the visit short, whether visiting in the hospital or at home, and you should go along with him. Encourage your child to think about some news his friend would like to know—the names of friends who have asked about him, who won the soccer game, or how practice for the spring concert at school is progressing. Your child may ask his friend about how he's feeling but shouldn't weary him with too many questions.

Tell your child not to make negative comments about his friend's appearance: "Wow! I didn't know you'd swell up like a balloon!" or "Do you think you'll ever be able to walk again?" Remind him not to tell disastrous stories about other people he knows who faced a similar circumstance: "When my aunt had your problem, she had to have her leg amputated."

Help your child pick out a gift for his friend. Books, magazines, small toys, and candy can be good ideas (but check with the patient's parents to make sure candy is okay). If candy is all right, put some in a container, and your child's friend can offer it to his visitors. If your child chooses flowers, they should be in a container so that the patient doesn't have to worry about finding a vase.

Don't stay more than twenty minutes. Your child should know that people who have had surgery or who are sick sleep many hours a day. They can enjoy the company of others only for brief periods.

Activity

The next time one of your or your child's friends is sick, make some chocolate chip cookies, gather together videos from your collection that the other person might enjoy borrowing, and go for a brief visit.

DECEMBER 8

Relating to people with disabilities

People with disabilities are, first of all, *people*. That is how they want to be seen—as people, not lumped together in a separate group called "disabled." In fact, they prefer that no one use the term *disabled*. Help your child think about the things he has in common with someone he knows who has a disability—he'll be able to relate more comfortably.

If your child is quite young, his first reaction to meeting a person with a disability may be to stare. He might blurt out, "What's wrong with that man's face?" or "Why can't that lady walk?" In a low voice, let him know that you'll explain to him later. Don't go into an explanation or ask the person with the disability what happened. If the person heard your child's question, briefly apologize on your child's behalf.

Help your child to understand that people with disabilities hope to live lives that are as normal as possible. They don't want to create a scene everywhere they go, and they shouldn't have to explain their challenges to total strangers.

Most people with disabilities aren't opposed to conversing with friends about the difficulties they face. They just don't want to make this the only topic of conversation—any more than your child would want people constantly to ask him about an unusual physical feature.

Remind your child that a person who has one disability doesn't necessarily have another. A person who can't see may hear perfectly well, and there is no need to shout when conversing. Nor should your child equate physical disabilities with mental disabilities. Assume that a person who has a hearing problem also has normal intelligence.

If there is a student with a disability at your child's school, his teacher should take time making sure the class understands the extent of the child's abilities and disabilities. If she doesn't, here's how you can explain it: "Nathan is not able to walk, so you will always see him in a wheelchair. However, he hears perfectly well, sees perfectly well, and is a good student. He is able to get around very well by propelling his chair himself. Please don't push it or touch it without warning him. Emotionally, he's like you in every way. He hopes you will be his friend."

Activity

Give your child the opportunity to empathize with what it is like to be without sight or hearing. Blindfold yourself and your child for an hour, or plug your ears for an evening. Discuss with your child how it felt. Did he rely more on other senses? What couldn't he do with the disability? What took him longer to accomplish?

DECEMBER 9

People with visual problems

When your child encounters a person with vision loss, she should keep in mind that the person is most likely just like her in every other way. Because we rely so heavily on nonverbal messages, most people say that their vision would be the sense they would least like to lose.

Give your child the following tips in helping someone with poor sight:

- *No surprises.* Your child should announce her presence in the room by saying hello. When she leaves the room, she should say she's leaving; she shouldn't just disappear, leaving the person talking into the air.
- *Offer an arm.* Your child shouldn't grab the arm of a blind person, but should let the person take her arm.
- *Speak from the perspective of the other person when giving directions.* Say something like "On your left there are three steps down" or "Heather is on your left and Brandon is on your right."
- *Treat others as capable people.* Unless asked, your child shouldn't try to do things for a blind person that she wouldn't normally do for another person. For example, when eating, don't cut the person's food or butter the bread. Verbal hints are often welcome, however: "Salt and pepper are to your left, and you have a glass of iced tea to the upper right of your plate."
- *Ask.* If your child isn't sure how much to help, it's okay to ask.
- *Don't touch a guide dog.* The blind person's life depends on this dog, who must be constantly alert for his master and shouldn't be distracted. He is not a pet and should not be touched or called to.

Activity

Have your child give you directions as you walk through your home, assuming that you can't rely on your vision. Then go outside and do the same thing. Encourage him to describe distance accurately, tell whether or not a walk slopes up or down, and use your right and left in his descriptions.

DECEMBER 10

People with hearing loss

People with hearing loss—especially those who weren't born deaf—may feel isolated and frustrated when they are in groups. If there are many voices coming at them at once, the sounds get jumbled as they are transmitted by a hearing aid. Some people may never guess that the person has a hearing loss because of the invisible nature of the disability. Others may be surprised to discover it, and withdraw in embarrassment.

Many people who are born deaf relate quite strongly to the deaf community and do not feel in the least that they have an impairment or disability. Explain to your child that acting with pity or condescension, as if the deaf person is horribly impaired, will offend most congenitally deaf individuals.

If your child wants to communicate with someone who has a hearing loss, learn how the person prefers to communicate from a distance. There are phone relay services in which an operator acts as middleman, transcribing the spoken words of a hearing person into a typed message for a person with hearing loss. Today, many people with hearing problems rely on e-mail.

To show consideration in relating to a person with hearing loss, your child should:

- *Get the person's attention* by touching a shoulder or waving a hand. Always try to communicate directly rather than through a companion.
- *Look directly at the person when he speaks,* keeping his face in the light so it can be easily seen. Many people with hearing

301

loss can read lips. Your child shouldn't use exaggerated lip movements or hide his face behind a hand. He'll soon be able to tell whether or not he is being understood.

- *Speak in a normal tone of voice.* Hearing aids distort shouting.
- *Repeat what he has said.* Be patient and understanding. Communicating may take longer, but it will be worth the effort.
- *Write the message* if communication seems impossible.
- *Don't underestimate the importance of facial expressions.* If the person can't read lips, he knows that a smile communicates friendliness and raised eyebrows indicate a question.

Activity

Get a book on American Sign Language (ASL) out of the library. Help your child learn the ASL alphabet. When you are at a public meeting with your child, point out to him any interpreters for deaf people whom you happen to see.

DECEMBER 11

People in wheelchairs

The wheelchair is the personal property of the person who has a disability. He relies on it, and he may even consider it an extension of his body. Here are tips to help your child show courtesy to an individual in a wheelchair:

- *Get on eye level to talk with someone in a wheelchair.* Tell your child to pull up a chair if the conversation will last more than a few minutes, or get down on his haunches if it will be brief.
- *Avoid touching the wheelchair without permission.* Your child shouldn't push, lean on, or grab it. He should remember that the wheelchair serves as the person's legs and feet. Your child wouldn't want someone to hang on to his legs.
- *Don't assume the person is sick.* Wheelchairs may be used in hospitals to help sick or injured people get around, but for people with disabilities, they take the place of walking. The person who can't walk may be healthy in every other way.

- *Don't imagine that the person never gets out of the wheelchair.* Wheelchairs provide personal assistance in getting around. They're like a bicycle or a car—the person isn't bound to the wheelchair all of the time.
- *Move an empty wheelchair only when given permission by the person who uses it.* It can be very frightening for a person with disabilities to find that the wheelchair is gone.
- *Arrange furniture so that there is enough space for a wheelchair to pass through.*
- *Avoid playing with wheelchairs that are available in public buildings.* Children shouldn't take a spin in the wheelchair in the hospital lobby, for example.

Activity

Talk with your child about words that should be avoided because of negative connotations: *cripple, defect, wheelchair-bound,* and *handicapped.* Rather than speaking of "the disabled," they should try "a person with a disability." Remember, whatever the physical disability someone may have, he or she is a person first.

Body Basics

❧

Gentle coaching in hygiene is a task that falls to each parent. You'll notice your youngster playing in the dirt or eating with fingers and may fear that your efforts will never be fruitful. In time they will. While you'll probably need to continue prompting your child to brush, comb, and wash through early adolescence, by the teenage years your job will be over!

DECEMBER 12

Dress appropriately for the occasion

Over the years, we've become less formal in the way we dress, but people still notice what we wear. Encourage your child to pay some attention to the clothes he chooses.

Have your child imagine going for a medical checkup and finding the doctor in blue jeans and a Mickey Mouse T-shirt. Ask your child to think about what would happen if he attended a trial in a courtroom where the judge presided in a warm-up suit. What if he entered the sanctuary of a church only to find the pastor in sandals and cutoff shorts?

Your child will probably laugh—such clothing would be surprising and out of place. These professionals could do their jobs in this attire, but people would have a hard time ignoring how silly they looked.

Of course, some of the value of clothing is simply practical. People get dressed because they need to cover themselves and protect themselves from the weather. If these were the only reasons to get dressed, the doctor, the judge, and the pastor would be just fine.

But clothing also has a symbolic function. What a person wears creates a certain impression. For example, your child may think that no one will notice if he wears old sneakers to a piano recital. After all, he's wearing shoes! But because it's appropriate to dress up for a recital, old sneakers are out of place in this situation.

By about the age of five, your child should begin to understand that his clothing makes a certain statement and that dressing appropriately shows respect for others. Let your child help choose what he will wear by this age (sometimes earlier if he has strong opinions), although you can retain veto power if it's not a good choice. Still, as long as it's not inappropriate, no child should be forced to wear clothing he absolutely hates. Here are some guidelines for helping your child pick the right item from the closet:

1. Dress the way others do. Wear play clothes at a birthday party and dress up for a wedding. If you aren't sure what others will wear, don't be afraid to ask.
2. Wear clean clothes.
3. Don't try to outdo others by wearing very expensive clothing.

Activity

Have your child cut pictures from magazines or catalogs of different kinds of clothing. Group them according to when they would be appropriate to wear. Some occasions to consider are school, a tea party, a hike, a wedding, graduation, a birthday party, visiting Dad's office, church, a concert, and a funeral.

DECEMBER 13

Jewelry

Your daughter can rely on advice mothers having been giving for years: Put as much jewelry on as she thinks would look nice and then take one piece off. She'll look special but won't be dripping with jewels. Or she may keep it even simpler: wear no more than three pieces unless she's going to a gala ball. Too much jewelry makes anyone look like a Christmas tree.

For the most part, boys avoid wearing jewelry. Styles do change from time to time, making it acceptable to wear something casual made out of a string of leather or natural fibers with a few beads, or occasionally a simple ring. Whatever the fads your son wishes to try, he'll eventually notice that his dad and other adult men most likely wear only a watch and a wedding band.

Girls have more options—there is lots of fun, casual jewelry available, and the styles seem to change monthly. Let simplicity, safety, and your family preferences guide your daughter's choices. Some families like to pierce their infant daughter's ears, while others wouldn't consider it until the girl is in her teens. Whatever her age, your daughter is safest sticking with small, close-to-the-ear earrings.

DECEMBER 14

It's easy being clean

Cleanliness might be next to godliness, but not all children have gotten this message. Keeping clean is hardly a natural instinct for children—every parent knows how kids can be drawn to dirt, sticky foods, and worse. Constant reminders about cleanliness are the key to getting your child through those years when she would happily scoop peanut butter out of a jar with her fingers, walk through a mud puddle in her sneakers, and put off taking a bath for a week.

At adolescence, your child probably will become so keen on being clean, she'll nearly rub her skin raw. Until then, remind her that keeping her body clean is her responsibility, and it makes her a more desirable person to be around. It's also a matter of staying healthy.

Your child should keep hands out of her nose, ears, and mouth, because fingers carry dirt and germs from everything they touch. Remind her to *always* wash her hands before and after eating, before setting the table or handling food, and after going to the bathroom. She also should keep hands clean after playing outside, working with crafts, or doing chores at school or at home.

Activity

Help your child organize her toiletries. Simple plastic baskets to hold shampoo, shower gel, and lotion can keep the bathroom neat. If the bath is seen as an important ritual, your child will come to understand its importance more quickly. Have a plan for used towels: They need not be washed after each use, but they should be hung in a place your child recognizes as her own. Add deodorant to the toiletry collection at the beginning of fifth grade.

DECEMBER 15

Perfumes

Perfumes, scents, colognes, body splashes, and various lotions are widely used, even by elementary-school girls (boys typically want to wait until middle school to start to splash on the fragrance).

But scents are never meant as cover-ups. The idea isn't to drench oneself in Old Spice and avoid a shower after soccer practice. Instead, scents should go on in moderate amounts after a bath or shower.

After-bath splash is light and evaporates rather quickly, so it can be used with more freedom. Cologne is a bit heavier than a splash and should be placed on a couple of spots only, not splashed over the body (the wrist and neck are good spots for cologne). Perfume is the strongest scent and must be used with care. It can overwhelm those nearby because the wearer of a scent becomes accustomed to it and eventually doesn't even smell it. There are people who are allergic to fragrances and who do everything they can to avoid them.

Activity

Take several coffee filters and cut them into strips. When you shop for a scent with your child, have her spray a sample onto the paper strip, wave it in the air to catch the aroma, and write the name of the scent on the strip. Use a number of tester bottles to collect different fragrances on the strips. Take the strips home and let your child take her time deciding which is her favorite. Join her in the activity and pick a new fragrance for yourself, too.

DECEMBER 16
Grooming in public

Good personal grooming is important for many reasons—it's healthy, it's good discipline for your child, and it makes her a nicer person to be around. But remind her that grooming is always a private matter. A child should never groom herself in public in any way.

Tell your child never to use a brush or a comb in public, especially in a restaurant—always go to the rest room to fix hair. In fact, your child shouldn't even *touch* hair in public. Help your child get accustomed to this by keeping combs and brushes confined to the bedrooms and bathrooms of your home. Urge your child never to brush hair in the kitchen—to avoid possibly finding hair in the food.

Stress the big three that should never be picked in public: her nose, her ears, and her teeth. Never, ever. It looks terrible, and it's anything but sanitary.

The sound of nails being clipped should never ring out in a movie theater, a restaurant, or an auditorium. It should be confined to the bathroom, and your child should be certain to leave the bathroom clean when she's finished.

Fresh breath

Children are sensitive to the breath odors of others. To the chagrin of their parents, they might even express their disgust in front of the person, wrinkling up their noses and honestly proclaiming: "Your breath stinks!" A parent should gently explain that while we can readily detect breath odors on others, we are rarely aware of our own. For children, a few daily habits should do the trick.

Brushing teeth in the morning and evening, flossing by third or fourth grade, and learning how to rinse the mouth with mouthwash are all important ways to control mouth odor. All of these help to rid the mouth of bacteria that cause bad breath and also contribute to tooth decay. During his brushing routine, encourage your child to gently brush the soft tissues in his mouth as well—his tongue, the inside of his cheeks, and the roof of his mouth. This adds to the invigorating, fresh taste and gets rid of bacteria.

Your child shouldn't talk to an older person about his breath, however. Explain that this is the obligation of the older person's friends. He may tell a friend about offensive breath, but ever so kindly. It's better to talk to a friend about it than to discuss it with others. It's embarrassing at first, but in the long run the friend will be grateful.

Sneezing

Aaaaachoo! You hear it and you cringe, envisioning hordes of germs being released into the atmosphere. Did your child cover her nose and mouth? Did she turn her head away from others? Is another outburst imminent?

Your child isn't expected to stifle a sneeze and burst the blood vessels in her eyes. But she should grab a tissue (or a napkin if that's the only thing available) to make sure she contains the eruption. If her hands are full, your child can bury her face in her sleeve at the inner elbow. A simple "excuse me" should be the only mention your child makes of the sneeze.

If your child is in a public place such as a concert or movie and she knows from experience that she's about to sneeze repeatedly, she should leave the audience.

Your child may hear "gesundheit" or "bless you" after a sneeze. This is an ancient, automatic remark based on the old superstition that the soul can leave the body during a sneeze. Because ancient belief held that sneezing brought you close to death, the habit of blessing the sneezer became a tradition. It's polite to thank a person who offers a "gesundheit," and then no more needs to be said.

It's important to remind your child to wash her hands after catching a sneeze, because they're sure to transfer germs to food, doorknobs, or other hands.

DECEMBER 19

Oh, no, I've gotta go!

Going to the bathroom isn't a good topic for the dinner table, but that doesn't mean it should never come up. Your child should understand that it's a necessary part of life.

If you're dining away from home and your child hasn't been told which bathroom to use, he should ask. Don't assume that every bathroom is available for use—sometimes families reserve a bathroom for adults only. He should also clean up after himself; if paper towels are available, wiping water drops from the sink is a nice gesture. And, of course, it's essential to flush the toilet.

Although your child should leave the bathroom neat, he doesn't have to erase any trace of having been there. If he used a linen or terry hand towel, he should fold it loosely and place it on the counter or on a towel rack. He shouldn't try to fold it perfectly so that it appears not to have been used—that's what it is there for, even if it's very beautiful. Paper hand towels get thrown away after they've been used.

Activity

Place a roll of paper towels, a sponge, or a squeegee in your child's bathroom so that he can get in the habit of wiping water drops from the sink or shower when he has finished.

DECEMBER 20

Posture communicates

You've probably been telling your child to stand up straight ever since he was a toddler. Maybe you simply didn't want him to appear sloppy, but good posture also communicates interest and respect. It's especially important when your child is with adults.

Have your child stand with his feet a few inches apart, with his weight on the balls of his feet rather than on his heels. This way he's leaning forward rather than slouching back. He should draw his shoulders up and back, pulling in his stomach and pushing his chest out a bit; this makes him appear confident, alert, and engaged. Your child should put only one hand in his pocket (having both hands thrust deep into pockets rounds the shoulders, hides the hands, and communicates lack of confidence). The chin should be held parallel to the floor, not in the air or hugging the chest. This way, your child can establish eye contact and not appear haughty or droopy. When the chin is down, so are the eyes, communicating shyness or lack of interest. Catching the eyes of others and greeting them with a smile is friendly body language. It helps your child appear warm and approachable. When he walks, your child can add purpose to his gait by picking up his feet. Shuffling makes him appear aimless and bored.

Activity

Get a helium-filled balloon with a long string attached. Ask your child to imagine that the balloon is attached to his head with the string running down through his backbone. The sensation he imagines of the balloon tugging him upward reminds him to "stretch up" into good posture.

DECEMBER 21
Chewing gum

While some manners experts advise never chewing gum, the realistic parent is going to set some guidelines for it. A rule for reasonable parents is "You can chew gum, but only when no one else can see you." That eliminates public occasions such as school, church, weddings, plays, or private lessons.

The worst thing about chewing gum is how it looks. The second problem is that many children don't know what to do with the gum once it has been chewed. It doesn't belong on the floor, in a cup, under the table, or behind the ear. It shouldn't be stuck on the side of a plate to chew after dinner. It needs to be disposed of. Wrap it in a small piece of paper and put it in the wastebasket (don't put it in the toilet).

If your child is going to chew gum, he should chew it at home or when he's outside, such as at a sporting event. He should keep the piece so small that it doesn't make his cheek bulge, and he should always chew with his mouth closed. (Someone has said good manners is the sound *not* heard while eating soup. The same is true for chewing gum. It's also the sight not seen!)

And if your child pops a stick of gum in his mouth, he should also offer one to friends who are with him.

DECEMBER 22
Coughing or sneezing at the table

It's never pleasant eating with someone who has a cold. And eating isn't all that pleasant for the person with the cold, either, since any help his taste buds normally get from his nasal passages is completely blocked. Food just doesn't taste as good.

As long as he can eat fairly quietly, your child may join others at the table if he has a cold. But if sneezing or coughing take over, it's time to ask to be excused. He should cover the nose and mouth in any way he can—with his napkin or his hand—when he first coughs or sneezes, and he should always turn his head away from the table. Whether or not this truly keeps those microbes from flying into the air, who can tell? But it looks much better than sneezing right onto the table.

If the sneezing or coughing persists, he should go to the bathroom until it is over. Before returning to the table, remind him to wash his hands.

DECEMBER 23

If your child's nose is running at the table

Your child's nose may begin to drip when he's eating something too hot or spicy. If this occurs frequently, he should bring a tissue to the table and keep it in his pocket or on his lap. If he can take care of the problem by turning his head to the side and quietly using the tissue, he doesn't need to leave the table. But if taking care of things is going to require a loud honk, he needs to excuse himself.

In the absence of a tissue, it's better to touch his napkin to his nose to catch the drip than to sniff or run his index finger along his nose. He shouldn't blow his nose into his napkin, cloth or paper.

DECEMBER 24

What to do with a belch

Food doesn't always go down as smoothly as we might hope, nor does it necessarily settle in our stomachs never to be heard from again. As much as we'd like to squelch every belch, sometimes it just isn't possible.

Tell your child to relax. An occasional belch isn't the end of the world, as long as it is relatively quiet and *not* intentional.

However, it is never acceptable to engage in a belching contest, even during a birthday party or a baseball game.

To take some of the shame out of a belch that just can't be held in, tell your child to cover his mouth with a napkin or his hand to muffle the burp, and then say "excuse me." There's no need to explain all about a sensitive stomach and the unsuccessful remedies that have been tried. The less attention called to the situation, the better. If your child feels more burping coming on, he should excuse himself and find a bathroom.

DECEMBER 25

Wearing a name tag

Name tags identify us, make us seem more approachable, and increase the likelihood that we'll make new friends. They are a great idea for any occasion when people are together who don't know each other well. It's embarrassing to be around people who look familiar to us, whom we know we've met before, but whose names we can't remember. Name tags eliminate the embarrassment.

When your child is asked to wear a name tag, he should go ahead and wear one. Adults will be able to identify him more quickly, and other kids will know his name, too.

A name tag goes on the right side. That puts it directly in the field of vision of someone who is shaking your child's hand. He should put it on straight, up near his shoulder.

Tell your child it's okay to ask for his tag to be changed if his name is spelled incorrectly.

Activity

Create brightly colored name tags for children at a birthday party if they don't know each other well. Coordinate them with the theme of the party and use different-colored tags to assign children to teams for games. Make them out of adhesive-backed paper or put a long piece of ribbon on the tag and have the children hang them around their necks. Have extra blank tags in case a name is spelled incorrectly.

DECEMBER 26

Hands

Hands are an important means of self-expression. They are a key part of body language, at times communicating as much as spoken words, and sometimes even contradicting the words we say. For example, your child may tell you she feels okay about letting a friend borrow her favorite doll, but if her hands are clenched, she's really telling you she isn't wild about the idea.

Encourage your child to keep her hands still—in her lap if she's sitting, with one on top of the other. If she's at the table, she shouldn't drum them.

Hands shouldn't be hidden in the pockets. Years ago, social rules dictated that hands stayed in full view to let others know a weapon wasn't being concealed. Today, having the hands in view still communicates trustworthiness.

Hands that are in full view should be clean, with neatly clipped nails. Even though fashion favors long nails for adults, kids always look best with short nails. Place a nail brush in your child's bathroom to be used regularly along with the toothbrush.

Other ways for children to control their hands:

1. Keep them out of their hair.
2. Don't study them in public.
3. Keep them away from their face.

Activity

Get a book from the library that shows how to use your hands to make shadow figures on the wall. Help your child create some of the figures and show her how creative she can be with her hands. Talk about how her hands are communicating with others even when she might not be thinking about it.

DECEMBER 27

Choking

There are two kinds of choking. In the first, food or drink goes down wrong and irritates the airway, causing a fit of coughing. The face gets red, the eyes water, and the one choking is generally miserable. This isn't a life-threatening choking situation. The best approach is not to stare at the one choking. If your child is the one who's choking, he may leave the table until he has regained his composure.

The second kind of choking is the silent (and potentially deadly) one. This person's airway is completely blocked, and he can't breathe or speak. He'll probably signal that he's choking by grasping his throat. One young girl's eyes got wide and her hands flew into the air repeatedly when a cookie lodged in her windpipe.

Your child should know how to help someone who's choking—he either calls for help or performs the Heimlich maneuver. If he's alone and chokes, he can perform the Heimlich maneuver on himself by pushing firmly on his abdomen or leaning hard over the back of a chair to pop out the food.

TIP

Taking small bites and chewing food well go a long way in preventing choking!

DECEMBER 28

Visiting the doctor

Visiting the doctor is part of life, but it isn't always fun. Help prepare your child for a smooth visit by talking about what to expect. Today consumers have many choices in health care, so offices have become much more child-friendly. There are fewer stark white uniforms and more brightly decorated patient rooms. Often the waiting rooms are designed as playrooms to divert a child's attention away from more sober thoughts. Explain to your child that a good patient:

- Gets to his appointment on time.
- Waits quietly in the waiting room.
- Answers questions the nurse or doctor has for him (if he doesn't know what to say, you can help him).
- Understands that the doctor cares about him and will make every effort to make him comfortable.
- Knows it's okay to cry if he's in pain, but doesn't become hysterical just imagining what might happen.
- Says thank you for any small gift he may be given after his appointment.

Activity

If your child's doctor has a bulletin board displaying cards, letters, or drawings from patients, have your child write to his doctor. He can look for his letter at his next appointment.

DECEMBER 29

In the hospital

Most adults want to know everything they can about the procedures they'll undergo in the hospital, how they'll feel when they wake up from anesthesia, and what to expect as they recover. The same is true for a child. When your child goes to the hospital, the information she receives will affect her experience and her behavior.

Your child will take most of her cues from you. Focusing on the positive in your conversation will help, as will your calm presence with her in the hospital. Let her take along a favorite stuffed animal, and plan to spend at least the first night with her. Assure her that the nurses who will care for her love kids, and that she'll be able to ask them for help if she needs it. Tell her what a good doctor she has, and mention something she can look forward to when she has recovered. Your child shouldn't have to endure an unruly roommate. If her roommate is noisy, constantly has visitors, or has the TV on all day, you may ask to have your child transferred to a quieter room. Being able to rest is a necessary part of getting better. If your child isn't too sick, encourage her to thank the nurse for small favors.

Activity

When your child is to be discharged from the hospital, bring a box of chocolates or a basket of fresh fruit for her to give to her favorite nurses. If she's tired and in some discomfort, this will help turn her focus to others. (And remember that nurses come in three shifts; if you leave a box of chocolates for nurses on one shift, it is a nice touch to leave some for those on later shifts as well.)

DECEMBER 30

Braces

If your child has a mouth full of braces, help him establish some good habits from the beginning that will have two positive results—other people won't feel sick when they look at his mouth, and his teeth will be in good shape when the braces come off. Give your child these etiquette tips for braces:

- Keep the braces clean. It's unappetizing to look at braces lined with lunch.
- Keep his fingers out of his mouth. Picking at the braces looks bad and carries germs into his mouth.
- Take out removable orthodontic appliances in private.
- Avoid the symphony of rubber band and wire noises. Try not to flick the tongue against these stringed instruments.
- Smile with confidence, knowing that a truly bright smile is just around the corner. Your child shouldn't let the teasing about "metal mouth" and "tinsel teeth" get him down. Braces are like the road signs at construction sites: temporary inconvenience for permanent improvement.

DECEMBER 31

Inappropriate touch

Most kids wish adults wouldn't pat them on the head. Gestures such as these are usually harmless, but if your child feels uncomfortable, tell her she won't be rude to move away.

Let your child know that it's okay for her to decide what is an appropriate touch for her. She has personal space—that area that includes her body and a foot or two around it. She doesn't need to allow into her personal space anyone with whom she's uncomfortable; she needs to respect her own instincts and know she's in control.

If she doesn't like a certain touch, she should say so. She doesn't have to say, "Get away from me!" when a boy puts his arm around her, when her dad's friend strokes her hair, or when someone tickles her, but she should move away and make her preferences clear. She could say, "I don't really like being touched. Please don't do that."

Let her know that she can always tell you when someone makes her feel uncomfortable.

_____ TIP _____

Don't hesitate to hug your children, even in their teen years. When kids experience appropriate touch, they'll be better able to say no to harmful touch.

In Conclusion

❧

This book was written to help make your job as a parent easier. It was meant to give you ideas and to make manageable a task that could seem overwhelming. Take heart as you patiently prompt and praise your children about their manners; in time you'll be pleased by the progress you see. And who knows—when your children are grown and endeavoring to civilize their own kids, they may thank you for your efforts.

About the Author

SHERYL EBERLY runs Distinctions, a company that presents manners instruction seminars to children, young adults, and businesspeople. She lives with her family in northern Virginia.